Philadelphia

GREATER PHILADELPHIA

CHAMBER OF COMMERCE

Get involved. Get results.

philachamber.com

Produced in cooperation with the Greater Philadelphia Chamber of Commerce

Philadelphia

By Kurt R. Niland
Special Introduction by Marion Laffey Fox
Profiles by Kody Rountree and Jim Dunham
Featuring the Photography of John McGrail

Beneficial
SAVINGS BANK

ace ina

ADVANTA

B101

BrandywineRealtyTrust

The Children's Hospital *of* Philadelphia
A pediatric healthcare network

Chester County Aviation

(Seal of the City of Philadelphia)

CROZER-KEYSTONE
HEALTH SYSTEM

DOYLE CONSULTING GROUP
INCORPORATED

Ewing Cole Cherry Brott
Architects • Engineers • Interior Designers • Planners

FOUR SEASONS HOTEL
Philadelphia

THE GRAHAM COMPANY
INSURANCE BROKERS AND CONSULTANTS

Independence
Blue Cross

Jefferson
Health System

Marriott
Residence
Inn

McDonald's

Philadelphia

Produced in cooperation with the
Greater Philadelphia Chamber of Commerce

Written by Kurt R. Niland
Special Introduction by Marion Laffey Fox
Corporate profiles by Kody Rountree and Jim Dunham
Featuring the photography of John McGrail

Community Communications, Inc.
Publisher: Ronald P. Beers

Staff for *Philadelphia*

Acquisitions	Ronald P. Beers
Project Manager—Sales	Mel Merk
Sales Associate	Marion Laffey Fox
Editor In Chief	Wendi L. Lewis
Managing Editor	Angela C. Johnson
Profile Editor	Christi Stevens
Design Director	Scott Phillips
Designer	Christi Scruggs
Photo Editors	Angela C. Johnson and Christi Scruggs
Contract Manager	Dana Wallace
Sales Assistant	Brandon Maddox
Accounting Services	Stephanie Perez
Print Production Manager	Christi Stevens
Pre-press/Color Separations	Artcraft Graphic Productions
Print Production	Walsworth Publishing Company

CCI

Community Communications, Inc.
Montgomery, Alabama

David M. Williamson, Chief Executive Officer
Ronald P. Beers, President
W. David Brown, Chief Operating Officer

A special thanks to Nick Katsikis of Residence Inn for his support during this project.

"Puma" statue by William Zorach (1954) in the Azalea Garden on Philadelphia Museum of Art grounds.

Contents

Part One, 14

1 Cradle of Liberty

The Philadelphia story is dramatic and rich. Visitors and residents here follow in the footsteps of George Washington, Benjamin Franklin, Thomas Jefferson, and all the signers of the Declaration of Independence. The city tells its unique tale, gently unfolding with time.

2 Workshop of the World

As a resource for the finest eighteenth-century handcrafted goods, nineteenth-century Philadelphia was called the "Workshop of the World." Today, the city is a central business hub, alive with exciting enterprises and opportunities for established industries and emerging technology.

3 A Cultural Masterpiece

Philadelphia has been allied with the visual arts from its inception. Today, its stunning collection of more than 100 museums, libraries, and repositories of rare artifacts dedicated to almost every imaginable subject is considered one of the most important in the country and, in some cases, in the Western Hemisphere. The opening of the Kimmel Center for the Performing Arts provided a state-of-the-art venue for the Philadelphia Orchestra, Pennsylvania Ballet, The Opera Company of Philadelphia, and many more.

4 Let Us Entertain You

Special events keep people here busy, with nonstop activities beginning with the high-stepping Mummers Day Parade on New Year's Day and continuing with Veterans' Day and Thanksgiving Parades. Philadelphians enjoy having a good time at local flower and dog shows, and daily outings at the zoo and other attractions.

Part Two, 214

10 *Networks, Energy & Transportation* 216

11 *Manufacturing & Distribution* 228

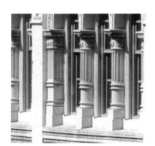

12 *Business & Finance* 236

13 *Professions* 260

Foreword

If William Penn could return to Philadelphia today, he most likely would be amazed and probably excited by what he saw. Penn's "greene Country Towne" has turned into a world-class thriving metropolis—the fifth largest city in our country, centrally located in the eastern corridor. We believe most gratifying to William Penn would be his observation of the preservation and unique display of his many contributions to the city.

The *Philadelphia* book brings to you the reader, a total overview of the city's thriving region. Included you will find the foundation of a rich historical perspective along with a classic mix of the present day sites and activities.

Everything that represents the area as a wonderful place to live and do business is presented in the *Philadelphia* book. You will learn about the cultural activities and museums, entertainment, neighborhoods, educational institutions, and diversity of the region.

Whether you want an overview of the region's incredible transportation network, or marketplace and development opportunities for established industries and emerging technology, everything is outlined in the following pages. If health care or education, financial and business, or professional service companies are your interest, you will find them in abundance as the region's primary economic base.

Philadelphia is a city of neighborhoods. The broad ethnic richness of these neighborhoods both in the city and outlying areas provides residents many choices of where to live: in a sprawling rural farm area, tranquil suburbs, the bustling city, a townhouse, and everything in between.

Please enjoy the *Philadelphia* book as a compilation of the many factors contributing to one of America's most livable cities and the diversity of businesses that keep the region a vibrant and strong segment of our great nation.

—*The Greater Philadelphia Chamber of Commerce*

The Philadelphia Museum of Art is sometimes referred to by locals as the "Parthenon on the Parkway."

(Following page) The historic Schuylkill River is a beautiful gateway to the city of Philadelphia whether for commerce or recreation.

Part One

Introduction

*I*f Philadelphia is often called a "World-Class City," it is an appropriate moniker. The fifth largest city in the country truly has it all.

I recall being stirred by the city when I came as a young child with my family to visit such stellar sights as the Liberty Bell, the Philadelphia Zoo, the Franklin Institute, and the Philadelphia Museum of Art. We learned American history first-hand on horse-drawn carriage rides through Society Hill and during strolls through old cemeteries where we searched for graves of signers of the Declaration of Independence. There were memorable picnics in Fairmount Park's violet-strewn fields, ambles through the battlefields of Valley Forge, and shopping forays in the Italian Market. Each visit not only made an indelible impression, it created a longing to return. Years later, when I enrolled at the University of Pennsylvania, my palpable excitement was enhanced by the realization that I could at last call Philadelphia my home.

The city boasts more "firsts" than any other city in the country and its endless list of attributes continue to represent boundless opportunities for personal growth as well as a satisfying way of life. Considering them all means enumerating a myriad of things that range from electrifying cultural opportunities to a stimulating business and economic climate. A reverence for the past insures the preservation of historic elements that draws visitors from everywhere. Entertainment? Countless choices. The list goes on, but, because Philadelphia is a place that has only recently begun to shed its historic modesty, self-appointed cheerleaders such as I feel compelled to introduce you to this pedigreed town, where my favorite places are not necessarily its most famous. Yet each underscores the specialness that distinguishes Philadelphia—home of the Liberty Bell and Independence Hall, Philly cheesesteak and soft pretzels, high-stepping Mummers and Schuylkill River Boathouse Row—from almost anyplace else.

For starters, Philadelphia was laid out by its founder, William Penn, in 1640 as a walkable, navigable grid of streets. Situated between the busy Delaware and languid Schuylkill Rivers, ninety miles from New York and 145 miles from Washington, it boasts an enviable location. Like a dazzling ribbon, it unravels along cobbled streets, past centuries-old houses, through the largest municipal park in the country into bustling ethnic neighborhoods. It continues through verdant arboretums thick with specimen trees and hidden gardens into rolling battlefields framed by distant covered wooden bridges, and leafy suburbs connected by an extensive network of interstate, local highways, and country roads.

America's Most Historic Square Mile is an actual compendium of more than a dozen of the nation's most revered historic sites that include the Liberty Bell and Independence Hall; Carpenters' Hall and the Second Bank of the United States; Christ Church, where George Washington and many of the signers of the Declaration of Independence worshiped; and the Christ Church

Burial Ground where more Revolutionary War heroes are buried than any other non-military cemetery in the nation. Nearby, the National Historic Landmark on Elfreth's Alley of thirty-three Colonial and Federal houses celebrates the oldest continuously occupied street in America. After strolling here, it is fun to explore other residential streets in Old City and Society Hill to get a bird's eye view of the lovingly preserved venerable steepled churches, tiny mews, and walled cemeteries that have been here since the early eighteenth century. The National Constitution Center, opening in 2003, honors the document that sets America apart from the rest of the world.

As America grew, so Philadelphia prospered. As the largest English-speaking city in the New World it was only second to London in activity and scope. Early land grants for those seeking religious freedom accounted for attracting significant blocks of Swedish, German, Dutch, and Welsh settlers to the region. In the nineteenth century, the flood of immigration of Southern and Eastern Europeans such as Poles, Ukraines, Slavs, Russian and German Jews, and Irish fleeing the Potato Famine altered the social fabric of Philadelphia forever. Later, more ethnic neighborhoods crystallized around the arrival of Puerto Ricans, Chinese, Koreans, Vietnamese, Mexicans, Latin Americans, and West Indians, who further enriched the area with

▲ **Independence Hall has stood the test of time and several restorations since the early 1800s, including a new clock and bell prior to the 1876 Centennial.**

their cultures. How logical that two hundred years later the evolving tapestry of diversity was consistent with William Penn's original plan.

Philadelphia is not only about ethnic neighborhoods. The Center City business and financial district is exciting in form and function. Characterized by a distinctive skyline of high-rise buildings, the area wordlessly defines a dramatic departure from the long-standing tradition or "Gentleman's Agreement" that previously limited new buildings

▲ Part of the Philadelphia Museum of Art's Grounds Tour, the Fountain of the Sea Horses, located on Kelly Drive, is a 1926 replica of the 1740 original.

to a height less than the 491-foot-high City Hall Tower. The charming idea once allowed the statue of William Penn to effectively preside over the city, while stubbornly restraining upward growth. At the same time, it propagated the impression that this insignificant-looking district of low-rise buildings was nothing more than a smallish place stuck in a time warp.

That is, until 1986, when developer Willard S. Rouse challenged the soundness of the out-moded custom with the proposal of constructing soaring, glass-fronted skyscrapers in this area. While his progressive vision was cheered by some, it was hotly challenged by others. The solution? Eventually, both sides agreed to a "low zone" or "view corridor" with height restrictions immediately around City Hall, as well as the abolition of the ban against skyscrapers beyond the tight little area.

Today, the exhilarating presence of Liberty One, Liberty Two, Mellon Bank Center, and the Bell Atlantic Tower anchor the vibrant business community. Nearby, the sprawling 1.3-million-square-foot Philadelphia Convention Center sets the scene for countless conventions, trade shows, and special exhibitions such as the Museum of Arts and Craft Show, and the Philadelphia Flower Show—the largest horticultural show of its kind in the nation. It also incorporates and showcases the historic Reading Terminal Market and Train Shed into accessible tourist destinations.

However, this city is not only about bricks and mortar. Many Philadelphians feel its very fiber is woven from cues left by the historic greats who lived here and shaped its future. After all, it was home to everyone from George Washington to Thomas Jefferson, Dolly Madison, John Hancock, Betsy Ross, and Samuel Powell, to name a few. But, among them all, Benjamin Franklin's remarkable persona consistently emerges as that which singularly left its mark everywhere we look. Few realize that Franklin rose from rags to riches, pointing the way for the common man to achieve a robust life of liberty and happiness long before those words were used in the Declaration of Independence. Born in Boston on January 17, 1706,

the young printer fled to Philadelphia in l723 when he was only seventeen years old. Over the course of his lifetime, he invented many things that are still useful today, such as the Franklin stove, lightning rod, and bifocals.

But it was Franklin's adopted home, the "City nearest the Centre" of the Colonies, that benefited most from his genius. As an early promoter of Philadelphia, he eventually observed it become the meeting place for the most important nation builders of the day. Concurrently, he was responsible for improving its resources. He updated the city's lighting, created street-paving patrols, founded its general post office, philosophical society, academy, churches, and Pennsylvania's first synagogue. His *Poor Richard's Almanac*— served up "scraps from the table of wisdom."

Consider the fact that much of what Franklin concentrated on continues to thrive today. His concept of an "Ingenious Acquaintance into a Club for Mutual Improvement," initially called the Junto, eventually became the American Philosophical Society. His Junto's "first Project of a public nature," pooled subscription resources to create a collection of books for common use. Today, contemporary Philadelphians enjoy the enormous facilities of what has evolved into the thriving Library Company of Philadelphia.

Franklin's brilliant idea of matching funds launched the opening of Pennsylvania Hospital, where subscribers who donated 2,000 pounds sterling witnessed their funds matched by the Pennsylvania Assembly. Consistent with Franklin's idea of matching funds, modern-day Philadelphia is a place renowned for creative and generous philanthropy. Dozens of foundations regularly infuse local institutions with millions of dollars each year to expand innovation and initiatives, scope and vision. They help nurture and create vibrant new programs that benefit the city and region in dynamic ways. Too innumerable to mention, these philanthropic organizations, such as The Pew Memorial Trusts, Independence Foundation, William Penn Foundation, Philadelphia Foundation, and Annenberg Foundation, continue to propagate the idea that making a difference has always been an important Philadelphia concept.

"This is the Age of Experiments," Franklin said of his time in life, and during eight long transatlantic voyages he charted the flow of the Gulf Stream and listed under "these new wonders" inventions like a handcrafted machine that produced static electricity. At the Society of

the Arts in London, he helped judge which artists and inventors should be rewarded for their genius. Today, that society grants Franklin medals to those who promote Anglo-American relations. In his memory, the Franklin Institute continues a 177-year Philadelphia tradition of publicly recognizing extraordinary achievements in science. Each year, under the auspices of the Institute's Committee on Science and the Arts, Benjamin Franklin Medals and prestigious Bower Awards are conferred to outstanding individuals who excel in six specific areas. Predecessors of contemporary laureates include Albert Einstein, Marie Curie, Thomas A. Edison, Alexander Graham Bell, David Packard, Rudolf Diesel, Irwin Jacobs, and Paul Baran, to name a few. In the last century ninety-eight Franklin Institute Laureates also have been honored with one hundred Nobel Prizes.

Philadelphia is a city of philanthropy and a preserver of culture and the arts. To that end, the city boasts more than a hundred museums, many of which appear on "Museum Mile," an elegant area that swirls around the Swann Fountain to mimic the very best of nineteenth-century Parisian architecture. Among its internationally renowned institutions, this area is solidly anchored by the highly acclaimed Philadelphia Museum of Art, known affectionately as the "Parthenon on the Parkway." Immortalized in the film starring Sylvester Stallone, *Rocky*, the museum is a paragon in the world of art and collections. Rising elegantly from its site on Fair Mount, a hill that once contained the city's first reservoir, the columned structure flaunts a golden-ochre facade and gabled blue-tiled roof. Inside, the repository of some of the greatest collections in the world consists of more than three hundred thousand works of art and antiquities and various permanent collections that span two thousand years.

Nearby, the Rodin Museum boasts the largest collection of Rodin's work outside Paris. The tiny museum is not far from the world-famous Franklin Institute, where thousands of visitors revel in the science exhibitions, ride locomotives, "fly airplanes," and walk through an enormous thumping heart. Across the street, The Academy of Natural Sciences is the oldest science research institution in the Western Hemisphere. It is also the place to marvel at the enormous skeleton of Tyrannosaurus Rex in its popular permanent exhibition called Discovering Dinosaurs.

Of course, no visit to the area would be complete without a stroll through the galleries of the venerable Pennsylvania Academy of the Fine Arts. America's oldest art school and museum, founded in 1805, was moved to its present location in the 1870s when the exuberant Frank Furness Building was opened to coincide with the 1876 Exposition in Fairmount Park. If aspiring artists come from everywhere to study within its hallowed halls, the Academy's collections also magnetize devotees. Included are important works by Charles Wilson Peale, John Singer Sargent, and Mary Cassatt.

In West Philadelphia, the University of Pennsylvania Museum of Archaeology and Anthropology is considered one of the world's finest museums of its kind on a college campus. Established in

 19

▲ **Joan of Arc by Emmanuel Fremiet (1890), an impressive sight on horseback, can be seen on the Kelly Drive tour.**

1886, it is dedicated to the understanding and study of the history of humankind. The popular Egyptian wing features the only Egyptian temple constructed in a museum as well as countless important mummies. In contrast, the Institute of Contemporary Art enjoys a well-served reputation for encouraging unproven artists on the cutting edge of the art world. Those it granted early exhibition space to include Andy Warhol, Robert Mapplethorpe, and Laurie Anderson.

Music is part of the very fiber of this first-class city. Considered a world-class venue for the performing arts, the city is home to the Philadelphia Orchestra, Pennsylvania Ballet, The Opera Company of Philadelphia, Academy of Vocal Arts, and Curtis Institute of Music. Anchor of the Avenue of the Arts, the venerable Academy of Music is raising its roof to accommodate new venues and, as the Grand Old Lady of Locust Street is still very grand, the hall anticipates a renewed lease on life.

Nearby, the newly opened Kimmel Center for the Performing Arts or Regional Performing Arts Center is a very different kind of architectural showcase. Occupying an entire city block of 2.3 acres, the landmark structure designed by architect Rafael Vignoly exudes glittering attitude and stylish urbanism. The Center houses Verizon Hall and the Perelman Theater as two freestanding venues beneath a glistening glass roof that soars one hundred fifty feet above a great indoor plaza.

The twenty-five-hundred-seat Verizon Hall is officially the new home of The Philadelphia Orchestra, as well as Peter Nero and the Philly Pops®. The smaller and more intimate six-hundred-fifty-seat Perelman Theater is home to PHILADANCO, the Chamber Orchestra of Philadelphia, The Philadelphia Chamber Music Society, and American Theater Arts for Youth, Inc., as well as chamber concerts by The Philadelphia Orchestra.

When Philadelphians are not attending performances, they are likely to be cheering on one of their sports teams. Philadelphia is one of a handful of cities with five professional sports teams and is one of very few American cities with countless parks and facilities

that encourage personal participation in sports such as tennis, racquetball, golf, and rowing.

As the second largest city on the east coast and the nation's fourth largest metropolitan area and retail market, Philadelphia is alive with enterprises that range from technology to research, health care to manufacturing. The legal profession supports more than sixteen thousand lawyers, and the business community is fueled by banks, brokerage houses, financial institutions, architecture and design firms, insurance and reinsurance firms, and advertising and public relations companies. One of the largest airports in the nation, which underwent a one-billion-dollar renovation, is expanding with new terminals, and the thriving regional rail system linking the suburbs to downtown is regularly filled with commuters.

It's not surprising with more than three hundred restaurants— many of which are considered national and international culinary shrines—that Philadelphia has been called the country's best restaurant city. In addition, the third largest downtown in the country boasts over two thousand retail establishments, two hundred jewelry stores, forty art and antiques stores, thirty-six bookstores, and many

auctions houses, including Freeman Fine Arts, the nation's oldest, founded in 1810.

Farther afield, the City of Philadelphia becomes the Greater Philadelphia Area, which includes adjacent Bucks, Montgomery, Chester, and Delaware Counties. Each is filled with historic sites and wonderful diversions. The Barnes Foundation on the Main Line in Merion Station, founded by Dr. Alfred Barnes, is a repository of early Impressionist, Post-Impressionist, and Early Modern masterpieces, African sculpture, and eighteenth-century Pennsylvania furniture. Across the river in Chestnut Hill, The Morris Arboretum of the University of Pennsylvania is worth a visit. Other not-to-miss places consist of The Mercer Museum in Doylestown, the Wharton Escherick House in Paoli, historic Yellow Springs in Chester County, and awesome Longwood Gardens, thirty miles west of the city.

The effect of Philadelphia's commanding presence on many of the outlying communities is undeniably urban. Many of the towns and cities in the port area, such as Camden, New Jersey, and Wilmington, Delaware continue to function not just as hubs of river transportation and commerce, but as key centers along the industrial backbone of the region. Camden recently underwent a rebirth with the help of a vigorous economy and the city of Philadelphia, along with a clear vision of the future. From the New Jersey State Aquarium, situated on Camden's waterfront directly across the Delaware River from Penn's Landing, to Camden's Children's Garden, to the Tweeter Center at the Waterfront, Camden has many opportunities for residents and visitors.

A little further south, the casinos and boardwalks of Atlantic City stretch out along the rolling ocean, providing Philadelphians a quick and easy escape for the day or weekend. Then, a short drive north of the city is another world removed from the urban bustle of Center City—Bucks County, a haven steeped in country charm and colonial heritage. The county seat, Doylestown, is a sterling example of historical preservation; street after street, architectural styles run the gamut from colonial to Victorian, creating a singular snapshot of the city's rich past. The Mercer Museum, a showcase of American industry and innovation before mechanization, houses some fifty thousand tools representing more than sixty trades in addition to exhibits of folk art and other Americana.

Of course there's more, but it would take volumes more than a mere introduction to list them all—so for the moment please share my personal delight in introducing you to my favorite city. Approach it with the care and respect that were inherent in its founding. Then enjoy the spirit, vibrancy, and soul of this truly special place that is clearly on the move. Whether you are lucky enough to live here, or simply passing through the City of Brotherly Love, welcome to one of the nation's most energetic, proud, and interesting cities.

—*Marion Laffey Fox*

What makes a leader?

*T*he dictionary defines leadership as a "foremost position"—the first, the head of the class. A leader commands, a leader influences, guides, conducts, escorts; a leader sets a precedent.

Within a community, leaders are those who are unafraid to step up to meet the challenges of today, and who have the foresight to plan for the needs of tomorrow. These are the visionaries, the individuals or groups that boldly take the next step, encouraging those around, "Come on! This way! Join me and see how much we can grow with each other's help!"

Perhaps nowhere is leadership more vital in a community than in the development of its business sector. The lifeblood of any city is its business community. A healthy, thriving business and industry base ensures jobs for citizens, tax revenue necessary for maintaining public property, city services and roads, and a healthy economy overall—which, in turn, is good for businesses. Everybody benefits.

All members of a community feel the influence of business leadership. It is evident in corporate sponsorships benefiting education, the arts, and the environment. Leadership is visible in a ready population of volunteers who donate their time and talents to assist those less fortunate in their community, making for a richer quality of life for all citizens. And, leadership is the force that inspires one to dream, to reach a little higher, to try a little harder.

Leadership is the force that makes Philadelphia special.

Conceived more than fifteen years before construction began in 1949, the Schuylkill Expressway links Fairmount Park to Valley Forge, making it one of the most vital routes in and out of Philadelphia.

Beneficial Savings Bank

"Leadership begins with a commitment to inspire the best in others, and the most effective form of leadership is example. For over 150 years, Beneficial Savings Bank has maintained a leadership position in and around Philadelphia by inspiring our own employees to help our customers achieve their financial goals. In turn, the men and women of Beneficial inspire each other to contribute to the improvement of the neighborhoods and communities in which we live and work. In one way or another, we all have a responsibility to lead and inspire."

George W. Nise
President & CEO
Beneficial Savings Bank

▲ Ringing Rocks Park in Bucks County is located on 123 acres. The name is derived from the boulder fields of rocks that ring like a bell when struck.

▲ The Philadelphia Zoo is home to almost 1,800 animals. The zoo's long history, amazing exhibits, and annual events make it a popular attraction.

ACE INA

"The dedication of ACE INA and its employees extends well beyond the business and its clients into the wider community. Through its philanthropic arm, ACE INA lends support to worthwhile educational and community organizations and cultural institutions. The ACE INA Foundation is actively involved in programs concerning youth, education, and the arts."

Dominic Frederico
Chairman and Chief Executive Officer
ACE INA Holdings, Inc.

Advanta

"The nature of Philadelphia is one of a small city grown large. In spite of its size and scale, there is a sense of community unlike any place in the world. This spirit of community that was so important to the foundation of our company, remains vital to Advanta's continued success in the future."

Dennis Alter
Chairman & CEO
Advanta

▲ The Wissahickon Creek is an important resource, both natural and recreational, for the neighborhoods through which it flows before it arrives at the Schuylkill River.

B101

"As broadcasters we not only have the ability to reach the public but a responsibility to use our voice to positively affect the society in which we live. David and I have always taken that responsibility very seriously and have done our best to drive positive change by using the station and its resources."

Jerry Lee
President and Partner
B101

▲ In the brutal winter of 1777-78, more soldiers perished at Valley Forge than the total casualties of both the Brandywine and Germantown battles.

Brandywine Realty Trust

"Most people truly want a sense of contribution by being part of something larger than their own world. One of the wonderful things about the art of real estate development is, not only does it encompass all the business processes important to financial success, but, more importantly, it has the ability to impact a neighborhood, a community, and a region."

Gerard H. Sweeney
President and CEO
Brandywine Realty Trust

Chester County Aviation

"The Philadelphia suburbs and Philadelphia in general are in an excellent position, one that allows for growth. As many of the Philadelphia companies find ways to expand along the 202 Corridor and into other surrounding counties, we can see our business growing and look forward to what the future holds."

Brian Campbell
President & General Manager
Chester County Aviation

▲ Enormous panels of stained glass windows at the National Shrine of Our Lady of Czestochowa depict Christianity's history in Poland and the U.S.

NAKED AND STARVING AS THEY ARE
WE CANNOT ENOUGH ADMIRE
THE INCOMPARABLE PATIENCE AND FIDELITY
OF THE SOLDIERY
WASHINGTON AT VALLEY FORGE FEBRUARY 16. 1778

▲ Today, the 3,600-acre Valley Forge National Historical Park attracts
visitors to its numerous historic sites, museums, and gardens.

The Children's Hospital of Philadelphia

"As the birthplace of pediatric medicine in America, The Children's Hospital of Philadelphia is a pioneer in pediatric clinical care, research, and education. For nearly 150 years, this institution has fostered clinical innovations and scientific breakthroughs that have advanced children's health around the world. Ranked as the best pediatric hospital in the nation by a comprehensive Child magazine survey, Children's Hospital is currently writing a new chapter in the chronicles of pediatric healthcare."

Steven M. Altschuler, M.D.
President and Chief Executive Officer
The Children's Hospital of Philadelphia

▲ **More than 250,000 people step back in time each year as they visit Betsy Ross' house—the birthplace of the American Flag.**

City of Philadelphia

"We are a city government that gets things done. Today, this government is more focused on quality of life issues than at any other time in its history. Through our Neighborhood Transformation Initiative, the City of Philadelphia is making over a $1.6 billion investment over five years to foster redevelopment in our neighborhoods. We are making our neighborhoods cleaner, safer, and more beautiful. We have forged a historic partnership with the Commonwealth of Pennsylvania to secure a better and brighter future for our public school students and every year in this city is dedicated as 'the year of the child' in Philadelphia to focus on our city's most important future asset, our children."

John F. Street
Mayor
City of Philadelphia

Crozer-Keystone Health System

"The Crozer-Keystone Health System is the major provider of health services and programs to the residents of Delaware County. With five hospitals and 1,100 associated physicians, Crozer-Keystone addresses the comprehensive medical needs of the majority of families in this community. Crozer-Keystone is also the largest employer in Delaware County with over 7,200 well-trained staff, dedicated to improving the health status of all those we are committed to serve. Working with our communities, we want to help create a healthy place to live and work, a sound environment in which to build and maintain our families."

Gerald Miller
President and Chief Executive Officer
Crozer-Keystone Health System

Doyle Consulting Group, Inc.

"The major hallmark of our success always has been that we have not only gotten some of the largest employers in our target market, but we also have maintained those relationships over a long period of time. The best barometer of success for any company is in the long term associations it develops.

"We will continue to exceed our client's expectations only by the virtue of our ability to deliver an innovative approach, exceptional service, and execution of their objectives."

Francis L. Doyle, III
Chairman and CEO
Doyle Consulting Group, Inc.

▲ Philadelphia's sculling tradition was born on the Schuylkill River. Rowing clubs ply five miles from the Manayunk train bridge in the north to the Schuylkill River Falls in the south.

▲ Since its founding 115 years ago, the Philadelphia Museum of Art has grown to house over 300,000 pieces of art in more than 200 galleries.

Ewing Cole Cherry Brott

"Ewing Cole's integration of technology and imagination allows us to translate our client's vision into physical space. Our philosophy of architecture is grounded in the belief that our design should help our clients fulfill their mission and attain their business goals. We design buildings that are beautiful, create a unique sense of place, and are specifically designed to meet the individual needs of each customer."

James A. Wilson, AIA
President
Ewing Cole Cherry Brott

First Union/Wachovia

"While building on the heritage of our legacy organizations, the spirit of today's Wachovia embodies something entirely unique. Our new brand is built on a rock-solid foundation—people. Our strength springs from a confluence of cultures, ideas and individuals working together to support shared goals and collective success.

"We touch the lives of almost one million retail customers and over 85,000 businesses here, from Philadelphia's largest corporations to individuals and grass roots community groups. As streams join to form rivers, the collective success of our customers, employees, and communities creates a stronger Philadelphia region."

Pamela L. Frey
Regional President
First Union/Wachovia

◀ 35

▲ Overlooking the Schuylkill River, the exterior and grounds of the
Philadelphia Museum of Art are attractions in their own right.

The Graham Company

"At The Graham Company, our reputation is reflected in the company we keep in terms of our clients and our staff. For over 50 years, we have been developing close, long-term relationships with world-class clients, and we have maintained a strong understanding of their businesses and challenges. Also, from the very beginning, we've recognized that if you attract, recruit, and train the very best people, you'll have a great organization."

William A. Graham, IV
CEO
The Graham Company

▲ An afternoon drive from the core of Philadelphia leads to picturesque estates and farmlands in surrounding counties, each with its own unique history.

Independence Blue Cross

"The Corporate Mission of Independence Blue Cross and its affiliates is to contribute to the good health of our members through financing the delivery of quality health care and allied services, effectively and efficiently managing the care provided to our members, and actively participating in shaping the evolution of the health care system."

G. Fred DiBona, Jr.
President & CEO
Independence Blue Cross

◀ 37

▲ Almost a million visitors per year tour the 1,050 acres of Longwood Gardens, with its forty indoor and outdoor gardens and 11,000 varieties of plants.

Jefferson Health System

"To remain the healthcare system of choice for the Delaware Valley, we must be vigilant about fulfilling our mission. We must continue to work hard, everyday to enhance the service-oriented culture for which Jefferson Health System members are known. We must protect our patients' rights and their access to healthcare. We must also improve our financial condition as a system, one member institution at a time, identifying areas where savings can be achieved without compromising quality."

Joseph T. Sebastionelli
President and Chief Executive Officer
Jefferson Health System

▲ The fifteen-by-forty-nine-foot replica of Maxfield Parrish's *Dream Garden* mural, displayed in the lobby of the Curtis Center, is comprised of 100,000 pieces of hand-fired glass consisting of 260 color tones.

Marriott Residence Inn

"We at the Residence Inn by Marriott take pride in our reputation as one of the finest hotels in the Philadelphia area. The relationships that we have developed with Philadelphia International Airport, the city, and the businesses in the area have been key in our past success. Because of these relationships, our luxury accommodations, and our outstanding guest service, we will continue to provide our guests with a 'home away from home'."

Nick Katsikis
General Manager
Marriott Residence Inn

McDonald's East Division

"Philadelphia and the Delaware Valley have always been a major market for McDonald's and we've found it to be the best location to center our east coast operations. We will continue to invest in this marketplace—financially with the restaurants and socially through Ronald McDonald House Charities, Ronald McDonald Care Mobiles, as well as the other civic and charitable organizations we support."

Henry Gonzalez
President
McDonald's East Division

▲ With exhibits such as antique car shows, Historic Yellow Springs has been preserved for the enjoyment of the community and everyone who visits.

▲ Colorful foliage highlights fall in Core Creek Park. Located in Bucks County, the park offers visitors a myriad of recreational activities through each season.

NovaCare Rehabilitation

"Although NovaCare Rehabilitation has more than 500 centers in 30 states, Philadelphia is one of our top markets. Our goal is to make a positive difference everyday for our patients, customers, and employees through excellence in clinical care and customer service. Our relationship with Philadelphia has allowed us to do this on a wide scale through partnerships with city organizations, area employers, professional sports teams, colleges and universities, insurance providers, and of course, the medical community."

Edward R. Miersch
President
NovaCare Rehabilitation

▲ Philadelphia's Center City link to New Jersey, the Benjamin Franklin Bridge
is as much a defining masterpiece as it is a critical link in transportation.

The Philadelphia Eagles

"You have to be willing to do whatever it takes to be the best; otherwise it's not worth doing. And you have to be willing to make aggressive, informed—perhaps controversial—decisions. That's the way to build a champion in any business.

"The people whom I refer to as 'championship makers' are extremely focused, demand excellence, and have a philosophy that they believe in and stick with.

"Prominently displayed in our headquarters is a quote to that effect from Charles Lindbergh: 'The important thing is to start…to lay a plan, and then follow it step by step, no matter how small or large each one by itself may seem.'"

Jeffrey Lurie
Chairman & CEO
The Philadelphia Eagles

▲ The development of Avenue of the Arts was a cooperative effort of the Commonwealth of Pennsylvania, the City, and many communities and organizations.

Philadelphia International Airport

"In every aspect of our operation we remind each visitor to our Airport of what a truly wonderful place Philadelphia is. This is demonstrated in our emphasis on Philadelphia area artists in our exhibitions program; the tremendous variety of Philadelphia shops and restaurants represented in our award-winning retail program; and the wealth of local talent we display regularly through our entertainment offerings. I believe Philadelphia is truly one of the great cities of the world and that this is reflected in Philadelphia International Airport."

Charles J. Isdell, Jr.
Director of Aviation
Philadelphia International Airport

Philadelphia Phillies

"Philadelphia is a special place—a major, world-class city with the spirit and warmth of a small town. We have unsurpassed attractions—universities, museums, and historical institutions, surrounded by intimate neighborhoods where everybody knows everyone else. Our sports fans have the same passion for our professional teams as a small town has for its local high school team. Similarly, we have a world-class business community, with a tradition of knowing and caring about each other. I am very proud, and extremely fortunate, to have lived and worked in Philadelphia my entire life."

David P. Montgomery
General Partner and President
Philadelphia Phillies

Public Financial Management

"Leadership is the art of making people think they can accomplish more together than they can as individuals. A leader needs to be able to draw on the strengths of individuals to create a team second to none. At PFM the quality most responsible for our success is our ability to work together in the diverse environment of 21st century America."

Mr. John White
CEO and Managing Director
Public Financial Management

▲ The nation's staggering debt and high inflation after the War of 1812 compelled President Madison to authorize the Second Bank of the United States in 1816.

▲ The stately old Customs Building towers over Philadelphia's historic district.

The Rubenstein Company, L.P.

"Many of our own very talented and highly motivated staff grew up and were educated in this terrific city. Others, who have relocated from out of state, remind me of a favorite saying, 'It is sometimes difficult to get people to relocate to Philadelphia; however, it is nearly impossible to get them to leave thereafter.' As a 'Philly'-based company, we have invested heavily here, backing our belief in the future of this City that we are proud to call 'Home'."

David B. Rubenstein
President & CEO
The Rubenstein Company, L.P.

Sunoco, Inc.

"Sunoco has been a part of the oil industry for more than a hundred years—through the rise of the automobile, the Great Depression, two world wars, oil shortages, and environmental challenges. But despite all of the changes that have occurred since the founding of Sunoco, the energy and other products we produce are still absolutely necessary to the American economy and way of life. We believe that America will continue to need petroleum products and chemicals far into the future. And as long as that holds true, Sunoco will be there to supply them."

John G. Drosdick
Chairman, CEO & President
Sunoco, Inc.

▲ Carpenters' Hall has served as a meeting place for the First Continental Congress, a hospital for troops, and an office for the Second Bank of the U.S.

Turner Construction

"For more than a century, Turner Construction has helped change the skyline of Philadelphia with our projects. Our status as a leader in the construction industry is a direct result of our dedication to excellence. This commitment to quality construction was the goal of our founder Howard Turner when he said, 'A promise made is a promise kept,' this commitment to quality can still be seen today in the actions of our leadership and staff."

John J. Fumosa
Vice President and General Manager, Philadelphia Office
Turner Construction

▲ The Liberty Bell, a well known icon of American history, received its name from a poem printed in the anti-slavery publication *The Liberator*.

Universal Health Services, Inc.

"Being a leader is more than just setting an agenda for the future of a company. Effective leaders must also establish goals to be achieved and standards of ethics to be followed. They must attract and retain the professionals needed and the capital necessary to accomplish the organization's goals. That will make it a success."

Alan B. Miller
President and CEO
Universal Health Services, Inc.

49

▲ Events in Philadelphia such as OpSail 2000 welcome visiting tallships from as far away as Lisbon, Portugal.

University of Pennsylvania

"The University of Pennsylvania, the country's first university, is proud to be located in Philadelphia, one of America's great cities and the birthplace of democracy. Our more than 20,000 students from around the country and the world, along with our extraordinary faculty, and talented staff, contribute to the richness and intellectual capital that has helped make Philadelphia a premier city that is truly on the move."

Judith Rodin
President
University of Pennsylvania

▲ Located on 650 acres, Tyler Arboretum, with an abundance of natural plant collections and several miles of marked hiking trails, is one of the largest and oldest in the nation,.

University of Pennsylvania Health System

"The University of Pennsylvania Health System continuously faces new challenges in the areas of technology, resource allocation, and payment issues. These challenges do nothing to dampen the outlook of UPHS's team members. Instead, they encourage innovation.

"We feel that the hard work, dedication, and resolve of the scores of men and women in our organization have helped us through a few very difficult years. All of us in the University of Pennsylvania Health System understand that excellence in patient care, research, and education depends on maintaining a sound financial foundation."

Robert D. Martin, Ph.D
CEO
University of Pennsylvania Health System

Wolf, Block, Schorr and Solis-Cohen LLP

"At WolfBlock, we're proud to have provided our clients with sound counsel since 1903. Through the hard work of many talented people, we've staked a clear leadership position in the legal community.

"Above all, leadership requires vision. Our forward-thinking approach allows us to serve as a catalyst for our clients.

"We are committed to a spirit of innovation, an unyielding appetite for work, an unwavering focus on ethics, and achieving exceptional results for our clients."

Mark Alderman
Chairman
Wolf, Block, Schorr and Solis-Cohen LLP

▲ The opening ceremonies of the Army-Navy football games are celebrated with military exercises including parachuting by the Navy Seals.

▶ A mounted police officer patrols the streets outside of City Hall with the statue of Major General John Fulton Reynolds standing guard behind her.

CHAPTER ONE

Cradle of Liberty

History is alive in Philadelphia—whether it's a reenactment of an historical event or new history being made. Visitors to the city frequently encounter the likes of Benjamin Franklin and George Washington when traipsing through Center City.

uropean settlement of the New World is the story of peoples seeking freedom from the shackles of religious and political inequities; it's the story of casting off centuries of Old World traditions to forge new freedoms in a land unfettered by monarchs and religious impositions. So it was when the Quakers, a relatively small but growing group of Christians in the British Isles, sought to climb out from under the pressures of the Church of England. Pressure to adhere solely to the Church of England peaked when England's Conventicle Act of 1664 outright forbade all religious gatherings and activities not associated with the Church of England.

The Quakers, who regarded all human beings as vessels of God, sought to emulate Christ by living humbly and simply, and to have a direct relationship with God. Their rejection of formal creed and a clergical hierarchy put them in a fundamentally severe opposition to the Church of England and, hence, England itself. The Quakers set

sail for the American colonies in the 1660s, settling primarily in New Jersey and Pennsylvania. Among these emigrants was William Penn, an Oxford graduate and son of Admiral William Penn. As payment of a debt owed to his deceased father, William Penn received from the crown a grant of territory in the Pennsylvania colony between the Delaware and Schuylkill Rivers in 1681. Once he arrived in Pennsylvania, Penn began carrying out his plans to build the "City of Brotherly Love." Recalling the bubonic plague in London in 1665 and a catastrophic fire that swept through the city a year later, Penn decided to design a "greene Country Towne" that would not succumb to such urban disasters. He chose the name "Philadelphia" in advance, determined the exact site for the city, drew a street plan, and designated plots for homes.

The Quaker brand of toleration and respect for all humans gave Philadelphia its seemingly magnetic force, attracting people of all

◀ **Irish-born Commodore John Barry was considered the "Father of the American Navy" by his contemporaries. The first to capture a British war vessel at sea, he was known for his humanity toward his men, as well as his enemies. His accomplishments include being credited with establishing a uniform signal system between ships and fighting the last naval battle of the American Revolution in 1783.**

▼ **Fifty-six delegates from all the American colonies except Georgia convened for the First Continental Congress at Carpenters' Hall on September 5, 1774, to discuss the escalating tensions between them and the Crown. Part of Independence National Historical Park, the building, still owned and operated by the Carpenter's Company, served as a guild for carpenters and their families in the colonial era.**

◀ 5 7

▲ Renewed pride in the American flag casts an even brighter light on the place where it was first sewn—the historic home of Betsy Ross. In the summer of 1776, Ross, a widow who was running her own struggling upholstery and sewing business, was approached by three representatives from the Continental Congress. History was made when the men showed Betsy a design of the new flag, and she demonstrated how to cut a five-pointed star with a single clip of the scissors.

races and faiths to the prospering city. Philadelphia was incorporated as a city in 1701. By 1720, the population crossed the 10,000 mark. The city's most famous resident, Benjamin Franklin, moved to Philadelphia from Boston in 1729, where he lived and legislated in the city for the rest of his life. As one of the most brilliant and influential thinkers of all time, Franklin helped establish the cultural and civic sophistication of the colonial city and later became instrumental in stewarding the American colonies to independence.

▲ "Proclaim Liberty Throughout All the Land unto All the Inhabitants Thereof. Leviticus XXV:X" The inscription on the Liberty Bell, housed in Independence National Historical Park, tells precisely of its purpose. The bell was rung on July 8, 1776, after the first public reading of the Declaration of Independence.

◀ While most visitors flock to Independence Hall to see the Liberty Bell, the park always is alive with demonstrations and reenactments of life in the colonies. Town Criers, the eighteenth-century equivalent of a news bulletin, kept townspeople informed on the latest political, social, and economic news.

By the middle of the eighteenth century, Philadelphia became embroiled, along with the rest of the colony, in rapidly escalating disputes and hostilities with the Crown. Philadelphia's status as the largest city in the American colonies, together with its strategic location and urban sophistication, made it the perfect location from which a nation's history would unfold. In 1774, an intercolonial assembly of delegates met at Carpenters' Hall in Philadelphia to draft a course of action in response to the "Intolerable Acts" passed by England as a punishment of sorts for the Boston Tea Party. The congress issued a petition to King George III called the *Declaration of Rights and Grievances* in an attempt to restore a level of harmony between the Crown and the colonies. The Second Continental Congress planned to

▲ More than three centuries of change have done little to alter the face of Elfreth's Alley, America's oldest residential street. Though deeply set in the vibrant pulse of modern Philadelphia, the street and its thirty-three houses have changed little since the first brick was laid in 1702. Sea captains, shipwrights, and colonial artisans originally inhabited Elfreth's Alley. Later, immigrants and laborers occupied many of the homes. Today, upscale urban professionals have chosen this historic neighborhood as their own.

reconvene on May 10, 1775, in Philadelphia if England failed to respond satisfactorily to the petition. Before that date, however, British soldiers invaded the Massachusetts colony and the siege of Boston was underway. On July 2, 1776, Thomas Jefferson penned the Declaration of Independence in Philadelphia. It was adopted by the Congress on July 4, and read to the public on July 8. Thereafter, the Liberty Bell was rung. Its resonance originated in Philadelphia, but it was a sound that transcended all space and time.

The following decade found Philadelphia the focus of attention in all the Western hemisphere. Marching twelve men deep, the Continental Army made an impressive display as it progressed through Philadelphia on August 24, 1777. It moved down Front Street and then west on Chestnut. The British were encroaching on Philadelphia and invasion appeared imminent. The Continental Army met the redcoats at Chadds Ford on the Brandywine Creek on September 11, and the two armies engaged in battle. General George Cornwallis and his army of eighteen thousand men effectively pushed General George Washington's men, numbering approximately eleven thousand, into retreat. News of the defeat quickly reached Philadelphia, twenty-five miles northeast, and set residents in a rush to scour the city of army supplies and anything else that might be endangered or used to the benefit of the British. It was at this time the Liberty Bell was lifted and carried to Allentown for safekeeping.

Philadelphia's capture dealt a severe blow to the Revolution, and for a time even Washington thought the American cause would fail. Though it may have faltered, Washington's vision of independence for the colonies never failed. His determination to see the American cause succeed inspired him and his troops to endure the harsh winter of 1778 at Valley Forge. It wasn't until the United States ratified an alliance with France that the British clutch on Philadelphia weakened.

In 1782, once independence was won and relations with England were mended, Philadelphia and the rest of the new nation faced the task of restoring normality to the area while forging the

◀ 61

▲ Every town and city has a popular gathering spot—a coffeehouse, bar, or restaurant where locals meet, politicians debate, and businessmen negotiate. So it was in the eighteenth century when Adams, Franklin, Jefferson, Revere, and Washington gathered at the City Tavern (also known as the Merchant's Coffee House). The Tory sympathizers even reveled here when the British occupied Philadelphia. The original tavern was destroyed by fire in 1854, but the building was reconstructed in 1975.

▶ Physick House, an imposing four-story brick house built in 1786 by wine importer Henry Hill, was the home of Dr. Philip Syng Physick from 1815 to 1837. The father of American surgery, Dr. Physick was one of the doctors who bravely stayed in Philadelphia during the yellow fever epidemic to care for those stricken by the disease. The Federal-style Physick House is the only freestanding house in Society Hill.

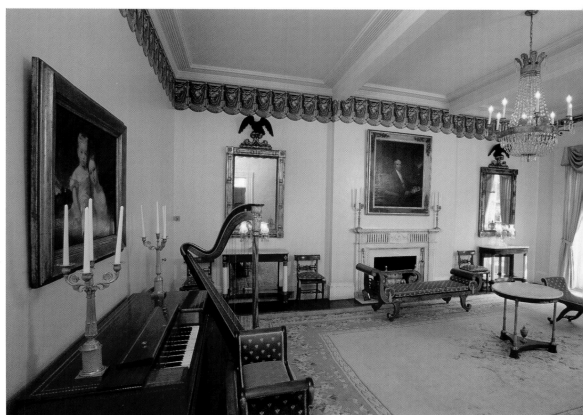

▲ (and Opposite) In 1855, city officials dedicated a vast tract of land along the Schuylkill River for public use as a park, partly to protect the purity of the city's water supply. Encompassing 4,180 acres, Fairmount Park is the nation's largest landscaped park. Among its many features is a group of eighteenth- and early nineteenth-century houses and mansions, established as country retreats by prominent Philadelphians and now preserved by a number of civic and private organizations as inspiring examples of the city's earlier heritage.

social, political, and intellectual charters and institutions of the new republic. Although it served as the seat of the Continental Congress, Philadelphia officially became the first capital of the United States in 1790 and remained as such until 1800.

The nineteenth century presented several new challenges for Philadelphia. Yellow Fever epidemics had ravaged the city in 1793, 1794, 1796, 1797, and 1798 and reemerged in the 1800s, with outbreaks of Cholera, Typhus, and Small Pox also posing immense challenges to the city's medical professionals.

Waves of immigrants arrived in the city: people left Ireland in scores during the potato famine, arriving in Philadelphia at roughly the same time as waves of Germans escaping political turmoil. By the middle of the century, one-third of the city's population was foreign born, with approximately 75 percent of them hailing from Ireland and Germany. Waves of Jewish immigrants—mostly small merchants—arrived from Central and Eastern Europe, attracted to the Jewish neighborhoods of Philadelphia already established in the previous century. Blacks escaping the tyranny of slavery from the American South continued to arrive in the ethnically tolerant city as they had done for nearly a hundred years. The newcomers provided the manpower needed for the Industrial Revolution now underway in Philadelphia. In fact, the urbanized part of Philadelphia County swelled to more than half a million inhabitants by 1850, making it one of the world's truly enormous cities.

Since Philadelphia sat so close to the Mason-Dixon line, fears mounted as civil war loomed on the horizon. Sympathies were initially split between the North and South, mirroring in many ways

the tensions that arose between the Loyalists and Patriots a century earlier. Although business as usual was imperiled by the war, for the most part Philadelphia remained unscathed and industrious. In true Quaker fashion, the city had a key role in the abolitionist movement both politically and ethically. Philadelphia also played a critical part as a material supplier of Union troops. The city's industrial function continued at an accelerated pace even after the war had ended.

In 1876, Philadelphia hosted America's first international fair in celebration of the nation's one-hundredth birthday. Following the precedent set by Ben Franklin, many social and civic clubs continued to form, bringing together people of like civic and intellectual interests, and enhancing the cultural life of the city. Among the most notable of these are: the Philadelphia Club, the city's oldest men's club; the Rabbit, established by members who paired their love of driving with a love of bucolic getaways; the Racquet Club, for members with a penchant for cricket, polo, tennis, and other competition; the New Century Club, benefiting "self-supporting women;" the Plastic Club, an art association for women; the Cosmopolitan Club, an

organization that sought "easy and frequent contracts" for artistically and intellectually talented women; and the Pen and Pencil Club, the oldest continually operating press club in America.

While such clubs upheld Benjamin Franklin's ideals of camaraderie and debate, they were also thread to strengthen the seams of an ethnically and intellectually diverse society. Immigrants from Europe and Asia continued to settle in Philadelphia, and like so many other ethnically diverse enclaves of America, witnessed their share of racial and ethnic tension. World Wars I and II, the Korean War, and the Vietnam War brought both unanimity and division to the nation, but each time, William Penn's vision of Philadelphia came through. Today, Philadelphia is one of the most well-preserved cities in the country, with each setback and triumph leaving its indelible impression. It is a city that perceives problems as challenges, and has a remarkable record of finding logical and timely solutions to the obstacles it faces. ℗

◀ Built between 1727 and 1754 and still possessing an active congregation, Christ Church stands as monument to unshakable faith through centuries of war and peace and to the timeless beauty of colonial architecture and craftsmanship. While not open to the public on a regular basis, Christ Church Cemetery is visible through the church fence. The fascinating cemetery and churchyard are the burial place of Benjamin Franklin and his wife, Deborah, seven signers of the Declaration of Independence, four signers of the Constitution, and many colonists young and old.

▲ The majestic Cathedral-Basilica of Saints Peter and Paul on 17th and Parkway is one of the most stunning structures in Philadelphia. The Roman-Corinthian style cathedral was completed in 1864 and still possesses an active Catholic clergy and congregation.

▲ (and Previous page) Valley Forge National Historical Park represents the staggering sacrifices made in America's fight for freedom and the unwavering dedication to the idea of liberty and self-governance. It was in Valley Forge that General George Washington's Continental Army trained to a level of military competence sufficient to overcome the British and gain independence in 1783. Washington's headquarters were located at Valley Forge.

▶ While much of Philadelphia is experienced in tours of historic buildings and stately museums, a lot of Philadelphia's past is brought to life with stirring re-enactments of both everyday life in the colonies and key historical events. Colonial and Revolutionary War-era reenactors can be seen throughout the Greater Philadelphia Area at most historical sites on important dates and in Center City year-round.

◀ (and Below) After Washington's troops were defeated at Brandywine, General William Howe led 20,000 British and Hessian (German) troops into Philadelphia to resupply, while a fleet of ships on the Delaware River held the British supplies. However, General Thomas Mifflin and his men took over and fortified the partially constructed British fort that patrolled the Delaware before the troops arrived. The British attacked Fort Mifflin, and it finally fell in November of 1777, but not before heavy British losses and the pivotal delay it caused them.

▲ Before 1834, merchants, seafarers, and other businessmen conducted business at the London Coffee House, and later, the City Tavern near the city docks. After the turn of the century, however, Philadelphia's business community grew in pace with the city's booming economy, and it was clear that a new center for business was needed. A group of trustees gathered to plan and construct the new Merchant's Exchange building on South 3rd at Walnut and Dock Streets. William Strickland designed the elegant Greek Revival building, which served as a commercial exchange building until it was purchased by Independence National Historical Park in 1952. INHP maintains offices there to this day.

▶ The Second Bank of the United States was authorized by President Madison after the War of 1812, when the U.S. was left with staggering debt and spiraling inflation. The bank's twenty-year charter helped stabilize the nation's volatile economy. Constructed between 1818 and 1824, the Greek revival building was modeled after the Parthenon in Greece. The stunning Portrait Gallery, a must-see for all visitors to Philadelphia, showcases the prominent faces and figures of eighteenth-century politics.

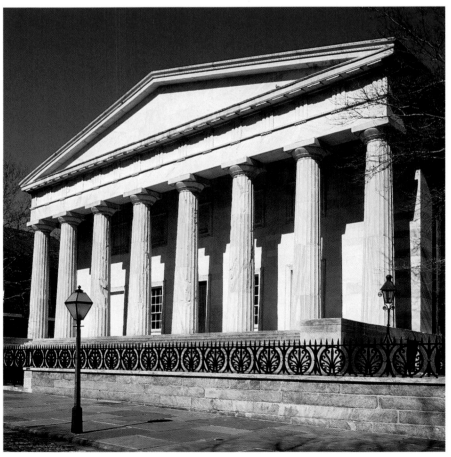

▲ Penn's Landing encompasses the spot on the waterfront of the Delaware River where city founder William Penn first set foot after sailing from England. As Philadelphia grew, Penn's Landing became the city's dominant commercial district. Today, the waterfront park is a hub of tourism and the site of cultural events that take place here throughout the year. A monument to explorer Christopher Columbus is but one of several features at Penn's Landing.

◀ In the venerable old Congress Hall, constructed between 1787 and 1789, so much American history unfurled. The Hall served as the meeting place for the U.S. Congress from 1790 to 1800. The House of Representatives met on the main floor and the Senate convened upstairs in the Senate Chamber (pictured here), where George Washington was sworn into his second term as President.

▲ Established by Congress in 1988 as an independent, nonpartisan, nonprofit organization, the National Constitution Center (NCC) seeks to promote awareness and increase understanding of the U.S. Constitution. As part of the NCC, the first museum ever devoted exclusively to the Constitution and its role in American society is under construction. The museum is scheduled to open on July 4, 2003, and will be situated on Independence Mall next to the Liberty Bell and Independence Hall.

◄ The new Independence Visitor Center at 6th and Market Streets heralded the ongoing improvements of Independence Mall, and is a conjunction of the Independence National Historical Park and Philadelphia Visitor Center. The 50,000-square-foot facility provides all the information visitors need for an enlightening and enjoyable visit to the park and all of Philadelphia.

▼ "When the wells dry, we know the worth of water," said Benjamin Franklin, who in 1801 proposed a common water system for the city. Inadequate facilities and pollution of the Schuylkill River were the main issues that motivated Franklin's idea. The site for the new facility—the first municipal waterworks in the country—was set at the foot of Faire Mount where the Philadelphia Museum of Art now is located. Subsequent expansion to keep pace with Philadelphia's exploding population resulted in construction of the world's longest dam and a pumping facility so spectacular it drew tourists from all over the world. The land and houses along the river that were purchased by the city to protect the water supply became Fairmount Park.

Philadelphia celebrates the tradition and heritage of the high seas through events that welcome tallships from throughout the world including the *NE Sagres* from Lisbon, Portugal.

CHAPTER TWO

Workshop of the World

Constructed in 1897 by the Fairmount Park Trolley Company, the
Strawberry Mansion Bridge recently reopened in 2001 after massive
restorations. The bridge extends over the Schuylkill River and is a glowing
model of Philadelphia's urban revitalization.

deals of tolerance and equality instituted by the Quakers in Philadelphia opened the city's doors to an international population, for it was here that people from all corners of the world could settle and prosper and still feel as if they were a welcome part of the community. With every trickle and wave of immigration came people with skills and talents, eager to earn their pay and contribute to the immense industrial engine that Philadelphia had rapidly become. Abundant natural resources provided fuel and raw materials; the city's port kept the region open to maritime trade; and, later, the railroads were hammered in place, extending Philadelphia's movement of materials and manufactured goods to New England, the Southern states, the Midwest, and the Pacific.

Philadelphia's transformation into an industrial giant occurred at an accelerated pace after the Civil War and during the early years of the twentieth century, thanks mostly to the almighty railroad. It was in Philadelphia that a brilliant young printer named Matthias Baldwin developed a way to double pressure in a steam engine—a feat that ended America's reliance on British-made locomotives forever. In fact, until his death in 1866, Baldwin had made fifteen hundred steam locomotives, and each one was better than its predecessors. Such advancements

78 ▶

▲ The Greater Philadelphia Area is an ideal home for businesses of all sizes. Airmatic, Inc., a leading distributor of industrial products, equipment, and services, is a prime example how small business can thrive in a city the size of Philadelphia. The company has remained a local, family-run operation since 1944.

▶ The 1.3-million-square-foot Pennsylvania Convention Center, situated in the heart of downtown Philadelphia, has played a critical role in the city's economy since it opened in 1993. The Convention Center's top-notch facilities draw more than five million people annually for meetings, shows, and other events. The need to accommodate and entertain the visitors set in motion the revitalization of downtown Philadelphia with the Avenue of the Arts project, the opening of the Kimmel Center, and myriad world-class hotels, restaurants, theaters, museums, galleries, and shops. The area around the Convention Center has since become a tourist destination in its own right.

◀ The Greater Philadelphia Chamber of Commerce has addressed the needs of the business community and the community at large for over two hundred years. One of its services is the annual Business Expo. Held at the Pennsylvania Convention Center, Philadelphia's Business Expo is the largest trade show of its kind in the region. The Expo provides an opportunity for hundreds of exhibitors to showcase their products to thousands of business leaders and executives.

enhanced Philadelphia's role as a crossroads of commerce; by 1874, the Pennsylvania Railroad was the largest corporation in the country and would stay that way for many years to come.

While Philadelphia had plants to manufacture almost every conceivable household item, textiles emerged as the dominant industry at the turn of the century. The city's proximity to its fashion-frenzied neighbor New York and its relatively close position to the cotton fields of the South were two factors contributing to this economic evolution. By 1904, nearly 20 percent of the city's 7,100 manufacturers produced textiles, employing nearly 40 percent of the workforce. John B. Stetson's big felt hats became an icon of the American West, and Philadelphia's carpets were coveted everywhere. Progress has its costs, however. The enormous success of industry in Philadelphia was turning Penn's "greene Country Towne" into a smoky proliferation of brick and concrete, and it would be several decades before massive attempts to clean up were underway.

◀ Since the Greater Philadelphia Area encompasses one of the busiest port systems in North America, the Philadelphia Coast Guard is a vital part of overseeing its safety and security. Prior to September 11, 2001, the Coast Guard concentrated on protecting the waters from illegal fishing and drug smugglers, while enforcing laws or rescuing those in peril. Today, the Coast Guard plays a crucial role in President Bush's Homeland Security plan by patrolling the waters near Philadelphia in search of anyone that might threaten the nation's safety.

▼ The Delaware River's contribution to the economy of the Greater Philadelphia Area can hardly be overstated. While the economy has moved from manufacturing to high-tech industries and life sciences, the river remains a key player in the movement of people and goods, whether for commerce or for recreation.

◀ 81

▲ In April of 2000, the Kvaerner-Philadelphia Shipyard began laying the keel in the production of its first ship at its shipbuilding facilities on the Delaware River in Philadelphia. Kvaerner has its origins in Norway, where it built its first gas carrier in 1955. Today, the company is one of the leading builders of cruise ships, LNG/LPG carriers, and container vessels in the world. Beyond Norway, the company's primary shipbuilding facilities are located in Finland, Germany, and Philadelphia.

Now that the nation has moved beyond the industrial era, steam-powered, coal-burning Philadelphia has become a hub for the technologies of tomorrow. Many of the same factors that contributed to Philadelphia's immense industrial success allowed it to evolve into one of the country's largest and most concentrated hubs for high-tech and biotech business. First, the city's location on the eastern seaboard midway between Washington, D.C. and New York makes it a viable location for a company of any kind to locate. Philadelphia

lies on the I-95 corridor, the "Main Street" of the East coast from Maine to Florida, and it also is transected by I-76, the main east-west route.

An extensive system of subway rails, trains, busses, and trolleys operated by the Southeastern Pennsylvania Transit Authority (SEPTA) allows commuters to be easily and affordably connected between home and office with more than one million passenger trips each day. The fifth largest transit authority in the country, SEPTA operates throughout Philadelphia, Delaware, Chester, Montgomery, and Bucks Counties. The Port Authority Transit Company (PATCO) Hi-Speedline moves passengers to and from Central City and the communities of South Jersey.

Shortly after its founding, Philadelphia became an important port city, and the Port of Philadelphia and Camden is currently the most

◀ (and Below) With the opening of Kvaerner-Philadelphia Shipyard's ship-building facilities on the Delaware River, Philadelphia is poised to become one of the world's leading shipbuilding cities. The Port of Philadelphia is one of the most active on the Atlantic Coast and the fourth largest handler of imported cargo in the nation, with more than 3,000 ships visiting the port each year to load and unload goods. Keeping the watery venues of the Delaware open to the world, the river ports in the Philadelphia region maintain the city's status as a major center of international commerce.

◀ 83

◀ Philadelphia is the fifth largest city in the U.S., and the Philadelphia metropolitan area is the fourth largest in the country. With the booming local economy continually attracting business to the area, new construction sites can be found in every part of the city.

▲ Investment firms and high-tech companies find an ideal business climate in Philadelphia due to the city's proximity to Washington, D.C., and New York City; its highly educated workforce; a flourishing community of business incubators; an entrepreneurial spirit; and a rich quality of life.

active port on the North Atlantic Coast for total cargo handled. By keeping the watery venues of the Delaware open to the world, the river ports in the Philadelphia region maintain the city's status as a major center of international commerce. The Delaware River Port Authority, which owns and operates the Ben Franklin, Betsy Ross, Commodore Barry, and Walt Whitman Bridges, also took over operation of the RiverLink Ferry system connecting Philadelphia with Camden, New Jersey. Additionally, the Philadelphia Regional Port Authority, operating the Port of Philadelphia, facilitates trade between Philadelphia and its major trading partners—the NAFTA countries, the United Kingdom, Japan, Chile, Germany, France, and Italy.

The world also arrives in Philadelphia through Philadelphia International Airport. The airport serves more than twenty-five million passengers annually with approximately a thousand daily flights. In recent years, the airport has kept pace with Philadelphia's rapidly expanding global market with greater than $1 billion in terminal expansion projects and improvements, the most recent of which was the construction of an 800,000-square-foot, 4-level international terminal with thirteen new gates. Built at a cost of $450 million, the new terminal opened in the fall of 2002.

While Philadelphia's transportation infrastructure—be it ground, water, or air—makes the city an ideal home for business, other aspects of the community have helped forge a path to a bright future in technology markets. Greater Philadelphia has one of the highest concentrations of academic institutions in the United States. The presence of two Ivy League universities—The University of Pennsylvania and Princeton—and nearly one hundred other top-rated colleges and tech schools amount to one of the most educated workforces in America.

Philadelphia's vast intellectual resources lure companies of all types to the area, but the effect has been most remarkable in the high-tech and biotechnology markets. With approximately a quarter million technology workers, Philadelphia ranks sixth in the country for high-tech employment. The area now serves as corporate headquarters to several important technology firms including SAP, Unisys, SunGuard Data Systems, Bluestone Software, Systems and Computer Technology, VerticalNet, Internet Capital Group, and several others. The conglomerate of technology companies in Philadelphia represents breakthroughs in hardware and software developments, information technology, and e-business.

After a two-and-a-half-year absence due to renovations, "Your Move" art has been reinstalled in the plaza of the Municipals Services Building on Broad Street. These enormous works of art—designed to be playing pieces from classic games such as chess, checkers, and dominoes—are interesting conversation pieces as well as art figures.

▶ Philadelphia's Antique Row stretches along Pine Street between 9th and 12th in the historic Washington Square district. Strolling amongst eras of art and furnishings, serious collectors and curious browsers alike find shopping on Antique Row interesting and unusual, much like a quick trip back in time.

▼ With its cobblestone streets, carefully tended gardens, quaint shops, boutiques and galleries, fine restaurants and cafés, Chestnut Hill is one of the Philadelphia's area's most attractive suburbs. Many of the independently owned stores along Germantown Avenue and other corners of Chestnut Hill have been owned by the same families for generations. The community is registered as a National Historic District.

▲ Situated in Fairmount Park, Valley Green Inn is open year-round except for Christmas Day, and offers a variety of amenities, including weddings and banquets, in a natural setting, while providing a peaceful respite in the bustling heart of Philadelphia. Like all of the premises in Fairmount Park, the Inn is owned by the city of Philadelphia.

With such a dense concentration of technology firms and a proportionally large number of workers employed as scientists, engineers, and other technology professionals, it's not surprising that Greater Philadelphia registers more wired households than New York, Los Angeles, Chicago, and several other major urban centers. Recent analysis shows that nearly 60 percent of Philadelphia's households are connected to the Internet—a number that continues to climb steadily each year.

Philadelphia's high-tech business community, together with its advantageous position as the home of some of the world's most groundbreaking medical colleges and hospitals, have positioned it as a global leader in biotechnology, life sciences, and pharmaceutical research and development. Philadelphia graduates more medical doctors than any other city in America, and nearly 14 percent of its workforce is employed in healthcare services. The city's numerous academic resources, its outstanding medical facilities, and the immense pool of skilled medical professionals create an ideal home for biotech firms and pharmaceutical companies. Currently, 80 percent of the world's largest pharmaceutical companies have operations in the Greater Philadelphia Area. A younger generation of firms engaged in the life sciences, spurred by unparalleled investments from bio-venture capital and billions of dollars in government

contributions, have made Greater Philadelphia home to one of the country's largest concentrations of biotech and pharmaceutical companies. In fact, 80 percent of the nation's pharmaceutical employment is located within a 50-mile radius of Philadelphia. As the birthplace of American medicine, Philadelphia is appropriately postured to lead the world in the medical technologies of the future. ℗

▲ Philadelphia company PlantGenix is a sterling example of the city's innovative bio tech and life sciences community. Founded in 1999, the company "harvests the power of plants" through scientific development and application. PlantGenix develops plants with longer, healthier lives, controlled aging and ripening, and the ability to produce and store chemicals and pharmaceuticals for use in agriculture, environmental safety, and medicine.

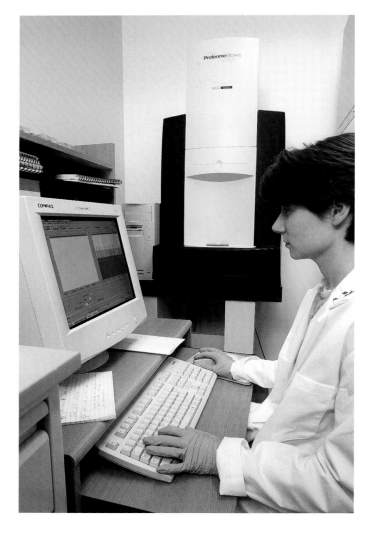

▲ Phillips Mushrooms Farms sells more mushrooms per year than any other farm in the U.S. The company began cultivating mushrooms in Kennett Square, Pennsylvania, in 1927. For more than fifty years, three generations of Phillips have pioneered the science of mushroom cultivation, making Kennett Square the "Mushroom Capital of the World." In 1980, the company began experimenting with growing shiitake mushrooms. Today, after divesting its white button mushroom operations, Phillips sells more than thirty million pounds of specialty mushrooms every year.

◀ Tastykakes, especially of the Butterscotch kind, are a Philadelphia legend. The bakery turns out 439,000 Butterscotch Krimpets every day (109 million a year). In fact, just one-third of that output would be enough to pave a three-foot-wide sidewalk with Butterscotch Krimpets all the way from Center City to Atlantic City. Aside from Butterscotch Krimpets, Tastykakes is known for its cupcakes, KandyKakes, pies, donuts, and coffee cakes (pictured).

▲ Rococo Restaurant is located in the lavishly refurbished National Corn Exchange Bank, a stately historical building on Chestnut Street. The "destination" restaurant opened in October of 1996 when downtown revitalization efforts were well underway. Such exquisite dining establishments led *Conde Nast Traveler* magazine readers to name Philadelphia as the "best restaurant city" in the United States.

▶ Located at One Avenue of the Arts, The Ritz-Carlton Philadelphia sits in the heart of the city's arts and entertainment district. The grand hotel occupies the former Mellon Bank Rotunda and Tower, two landmark historic buildings.

▶ (Opposite) Philadelphia's skyline underwent a colossal transformation when the towering skyscrapers of Liberty Place were completed—Liberty Place One opened in 1987 and Liberty Place Two in 1992. The stunning, sapphire-blue buildings were the first in Philadelphia to rise higher than the statue of William Penn atop City Hall. In addition to providing office space to a number of corporate clients, Liberty Place also contains more than sixty specialty shops, making it one of Center City's prime shopping destinations.

▲ Philadelphia International Airport serves over twenty-five million passengers annually with approximately a thousand daily flights. The Airport has kept pace with Philadelphia's expanding global market by allocating over $1 billion to terminal expansion projects and improvements.

▼ Philadelphia is serviced by Amtrak's high-speed Acela train, which rolls along the Northeast corridor from Boston to Washington, D.C., at speeds of 150 miles per hour.

▶ Utilizing the historic 30th Street Station, Amtrak is a vital form of transportation in the Philadelphia area, along with an extensive system of subway rails, trains, busses, and trolleys operated by SEPTA. Together, Amtrak and SEPTA keep commuters easily and affordably connected between home and office with more than one million passenger trips each day. The fifth largest transit authority in the country, SEPTA operates throughout Philadelphia, Delaware, Chester, Montgomery, and Bucks Counties.

▲ Interstate 476, officially named Veterans Memorial Highway but
commonly referred to as the Blue Route, provides a quick connection
between I-95 and I-76 and expedites traffic flow through and around
Philadelphia.

CHAPTER THREE

A Cultural Masterpiece

Completed in 1876 to memorialize the nation's first centennial
celebration, Memorial Hall in Fairmount Park is a splendid, modern
renaissance-style building topped with a four-sided dome and a statue of
Columbia. The Great Hall in the rotunda features lavish marble floors,
sculptured columns, and a shimmering glass ceiling. Today, the building is
used primarily to host large events from weddings to business functions.

f the arts community can be seen as a measure of a city's
cultural sophistication and maturity, then Philadelphia can
rightfully assume its place as a national treasure. It is a city steeped
in artistic antiquity yet its new creative force continually manifests
itself in myriad museums, galleries, theaters and other performance
venues, art festivals, and special projects.

Perhaps the city's steadfast dedication to the arts may be illustrated
with another Philly first: The Walnut Street Theatre—the country's
oldest theater and, in some respects, the oldest permanently established theater in the English-speaking world. That the theater flour-
ished in a disapproving Quaker community might be considered
remarkable in itself. However, the theater continued to enthrall
audiences even at a time when the newly formed nation was caught
between the aftermath of the Revolutionary War and the escalating
hostilities of the War of 1812. In fact, President Thomas Jefferson
and the Marquis de Lafayette attended a performance of *The Rivals*,
the first theatrical production staged in the theater, in 1812.
Subsequent wars and crises did little to disrupt the popular theater,
and nothing to stop it. Today, the Walnut Street Theatre has been
staging performances continually for nearly two centuries.

Skip ahead to 1990s, and Philadelphia's dedication to the arts
culminates in an initiative to advance the arts on a massive scale—
The Avenue of the Arts Project. The revitalization plan, already several years old by the time it finally gained momentum in 1992,
called for the relocation of several major arts institutions to a stretch
of South Broad Street in the vicinity of a new multi-million dollar
convention center. Just as planned, the newly renovated blocks of
South Broad became home to new museums, galleries, theaters,
restaurants, hotels, and stores, and successfully filled the city center
with people.

The cornerstone of the Philadelphia's downtown revitalization
efforts was a $265-million Regional Performing Arts Center (RPAC),
sponsored by city and state funds and generous gifts from individual
and corporate philanthropists. Like the Avenue of the Arts Project, the
Regional Performing Arts Center advocated the arts in downtown
Philadelphia, leading to a natural
merger of the two plans in 1996. As
RPAC neared completion, committee
leaders announced that the new theater
complex would be named The Kimmel
Center for the Performing Arts in honor
of the project's chief contributor,
Philadelphia philanthropist Sidney
Kimmel, the founder and chairman of the
Jones Apparel Group, Inc.

◀ **(and Above and Opposite) The 125-year-
old Philadelphia Museum of Art in Fairmount
Park showcases a stunning collection comprised of some 300,000 works of art. The
Museum has kept the community in touch
with the arts through one of the most impressive collections in the world and with its educational programs for students of all ages.**

▲ An image of the Philadelphia Museum of Art became embedded in the minds of many Americans when Rocky ran victoriously up its steps in the 1976 blockbuster movie. The very image, appropriately enough, not only symbolized Philadelphia's extraordinary artistic heritage, it also divined the enormous role that the arts would have on the city's future success. From film and theater to painting and sculpture, the arts aren't just appreciated in Philadelphia—they're celebrated. The arts are also one of main reasons why so many people visit Philadelphia every year.

After a star-studded gala with numerous performances, fanfare, and confettied ceremonies, the Kimmel Center opened to the public on December 16, 2001. Today, the center provides, by contract, a centrally located, permanent home to the Philadelphia Orchestra, The Opera Company of Philadelphia, the Pennsylvania Ballet, The Chamber Orchestra of Philadelphia, the Philadelphia Chamber Music Society, PHILADANCO, American Theater Arts for Youth, Inc., and Peter Nero and the Philly Pops®. With 450,000 square feet,

the facility covers an entire city block and includes the twenty-five-hundred-seat Verizon Hall, the six-hundred-fifty-seat Perelman Theater, the Merck Arts Education Center, and a number of gathering spaces for the public. Visitors also have access to the Center's Commonwealth Plaza, a rooftop garden, restaurant, bar, and café, and a number of other elegant alcoves and open spaces overlooking the colorful Avenue of the Arts. Considering Philadelphia's long-standing devotion to the arts, the Kimmel Center will undoubtedly entertain audiences for generations to come.

The strength of the arts is indeed an inherent part of life in Philadelphia, a colossal presence that is always seen and felt. At the very heart of the city's artistic community is the Academy of the Arts, both an historical landmark and the training grounds of tomorrow's talent. In many ways, the development of the Academy echoes the evolution of the Kimmel Center, nineteenth-century style. Fueled by civic support and contributions from the public, construction of the Academy commenced in June of 1855. Two years later, the "Grand

▲ The Rodin Museum, administered by the Philadelphia Museum of Art, houses the largest collection of Rodin's work outside of Paris.

◀ Constructed in 1897, Rudolph Siemering's Washington Monument is one of the city's most impressive and beloved examples of public art. The two fountains that flank the monument are named for Captain John Ericsson, an inventor, engineer, and descendant of explorer Leif Ericsson, and Eli Kirk Price, Jr., an attorney who helped establish the Museum of Art. The four fountains guarded by native American animals represent the Delaware, Hudson, Mississippi, and Potomac Rivers. The monument's thirteen steps symbolize the original colonies.

Old Lady of Locust Street" opened to the public as an opulent opera house with an exterior that was "perfectly plain and simple like a Markethouse." Today, it continues to celebrate its tradition of operatic excellence and stands as America's oldest opera house.

Year after year, Philadelphia's schools for the arts set the stage for some of the most brilliant music and stage careers. The Curtis Institute of Music, widely hailed as one of the finest conservatories in the world, prepares students to become solo performers, composers, and conductors to the highest level of professional excellence. Curtis Institute alumni can be found in just about every major orchestra worldwide, and one quarter of the principal chairs of orchestras nationwide are held by Curtis Institute graduates.

The Academy of Vocal Arts maintains the highest standards of excellence in training the opera singers of tomorrow. The Academy was started in the wake of the Great Depression when very few students dared dream of such a profession, let alone pay for and pursue such an education. However, Helen Corning Warden, a local socialite, launched the school in 1934, and set about to make such a dream obtainable for promising students.

The University of the Arts, another revered historical arts institution, continues its contribution to the arts community both locally and globally. In 1876, the Philadelphia College of Art and the Philadelphia Museum of Art were established in response to local demand for arts education. The Philadelphia College of Performing Arts (formerly known as the Philadelphia Music Academy) grew out of the original college and became a separate institution in 1950, expanding to include the Philadelphia Dance Academy in 1976, and launching the School of Theater in 1983. The College of Art and the College of Performing Arts joined in 1985 to become the Philadelphia College of the Arts, and later, in 1987, was renamed the University of the Arts. The University has recently added a new College of Media and Communication and offers degrees in communication, writing for film and television, and multimedia.

The demand for specialized training in entertainment media and communication grows as Philadelphia has itself become a shining star on the silver screen. Under the leadership of Sharon Pinkenson, the Greater Philadelphia Film Institute seeks to attract film and video production of all kinds to the region. The institute offers a complete range of services that facilitate the production of everything from movies, television programs, music videos, commercials, and more. Largely because of the Institute's successful efforts in promoting Philadelphia within the film industry, the city was named by *MovieMaker* magazine in its list of the "10 Best Cities in North America for Moviemakers." While Philadelphia's filmography is too extensive to list, recent Hollywood hits filmed here include *Unbreakable* (2000), *The Sixth Sense* (1998), *Beloved* (1997), *Fallen* (1996), *12 Monkeys* (1995), *Up Close and Personal* (1995), and *Philadelphia* (1993).

Whether on screen or on canvas, art provides Philadelphia with a palette of colorful opportunities. Indeed, any city visitor with art on the agenda may become a little overwhelmed by the city's countless art museums, but a good place to start is always the Philadelphia Museum of Art, a worldwide showcase of three-hundred thousand exhibits of fine and applied arts of all ages. The Philadelphia Museum of Art also administers the Rodin Museum, which houses the largest collection of Rodin's work outside of Paris. The Pennsylvania Academy of Fine Arts, founded in 1805 by painter and scientist Charles Willson Peale, sculptor William Rush, and a group of other local artists and businessmen, is the oldest art museum in the country and is considered to have one of the finest collections of American art from the eighteenth, nineteenth, and twentieth centuries.

104 ▶

▲ The center of American Indian life, culture, and heritage in the Delaware Valley is the American Indian Cultural Center, located on Chestnut Street, just a short walk from the Liberty Bell. The Center contains an exhibit of American Indian crafts and a Trading Post where visitors can browse and buy Native American art, crafts, and jewelry. A statue of Tamamend, the Lenape Indian chief who greeted William Penn on his arrival, stands at Front and Market Streets.

▶ The creation of sculptor Evangelos Frudak, *The Signer* honors the sheer courage and determination of those men who signed the Declaration of Independence and the Constitution, risking everything they had by publicly defying the crown. The statue stands in Independence National Historical Park at 5th and Chestnut.

Some may find it surprising that a city so oriented toward high-tech business, medicine, and biotechnology would abound with such an unabashed appreciation—one might say adoration—of the arts. However, the presence of so many art museums, theaters, galleries, and institutions for the performing arts in Philadelphia not only serves as a testament to the city's balance, but to the well-rounded quality of life it holds for all residents. ℗

▲ (and Right) Playing in Verizon Hall of the Kimmel Center, the Philadelphia Orchestra began a new season in its new home in 2002. By contract, the Kimmel Center provides a centrally located, permanent residence to the Orchestra, as well as The Opera Company of Philadelphia, the Pennsylvania Ballet, The Chamber Orchestra of Philadelphia, the Philadelphia Chamber Music Society, PHILADANCO, American Theater Arts for Youth, Inc., and Peter Nero and the Philly Pops®.

◀ (and Below) With 450,000 square feet, the Kimmel Center covers an entire city block and includes the 2,500-seat Verizon Hall (pictured below), the 650-seat Perelman Theater, the Merck Arts Education Center, and a number of gathering spaces for the public. Visitors also have access to the Center's Commonwealth Plaza, a rooftop garden, restaurant, bar, and café, and a number of other elegant alcoves and open spaces overlooking the colorful Avenue of the Arts.

(Following page) One of the world's finest museums devoted to archaeology and anthropology in the world is the University of Pennsylvania Museum of Archaeology and Anthropology. A profound sense of antiquity permeates more than thirty galleries showcasing artifacts from ancient Egypt, Greece and Rome, Mesopotamia, Asia, and Mesoamerica.

◀ 107

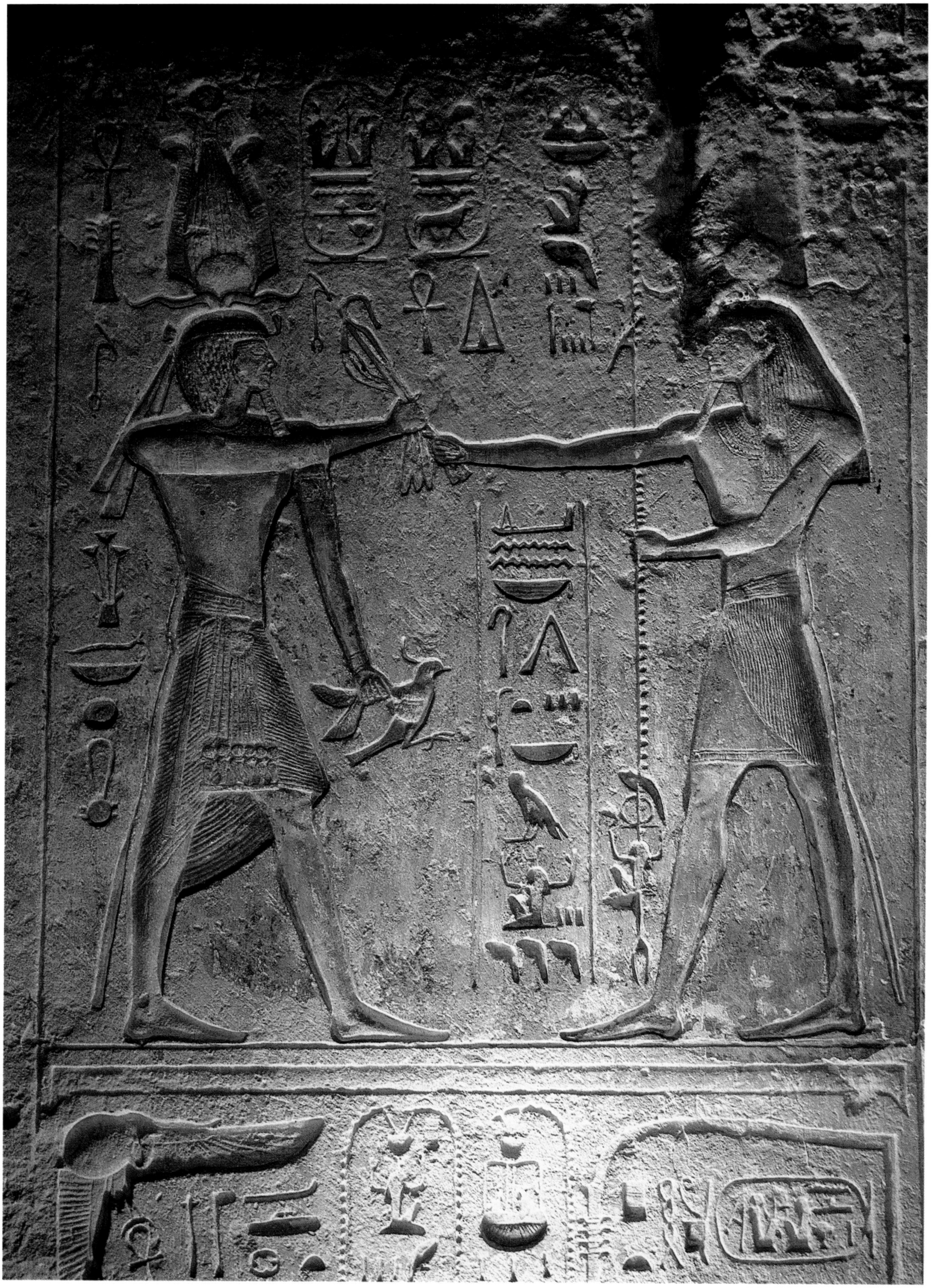

◀ The Pennsylvania Academy of Fine Arts, founded in 1805 by painter and scientist Charles Willson Peale, sculptor William Rush, and a group of other local artists and businessmen, is the oldest art school and museum in the country. Its collection of American art from the eighteenth, nineteenth, and twentieth centuries is one of the finest in the world.

▼ In 1805, the core curriculum for students at the Pennsylvania Academy of Fine Arts was the study of plaster casts of classical statues housed in the Louvre. Drawing of live models began around 1812. Here, art students at the Academy use an equine model in painting class.

▲ (and Right) The Rosenbach Museum & Library houses one of America's finest collections of rare books and manuscripts, including James Joyce's *Ulysses*, Charles Dickens's *Pickwick Papers*, and Joseph Conrad's *Lord Jim*. The historic townhouse is also home to an impressive and eclectic collection of art, artifacts, and eighteenth- and nineteenth-century furnishings, all of which were the property of two brothers, Dr. A.S.W. and Philip Rosenbach.

▲ Swedish settlers arrived in the Philadelphia area around 1639, years before William Penn's arrival. Today, the local Swedish community is still thriving and immensely proud of its heritage. Philadelphia's American Swedish Historical Museum opened in 1926 and is the oldest Swedish museum in the U.S. Its twelve permanent galleries offer visitors a glimpse of the fascinating history and traditions of Philadelphia's Swedish community.

◀ The African-American Museum opened in Philadelphia in 1976, and continues its purpose of collecting and preserving the material and intellectual culture of African Americans in Philadelphia, the Delaware Valley, the Commonwealth of Pennsylvania, and other parts of the Americas. Over 400,000 objects and displays document the African-American experience in all realms of life from family life to the Civil Rights movement, arts and entertainment, sports, medicine, architecture, politics, religion, law, and technology.

▲ (and Right) The Avenue of the Arts project called for the relocation of several major arts institutions to a stretch of South Broad Street in the vicinity of the new multi-million dollar Pennsylvania Convention Center. The Kimmel Center for the Performing Arts was established and the newly renovated blocks of South Broad became home to new museums, galleries, theaters, restaurants, hotels, and stores. Once again, the city center was full of life.

▲ Few cities in the world possess such an unabashed love of art as Philadelphia. On nearly every street, one will see a building, fountain, monument, museum, theater, or painting paying tribute to the human imagination and beautifying public venues.

◀ Splendor of Florence, a traveling showcase of artisans and artwork from Florence, Italy, opened to the public in Philadelphia in October 2001. Despite a postponement after September 11, 2001, the show attracted more than 15,000 people daily. The Philadelphia Museum of Art hosted the show's priceless art from the Uffizi Gallery, the highlight of which was a collection of Renaissance-era paintings of the Medici family.

▲ Not all theatrical companies embrace the tried and true. The Wilma Theater proudly considers itself to be "A theater company that combines the boldness of a space explorer with the precision of a master craftsman." Since 1973, the Wilma Theater has enriched Philadelphia's cultural scene with its avant-garde performances and its development of local artists.

◀ Pennsylvania Ballet is widely considered one of the finest ballet companies in the United States. The school and company have been a Philadelphia institution since 1963, and its troupe of forty dancers enchants audiences with performances of traditional favorites such as *The Nutcracker* and *Giselle* in addition to at least one world premier each year.

▼ The "Grand Old Lady of Locust Street" opened to the public in 1855 as an opulent opera house with an exterior that was "perfectly plain and simple like a Markethouse." Today, The Academy of the Arts continues to celebrate its tradition of operatic excellence and stands as America's oldest opera house.

◀ 115

▶ Fireman's Hall National Fire House & Museum is located in a firehouse that was built in 1876. The museum's exhibits, containing an impressive number of firefighting devices and other artifacts, demonstrate the methods of fighting fire that have been employed in the city as early as 1731.

▼ Philadelphia has a seafaring soul—one that is especially evident on the Delaware River waterfront. Independence Seaport Museum showcases the city's maritime heritage with 10,000 square feet of space dedicated to interactive exhibits, models, artifacts, and works of art.

▶ (Opposite) Visitors to Independence Seaport Museum at Penn's Landing can explore Admiral Dewey's cruiser *Olympia*, a cruiser built in 1892, and tour the *Becuna*, a submarine that served active duty in World War II.

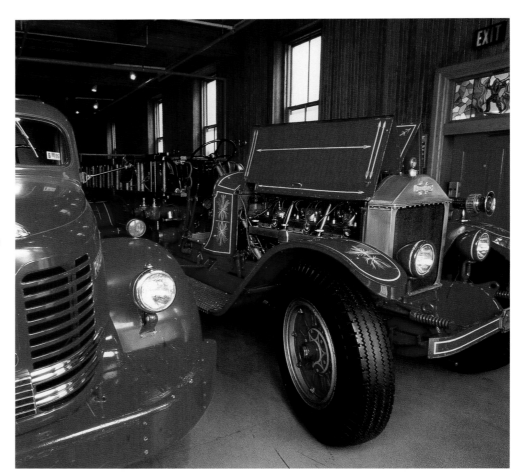

▲ Rocky racing up the steps of the Philadelphia Museum of Art has become an icon in American cinema, and another perfect example of how Philadelphia art and history are so intertwined.

▶ Philadelphia is Ben Franklin's city through and through. While trying to fathom the scope of his ideas and inventions can be exhausting, the city is full of tributes to some of his more famous accomplishments, such as his famous kite experiment and discovery of electricity.

▶ (Opposite) Pennsylvania's most revered Revolutionary officer, Major General Anthony Wayne, is memorialized in an impressive monument located in Fairmount Park on the grounds of the Philadelphia Museum of Art. The monument took nearly half a century to fund, but was finally constructed in 1937.

▲ Situated in the center of Logan Circle, the Swann Memorial Fountain,
also known as the Fountain of the Three Rivers, is named in honor of Dr.
Wilson Cary Swann, founder of the Philadelphia Fountain Society. Sculptor
Alexander Stirling Calder designed the fountain, which completed construc-
tion in 1924. The three native American statues represent the Schuylkill
River, Delaware River, and the Wissahickon Creek.

CHAPTER FOUR

Let Us Entertain You

One of the largest and most celebrated Fourth of July festivities in the
nation is Welcome America! The celebration, which includes free events,
concerts, fireworks, and many other patriotic activities throughout the city,
begins several days prior to July Fourth and usually ends the week after.

*E*very new year in Philadelphia starts with a flurry of fantasy, feathers, and fun as thousands of marchers take to the streets of Center City for the Mummers Parade. Scores of men, women, and children—numbering as many as thirty thousand in recent years—masquerade as comics, "fancies," alone or in brigades, while throngs of spectators cheer them on. Members of the locally popular string bands (also know as Mummers bands) dressed in astonishingly extravagant costumes fill the streets with traditional Mummers songs and the music Philadelphia loves. Beer and wine flow freely, spectators of all ages laugh, dance, or scratch their heads as the Mummers whirl down the streets. Here and there a policeman struts in time with the music, and Philadelphia becomes for a day something out of a child's wildest imagination.

Like Philadelphia itself, the parade is a result of not one culture or tradition, but several. Most Mummers and Mummer historians believe it originated as early as the 1620s in a southwestern corner of the city settled by Swedes and Finns, who celebrated New Years by shooting their guns and banging pots and pans en route to visit neighbors after Christmas. Not surprisingly, this flash of merriment that occurred like clockwork every year was not to everyone's taste, and in 1808 the event was deemed by legislature as a "common nuisance." Any law prohibiting the noisy tradition, however, was never enforced, and in 1859 the legislation was repealed. The Mummers Parade is now a Philadelphia tradition as inseparable from the city as Mardi Gras is to New Orleans. The Mummers Parade is perfectly Philadelphia, and there couldn't be a better way to launch a new year full of festivals, celebrations, special events, and scores of other opportunities for city residents and visitors alike to have fun.

Just as much of a local tradition, and one that seems entirely natural for William Penn's "greene Country Towne" is the annual Philadelphia Flower Show. Held at the Convention Center in early March, the show has attracted enough buyers, vendors, exhibitors, lecturers, and other experts to become the largest indoor flower show in the world. The Pennsylvania Horticultural Society, which formed in 1827 and is the oldest horticultural society in the country, held its first exhibition at the Masonic Hall on Chestnut Street in 1829. From those relatively small beginnings, the show grew to feature exhibitors from all over the U.S., Africa, Asia, and Europe. The weeklong event now draws over three hundred thousand visitors and has become a centerpiece of the city's culture and an instrumental part of its economy.

Celebrating the city's dynamic film industry and its important role on the world stage is the Philadelphia Festival of World Cinema, held each spring in a number of venues throughout the city. More than 200 feature films, documentaries, and shorts from every inhabited continent flicker on the city's screens for nearly two weeks each year. A smaller cinematic event, but one that shines a spotlight on Philadelphia's film community, is the Philadelphia Weekend Film Festival. Held each year at the Prince Theater and the Ritz-Carlton hotel, the festival honors the work of an outstanding

American director or actor, in attendance, with showings of five of the honoree's movies. Past festivals have celebrated the works of directors John Schlesinger, Alan Pakula, Norman Jewison, Lawrence Kasdan, Alan Rudolph, Sydney Pollack, Arthur Penn, Richard Brooks, and Philip Kaufman, and actors Kevin Bacon, Richard Dreyfuss, and Meryl Streep. These film festivals not only celebrate the creative genius of moviemakers worldwide, they effectively promote the city itself, illuminating the thousands of local filmmaking professionals and support services available in Greater Philadelphia.

The city kicks off the summer season with Jam on the River, a music and food festival held at Penn's Landing on Memorial Day

EAGLE ROSE
ROSA
EN EAGLE

weekend. Top musical performers descend on the Delaware River during the holiday and flood the air with jazz, zydeco and Cajun rhythms, reggae, country, and rock tunes. Food vendors, souvenir stands, art displays, and children's activities line the venues of the riverfront during the festival, giving guests a chance to meander and relax between their favorite acts.

As midsummer approaches, the birthplace of America gears up for its spectacular, thunderous Fourth of July celebrations. Several communities in and around the city host fireworks displays, outdoor picnics, parades, and other entertainment to celebrate America's birthday, but the largest and best known of these is Sunoco Welcome

▲ The annual Philadelphia Flower Show is largest indoor flower show in the world. Held at the Convention Center in early March, the show attracts buyers, vendors, exhibitors, lecturers, and other experts from around the world. The Pennsylvania Horticultural Society, which formed in 1827 and is the oldest horticultural society in the country, held the first flower show at the Masonic Hall on Chestnut Street in 1829.

America! Several national publications, including *USA Today* and *The Wall Street Journal* have named Welcome America! the premier Fourth of July celebration in the country. The festivities, which include free events, concerts, fireworks, and many other patriotic

activities throughout the city, begin several days prior to July Fourth and usually end the week after. To say that patriotism runs high throughout the city at this time would be a giant understatement. On the fourth, leaders of Greater Philadelphia First present the Liberty Medal to a person or organization whose leadership has made a positive difference in the world. During the Welcome America! festivities, Independence Hall, the Liberty Bell, Penn's Landing, and many other places so vital to the foundations of America assume an especially profound meaning for visitors and residents alike.

Thanksgiving Day is another festive national holiday in the city. It was in Philadelphia that the first Thanksgiving Day parade was held. The tradition, marked by a procession of elaborate floats and marching bands, was launched by Gimbel Brothers Department Store in 1920. Macy's, then a competitor of Gimbel's, started its own Thanksgiving Day Parade in New York City in 1924. While Gimbel's is no longer around, the annual parade lives on in Philadelphia and attracts thousands of spectators. For generations of Philadelphians, there simply is no other way to start the Thanksgiving holiday than to watch the colorful spectacle pass down Benjamin Franklin Parkway as children eagerly await the appearance of Santa Claus at the end.

Philadelphia's calendar of events and celebrations keep the city alive with new sights and sounds all year long, but the city's permanent

▲ (and Opposite) Philadelphia loves its parades. In addition to its world-famous Mummer's and Thanksgiving Day Parades, Philadelphia marks Independence and Memorial Day Parades with spectacular patriotic processions led by historical figures, bringing to life those who played such important roles in this country's past. First Troop Philadelphia and the Fife and Drum Corp are two common entities seen in many area celebrations.

attractions provide equally impressive venues of entertainment. Located in Fairmount Park, the Philadelphia Zoo is home to nearly two thousand animals and some of the city's most beautifully manicured landscape gardens. Chartered in 1859 and opened in 1874, the Philadelphia Zoo was America's first zoo, and it has provided an oasis of exotic plant and animal life in the heart of the city ever since. The zoo's history contains a long list of other firsts, including the first gorilla exhibited in an American zoo, but it's the institution's commitment to conservation and its efforts to boost public understanding of the natural world that are the most remarkable today.

Philadelphians also can explore the wilds of the deep at the New Jersey State Aquarium across the Delaware River in Camden. Inside the aquarium, visitors can view and walk through more than eighty exhibits containing over four thousand animals from five hundred species. Other nearby New Jersey attractions include the hair-raising rides of Six Flags Great Adventure amusement park in Jackson, the

▲ The Honor Guard of the Philadelphia chapter of the 82nd Airborne Division Association marches to the annual Veteran's Day memorial ceremony at Washington Square. When called upon, the chapter provides honor guards and burial details for local paratrooper veterans who have passed away.

world-famous casinos and boardwalks of Atlantic City, and the expansive sandy beaches and boardwalk amusement piers of Wildwood—all of which are favorite haunts of fun-seeking Philadelphians.

As the saying goes, big things come in little packages, and so it stands to reason that Philadelphia's shops, restaurants, and nightclubs offer some of the best ways to spend a day (or a night) of leisure. The streets of Center City bustle with shoppers towing bags from Banana Republic across the street to Tiffany and back again to Tower Records. Almost all big-name stores have a big presence in Philadelphia, imparting to the city streets a feeling that this is the world's biggest shopping mall. On a literal note, the country's second largest shopping mall sits just a few minutes west in King of Prussia. The King of Prussia Mall is not just a shopping destination for residents of the Philadelphia area, it is a destination in itself for shoppers from all over the country seeking myriad bargains under one roof and taking advantage of Pennsylvania's sales tax exemption on all articles of clothing.

Some of the country's finest dining establishments can be found in Philadelphia, too. In fact, *Conde Nast Traveler* magazine's readers ranked Philadelphia as the "best restaurant city" in the United States. Italian bistros, French cafés, Greek taverns, Moroccan eateries—you name it; Philadelphia offers a world of ethnic cuisine in addition to some of the finest traditional and new-American fare, cutting edge fusion cooking, seafood restaurants, and more.

Philadelphia may be ranked as the best restaurant city in America, but for beer lovers it's heaven on earth. The city has one of the densest concentrations of breweries and brewpubs in the country, including the oldest continually operating one—Yuengling Brewery, established in 1829. Philadelphia won't let connoisseurs down, either. Greater Philadelphia is home to scores of vineyards and wineries offering tours, winemaking lessons, and product sampling. Philadelphia held its first Wine Festival in May 2002, introducing the public to the winemakers and wines from more than sixty national and regional wineries.

Philadelphians need not travel far to find the best that life has to offer, be it their favorite band, a swim in the rolling Atlantic, a hike in the mountains, an exotic dinner, or a fascinating and fun-filled day at the zoo or the aquarium. With so much happening all year, boredom is certainly more a word than a reality in the Greater Philadelphia Area. ℗

▲ Several national publications, including *USA Today* and *The Wall Street Journal,* have named Philadelphia's Welcome America! the premier Fourth of July celebration in the country.

◀ Despite the absence of reservations, the Delaware Valley is home to several native peoples. Census reports show some eleven thousand people of Native American descent living in and around Philadelphia. The United American Indians of Delaware Valley, a nonprofit organization located in Center City, offers an array of services to the American Indians who reside in the Philadelphia area. The UAIDV's Fall Festival is just one of the ways the organization seeks to preserve its extraordinary and precious heritage.

▲ Philadelphia residents and visitors are able to enjoy a wealth of public art throughout the metropolitan area due in part to the city's "percent-for-art mandate."

▼ The Azalea Garden behind the Philadelphia Museum of Art trumpets the arrival of spring with its vibrant splash of color. The garden is part of the Museum Grounds Tour and includes many unique statues, as well as beautiful flowers and vegetation.

◀ (and Opposite) Located in Fairmount Park, the Philadelphia Zoo is home to nearly two thousand animals and some of the city's most beautifully manicured landscape gardens. Chartered in 1859 and opened in 1874, the Philadelphia Zoo was America's first zoo. The zoo's history includes a long list of firsts, including the first gorilla exhibited in an American zoo, but it's the institution's commitment to conservation and its efforts to boost public understanding of the natural world that are the most impressive today.

▶ Each year, the Kennel Club of Philadelphia holds its world-famous dog show, one of the oldest and most prestigious sporting events in North America. Winners from each of 130 breeds proceed to judging in seven groups—Sporting, Hound, Working, Terrier, Toy, Non-Sporting, and Herding. The top dogs from each group then compete in the main ring.

(Following page) By the mid-nineteenth century, one-third of Philadelphia's population was foreign born, and the Irish community was one of the largest and fastest growing. Today, the Irish community is still one of the most visible and active communities in the city, especially during March (officially declared as "Irish Month in the city") when the St. Patrick's Day Parade rolls through town.

◀ Philadelphia kicks off the summer season with Jam on the River, a music and food festival held at Penn's Landing on Memorial Day weekend. Top musical performers descend on the Delaware River during the holiday and flood the air with jazz, zydeco and Cajun rhythms, reggae, country, and rock tunes. Jam attracts thousands of visitors and celebrities such as Billy Bob Thornton.

▼ Every New Year commences in Philadelphia when thousands of marchers take to the streets of Center City for the Mummers Parade, a uniquely Philadelphian celebration. Scores of men, women, and children—numbering as many as 30,000 in recent years—masquerade as throngs of spectators cheer them on.

▲ Philadelphia held the first Thanksgiving Day parade, a tradition launched by Gimbel Brothers Department Store in 1920. The tradition, marked by a procession of elaborate floats and marching bands, was later rivaled by Macy's in New York City.

CHAPTER FIVE

The Melting Pot

Society Hill is Philadelphia's showcase neighborhood. Situated on the
eastern edge of the city near the Delaware River and just south of
Independence National Historical Park, the neighborhood is comprised of
tree-lined brick roads weaving through rows of stately colonial and
nineteenth-century homes, flowery gardens, and scenic parks.

𝓑arely any time had passed since Philadelphia's first foundations and streets were laid before the light of the community, like a lighthouse beacon, radiated across the water to attract people from all corners of the globe. This was a new city in the new world—a place with a welcoming name and promises of prosperity, or at least a better life. These were more than the governments and traditions of the old world could ever offer, and they were enough to persuade emigrants to cross oceans and continents, risking life and limb in their pursuit.

With each wave of immigrants that arrived, the face of Philadelphia changed. German immigrants began arriving as early as the 1690s, and by the late 1720s, the steady trickle of immigration from both Eastern and Western Europe had burst into a full-fledged flood. The rising tide of peoples from Europe and Asia formed a seemingly bottomless pool of manual labor into which local industries could tap. It wasn't until the nineteenth century that Philadelphia finally gave way to New York City as the country's principle immigration port, but the city continued to swell with new arrivals. Socially and physically, the impact of immigration on the city was enormous. New neighborhoods emerged as Philadelphia assumed a more cosmo-politan personality, yet so much of Philadelphia remained the same.

▲ (and Opposite) A relaxed, provincial aura encompasses Rittenhouse Square in the south western quadrant of the city. While situated in close proximity to bustling downtown streets and some of Philadelphia's most alluring restau-rants, theaters, shops, and museums, Rittenhouse Square has maintained its historical aura and relaxed provincial charm, and is home to some of the city's most prestigious addresses.

◀ South Philadelphia teems with the scents and sounds of Italy, especially in the Bella Vista neighborhood, where there is a bustling Italian market that is still run by the descendants of those who began hawking fresh meat and produce here at the turn of the twentieth century.

▲ As one of the oldest cities in America, Philadelphia is full of antique charm. Many sections of the city are marked by winding cobblestone alleys, carefully manicured gardens, and wonderful clusters of historical homes and stores.

The heart of Philadelphia, Center City, still contains the essence of William Penn's blueprint for the city. On the tract of land straddling the Delaware and Schuylkill Rivers, he drew a grid fashioned by thoroughfares named after trees (Mulberry, Walnut, Locust, Spruce, and Pine) running east-west, intersected by numbered avenues running north-south. The intersecting lines created roughly 175 blocks spreading outward from the city center at High and Broad. To maintain the wholesome, natural character of a "greene Country Towne," he established four verdant squares equidistant between the center of town and the river boundaries to the east and west. This layout is still apparent today, though it has been dressed

with bustling urban streets, towering high-rise offices, stately hotels, museums, and theaters, and a paradise of restaurants, stores, and galleries. Indeed, Philadelphia's "Old City" may be new, but it hasn't lost the charm and colonial soul of its early days as America's first planned city.

Philadelphia's showcase neighborhood is Society Hill. Situated on the eastern edge of the city near the Delaware River and just south of Independence National Historical Park, the neighborhood is comprised of tree-lined brick roads weaving through rows of stately colonial and nineteenth-century homes, flowery gardens, and scenic parks. St. Peter's Episcopal Church, where John Nixon, who first read the Declaration of Independence to the public, is buried, has been the neighborhood's dominant landmark since its construction in 1757.

To the west of Society Hill and south of Independence Hall sits the neighborhood of Washington Square West, one of Penn's original leafy

▲ An old Swedish church, Gloria Dei, echoes Philadelphia's rich Swedish heritage. Arriving in 1638, Swedish immigrants were the first to settle in Pennsylvania, and New Sweden was the first permanent European settlement in the Delaware Valley.

quadrants. This 36-block section of the city is a checkerboard of old brownstone homes and businesses, a labyrinth of cobblestone alleys, and a wonderful cluster of antique stores stretching between Eighth and Twelfth along Pine Street known as "Antique Row." Washington Square West may be one of America's most eclectic neighborhoods; its well-preserved edifices represent a mixture of Colonial, Federalist, Egyptian Revival, Greek Revival, Renaissance, and Victorian architectural styles.

Continuing west past Broad Street to Southwestern quadrant is Rittenhouse Square, named for Penn's original square

▶ Philadelphia's "Old City" may be tucked in the heart of a progressive modern city, but it hasn't lost the charm and colonial soul of its early days. Touring in a horse-drawn carriage is a unique way to experience the city's history first-hand.

that is the centerpiece of the neighborhood. A relaxed, provincial aura encompasses the neighborhood, even though it is located within easy walking distance to bustling downtown streets and some of Philadelphia's most alluring restaurants, theaters, shops, and museums, not to mention historical landmarks. The location and sheer antiquity of Rittenhouse Square have made it home to some of the city's most prestigious addresses.

Chestnut Hill, in the northwestern corner of the city, blossomed in the nineteenth century and has weathered time remarkably well, having retained most of its colonial and nineteenth-century townhouses and storefronts. Chestnut Hill's main artery is Germantown Avenue—in itself a fine example of just how well-preserved Philadelphia's neighborhoods are despite being in the throes of such a dynamic, rapidly changing and redeveloping city.

The northeastern section of the city, stretching down to Penn's Landing on the banks of the Delaware River, is known as Old City, and it is this quadrant that is recognized as America's most historic square mile. Elfreth's Alley, the oldest residential street in the country, contains thirty-three homes, each one as old as the country itself, if not older. The sheer historical significance of Old City is staggering, for it is where the most successful nation in the history of civilization was formed, where history continues to live in the very same buildings in streets in which it was made so many years ago. Residents of Old City can truly enjoy living in two different centuries, with all the modern amenities of big city living intertwined with the fabric of a colonial era.

While many of the city's neighborhoods can be defined by their historical significance, other neighborhoods in Philadelphia are bound more by purpose. Just as its name suggests, University City is an area dominated by college campuses, hospitals, museums, theaters, and a

144 ▶

proliferation of social and cultural institutions oriented toward a younger crowd but enjoyed by all. The area is not only popular among college professors, staff, and students, but anyone who enjoys a refined and culturally alert community whether or not he or she is a member of the surrounding academia. University City hugs the Schuylkill River on its eastern edge. While The University of Pennsylvania and Drexel University are located in the immediate area, residents have quick and easy access to a host of other colleges as well.

Tradition, especially the cultural imports pulled into town by the immigrant population, is another thread that defines many neighborhoods in the Greater Philadelphia Area. The mid-eighteenth century saw the greatest influx of German immigrants to Philadelphia; during the years 1749 and 1750, thirty-six ships bearing roughly eleven thousand German immigrants arrived in Philadelphia. Most of these immigrants settled in the northwestern stretches of town on the eastern banks of the Schuylkill River and in Germantown, which was founded in 1683 by thirteen Quaker families from Germany. So great had the number of Germans in Philadelphia become that it created some anxiety amongst the non-German population, who worried that Philadelphia would become exclusively a German city. Today, German culture and traditions still dominate many communities in Philadelphia.

Between 1845 and 1847, the potato famine in Ireland set in motion a tidal wave of emigration from Ireland. Scores more immigrants from Alsace, Poland, and Eastern Europe arrived on ships and imparted not only a tremendous amount of Slavic culture to the city, but added to already rapidly growing Catholic and Jewish communities.

▲ The three "big people" at Penn's Landing are the creation of American sculptor William King. *Stroll* is one of the most beloved and photographed works of art in the city.

▶ Sitting along the Schuylkill riverbanks and the Manayunk Canal, the National Historic District of Manayunk, just a few minutes west of Center City, has some of the best shopping and dining destinations in the area. From arts festivals to street music to cycling championships, Manayunk always offers visitors a fun-filled time.

To the slave population of the South, Philadelphia was in many ways the closest free city. The city had a black population numbering nearly twenty thousand in 1850—a number that continued to grow as the Civil War and a specter of uncertainty loomed on the horizon. The densest concentration of blacks was in Moyamensing in an area straddling South and Fitzwater Streets between Fifth and Eighth. By the 1890s, Philadelphia's black population was greater in number than any other northern city, and second only to Baltimore, Washington, and New Orleans.

In the thirty years preceding 1900, Philadelphia's Italian population swelled to more than sixty times its size—growing from roughly three hundred in 1870 to nearly eighteen thousand in 1900. Today, South Philadelphia teems with the scents and sounds of Italy, especially in the Bella Vista neighborhood, where there is a bustling Italian market that is still run by the descendants of those who began hawking fresh meat and produce here at the turn of the twentieth century. The South Philadelphia area is also home to the big sports

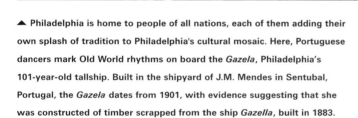

▲ Philadelphia is home to people of all nations, each of them adding their own splash of tradition to Philadelphia's cultural mosaic. Here, Portuguese dancers mark Old World rhythms on board the *Gazela*, Philadelphia's 101-year-old tallship. Built in the shipyard of J.M. Mendes in Sentubal, Portugal, the *Gazela* dates from 1901, with evidence suggesting that she was constructed of timber scrapped from the ship *Gazella*, built in 1883.

◀ As the nearest northern city to the South, Philadelphia became a haven for slaves seeking liberty. Today, the city's African-American community honors its colorful roots with celebrations such as the Odunde Festival and Marketplace, the African-American Cultural Extravaganza, and annual Kwanzaa festivities.

(Following page) Congregation Rodelph Shalom represents more than 200 years of Jewish-American history. The beautiful old synagogue on Broad Street is one of the oldest Reform Jewish congregations in the United States. Philadelphia's Jewish community has a long history in the city. William Penn's "Holy Experiment" extended welcome and toleration not just to Catholics, but to Jews as well. Historical records indicate that the first Jewish settler, Nathan Levy, arrived in Philadelphia by 1735. Philadelphia is also home to the National Museum of American Jewish History, the first and only museum in the U.S. to focus exclusively on the history of Jews in America.

complexes, the city's most outstanding restaurants, and the legendary Philly cheesesteak.

◀ 1 4 7

From a single Chinese laundromat that opened on 9th and Race in the late nineteenth century grew an entire Chinese community. Philadelphia's Chinatown developed especially fast after the Cultural Revolution swept mainland China in the early 1950s. Scores of Chinese citizens fled their nation's borders as the iron curtain closed around them. The community in Philadelphia gradually became a bustling hub of Chinese culture that today consists of more than fifty restaurants, fifteen grocery stores, and a colorful range of coffee shops, gift stores, beauty salons, bakeries, and a number of other authentic Chinese businesses. Chinatown, like many of Philadelphia's ethnic groups and neighborhoods, has its own organization, the Philadelphia Chinatown Development Corporation, that aims to protect the neighborhood boundaries from encroaching development while promoting it as a lively and viable place to live, visit, and conduct business.

Contemporary immigration indicates that the City of Brotherly Love—indeed, the City of Neighborhoods—remains a practical choice for modern immigrants who crave a sense of belonging to their community. While European and even Asian cultures are absorbed into the American mainstream, newer communities continue to grow as cultural strongholds, communities in which people share the same language, food, religion, and heritage. For example, El Centro de Oro, Philadelphia's Hispanic community, continues to grow in the northeastern end of the city known as Fairhill. Latinos from all over the Caribbean, Mexico, Central America, and South America today comprise the most rapidly developing cultural enclave of Philadelphia, adding yet another piece to the city's rich, colorful ethnic mosaic. ℗

FOR·ALL·PEOPLES

◀ Tradition, especially the cultural imports pulled into town by the immigrant population, is the defining thread of many Philadelphia neighborhoods. Be they Asian, African, European, South American, or from anywhere else, the ethnic communities of Philadelphia bring the world home.

▼ Philadelphia's Chinatown quickly became a bustling hub of Chinese culture after the Cultural Revolution swept China in the 1950s. Today, Chinatown consists of more than fifty restaurants, fifteen grocery stores, and a colorful range of coffee shops, gift stores, beauty salons, bakeries, and a number of other authentic Chinese businesses.

The Japanese House and Garden in the Horticultural Center of West Fairmount Park was planned and built for the city's Centennial Exposition in 1876. The garden represents one of the country's finest, most authentic Japanese gardens in the U.S. The garden, landscaped in the seventeenth-century Momoyama style, is a delight for visitors year-round. In the spring, cherry, dogwood, and plum trees blossom together with vibrant azaleas. In the fall, the trees become a vivid crimson and contrast brilliantly with the evergreens and pond.

CHAPTER SIX

An Educational Foundation

The Philadelphia Free Library, now with fifty-five locations and over ten
million items, was begun in 1731 by Benjamin Franklin. In the eighteenth
century, very few people had the means to purchase books, which were
extraordinarily expensive at the time. Franklin and other members of the
Junto, a philosophical association, knew that with their combined
purchasing power, books could be made available to all. Thus, the
Philadelphia Library Company was born. A Latin motto was chosen for the
library, meaning "to support the common good is divine."

If knowledge is power, then the strength of Philadelphia's educational system and the intellectual fuel it adds to the community are perhaps too immense to quantify. One only needs to consider the facts: within the Greater Philadelphia Area there are eighty-nine post-secondary schools, colleges, and universities, six medical schools, twenty-four teaching hospitals, and a number of schools devoted to other medical professions, including dentistry, pharmaceutical sciences, veterinary medicine, optometry, podiatry, and osteopathy. Five law schools in the region help bolster the definition of a "Philadelphia lawyer" as a particularly shrewd breed of attorney. More than fifty-five thousand students merit degrees from the city's institutes of higher learning each year—the largest number of them in sciences, health care, and medical technologies. Philadelphia, in fact, graduates more doctors per year than any other American city.

Such staggering dedication to education begins, of course, with a solid foundation of public and private schools, each in its own way upholding standards of excellence and forging paths into the future for today's youth. The city's magnet schools work to identify and encourage the particular talents and interests of each student in much the same way the area's vocational and technical schools

◀ 155

◀ **Founded in 1864 by the Religious Society of Friends (Quakers), Swarthmore College cooperates closely with Bryn Mawr College, Haverford, and the University of Pennsylvania. The shared resources and facilities of the colleges enhance the lives and studies of its students while working cooperatively for the common good, and year after year, Swarthmore College finds itself on the top-ten lists of America's best liberal arts colleges. The college's alumni reads like a list of Nobel Prize winners, government leaders, and other outstanding leaders.**

▲ **Philadelphia's historically staunch dedication to learning begins, of course, with a solid foundation of public and private schools, each in its own way upholding standards of excellence and forging paths into the future for today's youth. Each year, the School District of Philadelphia provides an education for more than 200,000 students through its 264 schools. The district also transports 33,000 plus students in the public, private, and parochial systems.**

◀ **Parents wishing to enroll their children in private school have access to a spectrum of schools with a worldwide reputation for academic excellence. A college preparatory school for boys of diverse backgrounds, The Haverford School provides a superior liberal arts education for junior kindergarten through grade twelve. In addition to the number of private, mostly college preparatory schools in the Delaware Valley, there is a wealth of parochial schools representing several denominations from which to choose.**

▲ The Academy of Vocal Arts maintains the highest standards of excellence in training the opera singers of tomorrow. The Academy was started in the wake of the Great Depression when very few students dared dream of such a profession, let alone pay for and pursue this type of education. Admission to the four-year, tuition-free program is extremely competitive. The thirty or so students admitted each year "are immersed in an intensive performance program led by some of the most dedicated and inspired teachers and creative artists in the world of opera."

prime students for specific careers. New publicly-funded schools run by private citizens provide still another option for parents. Known as "charter schools," these schools keep parents and the wider community involved closely in the classroom.

Parents who wish to enroll their children in private school also have access to a spectrum of schools with a worldwide reputation for academic excellence. Seeking a nonpublic school in Philadelphia is, according to independent school representatives, not a matter of finding what school is reputedly the best, but which school best fits a particular child, with class size, special curriculums, educational theory, co-educational divisions, and a number of other factors all part of the equation. In addition to the number of private, mostly college preparatory schools in the Delaware Valley, there is a wealth of parochial schools representing several denominations. Philadelphia contains the largest number of Quaker or "Friends" schools in the country, which carry on the spiritual, intellectual, and character building traditions of the city's forefathers. More than 200 Catholic elementary schools and

twenty-two Catholic secondary schools in Philadelphia and the surrounding counties offer local schoolchildren excellent, well-rounded educations, as do those affiliated with other churches.

In an effort to widen the availability of private school education to underprivileged children, the state of Pennsylvania approved $20 million in tax credits to companies donating scholarships to private and religious schools. Philadelphia's business community responded with enthusiasm, and the plan will allow thousands of local children to gain access to schools they could not otherwise afford to attend.

On the college level, Philadelphia's reputation for academic excellence is legendary. More than three hundred thousand students from every state and nation pursue coveted degrees in local universities. The University of Pennsylvania, while not the oldest institution of higher learning in the United States, is the country's first university. Founded in 1740, the University known as Penn grew out of founder Benjamin Franklin's idea to offer a school that would reach beyond the traditional margins of a classical education to offer courses in contemporary subjects; in his words, students should learn "everything that is useful and everything that is ornamental." The innovative university went on to establish the nation's first medical school, its first business school, the first university teaching hospital, and the first modern liberal arts curriculum. Penn's rigorous academic standards consistently place it in *U.S. News and World Report*'s list of the top ten universities in America. The picturesque campus is completely contained in its own 262 acres of West Philadelphia, an aspect that distinguishes it from its other Ivy League peers.

◀ The William W. Bodine High School for International Affairs provides an excellent education with a focus on international studies, and is the first public magnet school of its kind in the nation. The high school operates in partnership with the World Affairs Council of Philadelphia and offers a college-preparatory education to students with a common interest in social studies, foreign languages, and the dynamics of global society.

▼ William Penn Demonstration High School occupies a modern, state-of-the art building on North Broad Street. The school is affiliated with Temple University's Education Department and employs only the most innovative and effective methods of teaching while holding its students to the highest standards of academic excellence.

◀ 157

▲ Located on Philadelphia's artistically charged stretch of South Broad Street, the University of the Arts prepares students for careers in every field of visual and performing arts, including filmmaking, graphic design, and music, with classes as diverse as glass-blowing.

Two local colleges deeply rooted in the region's Quaker heritage are Bryn Mawr College, located eleven miles west of Philadelphia in the small town of Bryn Mawr, and Haverford College in neighboring Haverford. Dr. Joseph Taylor, a New Jersey physician and member of the Society of Friends, founded Bryn Mawr College in 1880 as the educational equivalent of all-male Haverford, but exclusively for young Quaker women. Its landmark achievement was the establishment of a graduate program that awarded women doctorate degrees—the first women's college in the country to do so. Today, Bryn Mawr and Haverford remain closely affiliated, with many facilities and resources of each open to the students of both colleges—a cooperation further broadened by close ties to Swarthmore College and the University of Pennsylvania.

Situated near Bryn Mawr and Haverford Colleges is Villanova University, a celebrated Catholic institution that upholds standards of academic excellence in the Augustinian intellectual tradition. Two Augustinians from Saint Augustine's Church in Philadelphia founded the college in 1842 as the Augustinian College of Villanova. The university's excellence is exemplified in current times by its ranking as the number-one northern university for its Masters programs— the twelfth time that *U.S. News and World Report* has named it such.

In 1891, Philadelphia financier and philanthropist Anthony J. Drexel contributed $3 million to establish The Drexel Institute of Art, Science, and Industry. The school's specific purpose was to provide technical skills and education to Philadelphia's working-class youth. More than one hundred years later, the university's mission remains much the same as it prepares students for successful careers in the sciences and the technologies.

The third largest provider of professional education in the country, Temple University offers associate degrees in four areas, one hundred thirty-three bachelor's degree areas, one hundred thirty-five master's degree areas, fifty-eight doctoral degree areas, and six first professional degree areas. From its relatively small beginnings in 1884, Temple has grown to become the thirty-sixth largest university in the United States, and one of Pennsylvania's three research universities. Temple enrolls more than thirty thousand students on five campuses in the metropolitan area, with the main campus occupying one hundred fourteen acres in North Philadelphia. The university's two international campuses are located in Rome, Italy, and Tokyo, Japan, with an additional instructional campus in Harrisburg.

Exceptionally talented students who wish to pursue a higher education in the arts will find unparalleled opportunities in Philadelphia. The Curtis Institute of Music and The University of the Arts are just two of the city's remarkable schools wholly dedicated to arts education. The Curtis Institute of Music provides an open-ended, tuition-free program of study for students whose merits meet the extremely competitive admissions criteria. Students at Curtis train one its students' passion for self-expression, and, in turn, nurture both the presence and the purpose of the arts in the world. The university enrolls approximately two thousand students.

Venture outside the classroom and onto the streets of Philadelphia, and you will find yourself in a living museum, where some of the nation's most significant historical sites and museums sit around every asphalt avenue and cobblestoned corner. Independence National Historical Park, located at 6th and Market Streets is the nation's most historic square mile, and the Liberty Bell are just two of the destinations that give visitors a true sense of the nation's struggle for independence. People of all ages can learn fascinating facts about animals, ecosystems, and natural conservation with a trip to the Philadelphia Zoo in Fairmount Park or take a crash course in marine biology and the sustaining forces of the world's waterways at the New Jersey State Aquarium in nearby Camden. Learn all about earth's forces and mechanisms at the Academy of Natural Sciences or the Franklin Institute, a hands-on science museum. With so many educational resources, it's plain to see that a lot of learning takes place outside Philadelphia's classrooms. ℗

▲ Girard College was founded in 1848 at the bequest of French philanthropist and millionaire Stephen Girard, who wanted part of his $6-million fortune to fund a school for orphans. Today, the private boarding school, located on 43 acres and situated in the Fairmount Park area, houses 600 students on campus. The college-prepatory school enrolls students in grades one through twelve.

on one with an instructor from the first class to the last and progress at their own pace. Curtis Institute graduates can be found in just about every major orchestra worldwide.

Located on Philadelphia's artistically charged stretch of South Broad Street, The University of the Arts prepares students for careers in every field of visual and performing arts, including filmmaking, graphic design, and music. The university also confers graduate degrees in twelve fields of study, most of them related to arts education and museum studies. For over one hundred and twenty-five years, the university has evolved and changed names several times, but it has always sought to encourage

▶ Founded in Wilmington, Delaware, in 1821, Widener University's eight schools and colleges offer exceptional education in liberal arts and sciences, engineering, hospitality management, human service professions, law, business administration, and nursing. The university's main campus is now located in Chester, Pennsylvania. Additional campuses are maintained in Wilmington, Delaware, and Harrisburg, Pennsylvania.

▲ La Salle University was founded in 1863 by the Christian Brothers, a Catholic order committed to the merits of teaching. The university offers undergraduate degrees in approximately sixty areas of study and graduate degree programs in thirteen areas. LaSalle contributes to the Philadelphia area's reputation for academic excellence, and has been ranked among the country's top universities by *Barron's*, *Money Magazine*, the *New York Times*, and *U.S. News & World Report*. Exemplifying the university's innovation and foresight is the nation's first e-commerce institute, which LaSalle opened in order to educate students of all majors about e-commerce as a powerful business tool.

▲ From its relatively small beginnings in 1884, Temple has grown to become the thirty-sixth largest university in the United States, and one of Pennsylvania's three research universities. Temple enrolls more than 30,000 students on five campuses in the metropolitan area, with the main campus occupying 114 acres in North Philadelphia.

▼ Villanova University is a celebrated Catholic institution that upholds standards of academic excellence in the Augustinian intellectual tradition. The university's excellence is exemplified by the success of its graduates and by its ranking as the number-one northern university for its Masters programs— the twelfth time that *U.S. News & World Report* has named it such.

▶ Eastern University (formerly Eastern College) has its beginnings in 1932, when it opened as a department of the Eastern Baptist Theological Seminary. Today, the university retains its affiliation with the American Baptist Churches, but is open to all evangelical Christians. Approximately 3,000 students, including more than 100 students from thirty foreign countries, are enrolled at Eastern.

▼ The Anne and Jerome Fisher Fine Arts Library is just one of fifteen libraries located on the University of Pennsylvania campus. The vast amount of resources and latest technology allow Penn's students to access a wealth of information from several locations on campus.

▶ (Opposite) Founded in 1740, the University of Pennsylvania grew out of founder Benjamin Franklin's idea to offer a school that would reach beyond the traditional margins of a classical education to offer courses in contemporary subjects.

▲ The country's first university, Penn established many of the nation's other firsts, including a medical school, business school, university teaching hospital, and modern liberal-arts curriculum. The picturesque campus is completely contained in its own 262 acres of West Philadelphia, an aspect that distinguishes it from its Ivy League peers.

CHAPTER SEVEN

A Healthy Tomorrow

Philadelphia is home to the nation's first Ronald McDonald House.
The house opened in 1974 after the daughter of Philadelphia Eagles football player
Fred Hill was diagnosed with leukemia. Dr. Audrey Evans, a pediatric oncologist from
the Children's Hospital of Philadelphia, worked with representatives of McDonald's and
the Philadelphia Eagles to garner financial support for this trailblazing project.
Over 200 Ronald McDonald Houses are now located in 20 countries worldwide, providing a
"home-away-from-home" for families of seriously ill children who are receiving treatment
at nearby hospitals.

*N*ot many visitors and tourists would think of putting a hospital on their itinerary of places to see, but in Philadelphia the oddity is justified. Pennsylvania Hospital, another of Benjamin Franklin's historical endeavors, was born years before the United States itself. Built in 1751, it was the nation's first hospital, a landmark highlighted by the recent celebration of its two-hundred-fiftieth anniversary. The original structure, Pine Building, is a National Historic Landmark and remains a section of the hospital, which has expanded in over fifty years of construction. The second floor of the hospital houses the hospital's library, where dark bookcases containing thousands of medical volumes peer from behind panels of hand-blown glass, silently but almost movingly testifying to the intense pursuit of medical knowledge that set Philadelphia on top of the world of medicine at such an early age. The surgical amphitheater and the Museum of Nursing History upstairs from the museum also document the earliest days of the hospital's pioneering staff. Considering the historical significance of Pennsylvania Hospital, one might be surprised to learn that it stills serves the community as a 500-plus bed, acute care facility.

For more than two centuries, Pennsylvania Hospital has been an educational partner of another one of Philadelphia's medical milestones: The University of Pennsylvania Health System (UPHS). The two institutions couldn't be more appropriately cooperative; while Philadelphia Hospital was the nation's first hospital, Penn opened the nation's first medical school. Penn launched its school of medicine in 1765. A little over one hundred years later, it opened the actual hospital and so commenced the nation's first teaching

hospital. Today, *U.S. News & World Report* notes Penn on its list of America's top ten medical schools.

Throughout its long history, Penn never has lost its pace as a pioneer of medicine. Its contributions to medical knowledge and developments in medical technology have significantly improved the lives of people the world over. Acknowledging Penn's achievements, *U.S. News & World Report* consistently ranks the hospital among the best in both the Delaware Valley and the entire nation. The most recent "report card" positioned UHPS as fourteenth in the nation overall. In specialty areas, UHPS ranked highest in the Delaware Valley for thirteen specialties and among the nation's top facilities in fifteen areas, including among the nation's top ten for cancer treatment. Cutting-edge research facilities, some of the worlds top medical experts, and a simple but steadfast devotion to medical progress have made UHPS centrally important in the field of research. Penn's research in the detection, treatment, and prevention of disease has led to breakthrough discoveries in cancer, genetics, imáging, and the neurosciences, to name but a few.

Early in its history, Philadelphia's doctors made the important distinction between physical and mental health. Friends Asylum, one of

▼ **(and Opposite) The Children's Hospital of Philadelphia opened its doors in 1855 as the first hospital in the United States providing health care exclusively to children. Since its opening, the hospital has garnered an impressive list of medical breakthroughs and firsts. Its dedication to excellence has recently led it to a $65-million expansion project that will double the size of its main campus.**

▲ Thomas Jefferson University Hospitals have enhanced the community's quality of life since 1825 with outstanding medical care. When the hospital separated from Thomas Jefferson University in 1995, the Jefferson Health System was established, and it is dedicated to enhancing the community's quality of life through advanced medical treatment and innovative healthcare research.

▶ More than 200 pharmaceutical and biotech companies have headquarters or maintain branches in Greater Philadelphia. Add to that conglomeration the city's 135 medical manufacturers, its 120 hospitals, plus its seven medical schools, and you have the nation's second largest concentration of healthcare resources, which provide outstanding medical care through commitment to research.

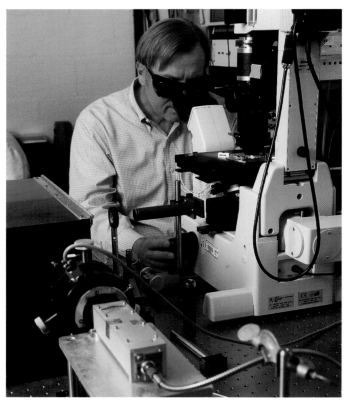

the first hospitals in the nation built strictly for the housing and treatment of the mentally ill, opened on a bucolic and picturesque stretch of land near Philadelphia in 1817. In accordance with their enlightenment principles, the Quaker founders believed such surroundings would be more healthful and restorative to patients than the typically inhumane and dungeon-like asylums found elsewhere in the country. The father of American psychiatry, Dr. Benjamin Rush, pioneered medicine in Philadelphia and laid the groundwork on which much of

modern psychiatry is built. His likeness, in fact, adorns the seal of the American Psychiatric Association to this day.

Philadelphia's founding doctors and hospitals, so fundamental to the history and personality of the city, continue to make an enormous impact on the quality of life in Philadelphia. While first-rate doctors and hospitals make Philadelphia a desirable place for anyone, healthy or not, in which to live, they also possess a magnetic draw for firms specializing in pharmaceutical and life sciences, biotechnology, and medical manufacturing. Currently, more than 200 pharmaceutical and biotech companies have headquarters or maintain branches in Greater Philadelphia. Add to that conglomeration the city's 135 medical manufacturers, its 120 hospitals, plus its seven medical schools, and you have the nation's second largest concentration of healthcare resources. As a crucible of medicine in the United States, it's not surprising that one in every five doctors practicing medicine in the U.S. was trained in Philadelphia, and that the number of practicing physicians in the area exceeds ten thousand.

The number of medical institutions and professionals in Philadelphia and the solid network of cooperation between them adds momentum to the city's ever-expanding medical marketplace. Today, 80 percent of the world's pharmaceutical giants have a presence in Philadelphia, including DuPont, GlaxoSmithKline, and Merck and Co. In fact, 80 percent of the pharmaceutical employment in the United States is contained within a 50-mile radius of

▲ Available twenty-four hours a day, year-round, PENNSTAR Flight program was established by the University of Pennsylvania's hospital. PENNSTAR can provide rapid, critical care air transport from accident scenes and trauma-related incidents within a 100-mile radius of the hospital. Equipped with the most advanced critical care system, the unit can provide complete in-flight treatment for up to two patients.

Philadelphia. The city also ranks fifth nationally for the highest number of small biotech firms, a status that attracts more than $2 billion of federal research money to Philadelphia every year.

Research dollars, in turn, not only fuel the local economy, but trickle down to the community itself, making quality care more abundant and more accessible. Take for instance, the city's younger generations and the local presence of one of the world's best children's hospitals. The Children's Hospital of Philadelphia opened its doors in 1855 as the first hospital in the United States providing health care exclusively to children. Since then, the hospital has garnered an impressive list of medical breakthroughs and firsts in the field of pediatric medicine. Demand for the hospital's services and its dedication to excellence have recently led it to a $65-million expansion project that will double the size of its main campus. The hospital's outstanding inpatient and outpatient services and its continually growing list of medical discoveries piloted it to become the number-one children's hospital in the nation, according to *Child* magazine.

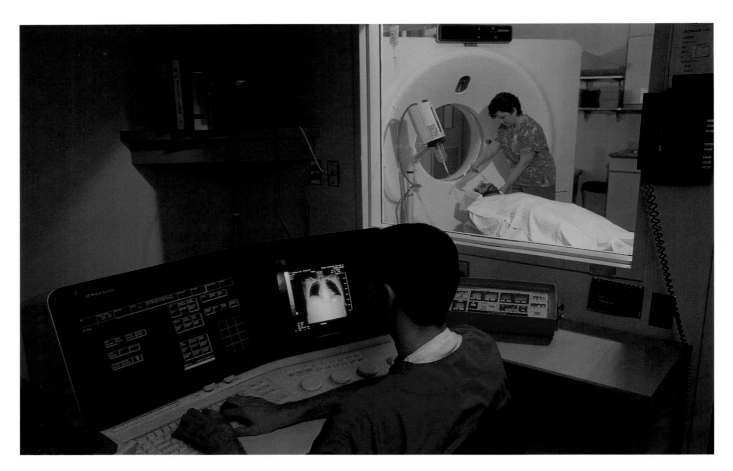

▲ Philadelphia's pioneering doctors and hospitals, so fundamental to the
history and personality of the city, continue to make an enormous impact
on the quality of life in Philadelphia. The area's support of research
facilities allows its healthcare systems to stay on the leading edge of
technology and medical breakthroughs.

In 1892, the Wistar Institute was founded in Philadelphia as the
first institute dedicated solely to medical research. The institute was
named for Dr. Caspar Wistar, a man of immense cultural sophistication and intellectual prowess. Like his namesake institute, Dr. Wistar
was prodigious in the realm of medicine. He authored the first
American anatomy textbook, served as chair of the Department of
Anatomy at the University of Pennsylvania, and became president of
the American Philosophical Society, a seat next held by his friend
Thomas Jefferson. Such legendary accomplishments echo those of
the Wistar Institute today. Its four areas of research—molecular
genetics, structural biology, tumor biology, and tumor immunology—
continue to yield advances that revolutionize medicine. Wistar scientists were among the first to develop the protein molecules that
can detect and destroy foreign invaders such as cancer cells; they
have identified key genes associated with breast, lung, and prostate
cancers; and they discovered a molecule known as human inter-
leukin-12, believed to have an immense impact on the body's
immune response to cancers and infectious agents including HIV.

Wistar and the region's other excellent bio-pharmaceutical
research institutes benefit from an influx of capital from both state
and private sources. The state committed nearly all of its recent
$11.3-billion tobacco settlement (to be paid in $397- and $459-
million annual installments over the next twenty-five years) to
medical research and health care. Hundreds of millions of dollars
have already been allocated to the state's healthcare and biotechnology industries, most of which are located in the Greater Philadelphia
Area. The impact of these payments on the city of Philadelphia will
be profound. Indeed, it already is. A new biotechnology incubator in
the city—one of three being created statewide—will expedite
biotech research and discovery. Millions also will be directed to university research, and millions more set aside as venture capital to be
applied as needed. These investments, in turn, are expected to
attract upwards of $180 million more annually in co-investments
from the city's numerous biotechnology venture firms. Philadelphia's
medical community will continue to receive cash injections for the
next quarter century, securing its future as a vital hub of medicine
and biotechnology. ℗

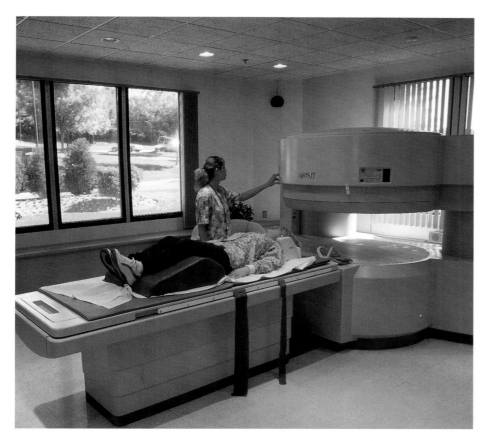

◀ (and Below) Philadelphia has forged the way in American medicine longer than the United States has been a country. One in every five doctors practicing medicine in the U.S. was trained in Philadelphia, and the number of practicing physicians in the area exceeds 10,000. Whether receiving an open MRI through advanced technology or undergoing the newest medical procedures at St. Mary's Hospital, Delaware Valley residents have access to the world's finest health care.

◀ 173

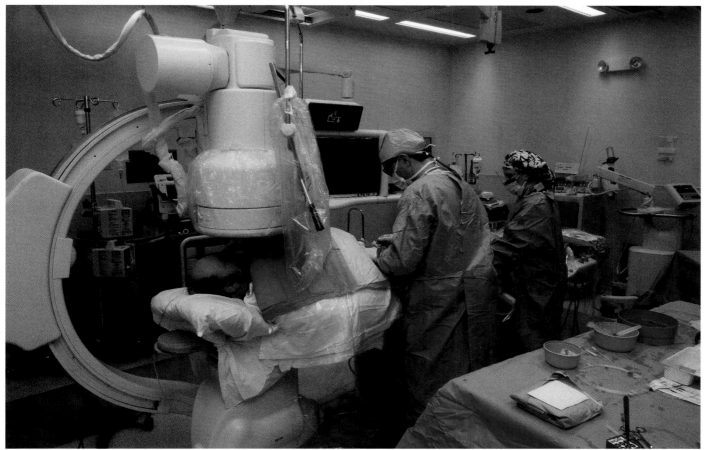

▲ NovaCare Rehabilitation, a division of Select Medical Corporation of Mechanicsburg, Pennsylvania, operates a number of rehabilitation facilities in the Greater Philadelphia Area.

◀ From preventative to rehabilitative medicine, Philadelphia area health care is advanced and accessible to residents. Patients needing follow-up care after surgery or injury have many choices for therapy at their disposal through local hospitals or private organizations.

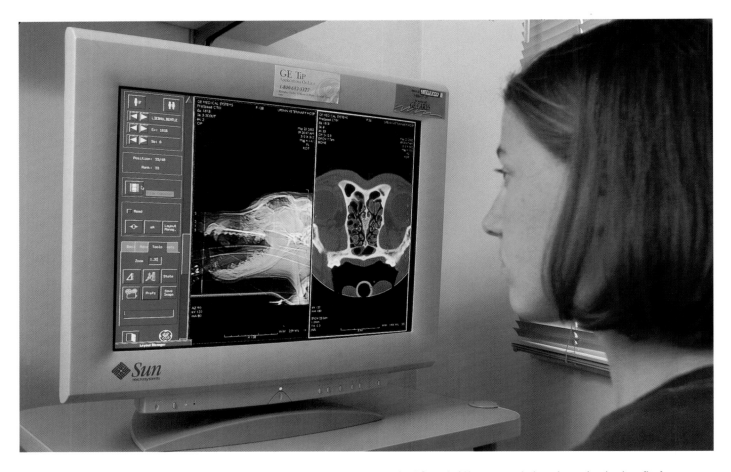

▲ (and Opposite) Humans aren't the only species that benefits from cutting-edge health care in Philadelphia. The Veterinary Hospital of the University of Pennsylvania (VHUP) sees more than 20,000 small animal patients annually, making it the country's busiest veterinary teaching hospital. Established in 1884, VHUP is the only school of veterinary medicine developed in association with a medical school. This unique affiliation led to the establishment of animal nutrition and genetics, the first such departments for animals in the country.

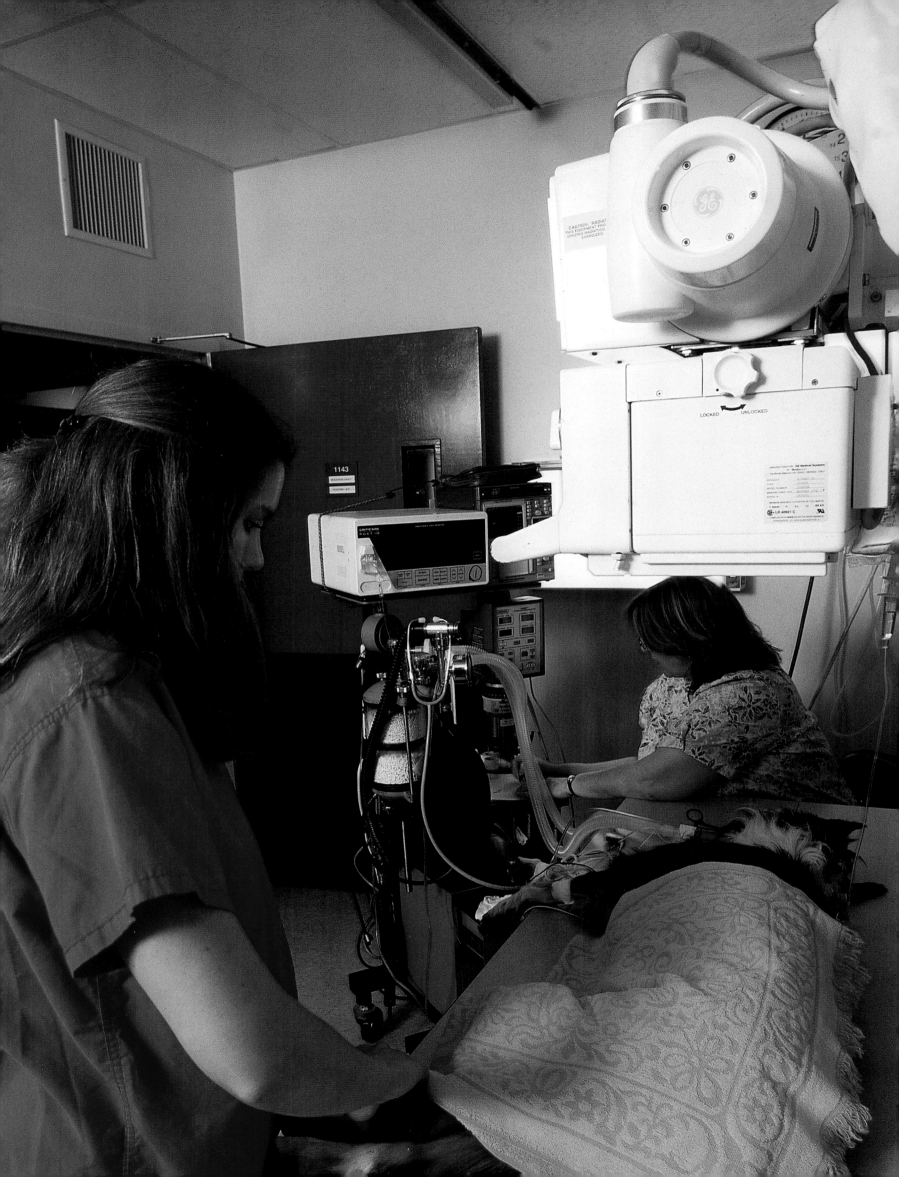

▲ Medical research and development in the Greater Philadelphia Area form a substantial part of the local economy. Research dollars, in turn, not only fuel the local economy, but trickle down to the community itself, making quality care more abundant and more accessible. For instance, the critical care telemetry unit at St. Mary's Medical Center allows the staff to monitor patients on individual computer screens.

◀ (Opposite) The number of medical institutions and professionals in Philadelphia and the solid network of cooperation between them add momentum to the city's ever-expanding medical marketplace and continually increases the quality of care for the community. These cooperative efforts are supported by the medical research teams at institutions such as the University of Pennsylvania.

CHAPTER EIGHT

Hi, Neighbor!

The counties surrounding Philadelphia are home to some of the
country's most impressive rural estates; however, not all of these were residential. Hopewell Furnace in Berks County was once a self-contained iron
plantation with a furnace complex and ironmaster's mansion in the early
nineteenth century. It was at Hopewell that the cannons for Washington's
army were cast. Today, the picturesque iron plantation is a Historic
National Site and popular tourist attraction.

Since its beginnings as William Penn's "holy experiment," even when it was just a utopian vision in the founder's mind, Philadelphia was destined to become a great metropolis in the New World. The fundamental American ideals of liberty and equality, so eloquently written into the Constitution, were a way of life in Philadelphia long before they became a part of the American record. To the north were the religiously austere and persecutive communities of Puritan New England. To the south lay a vast agriculturally rich society shackled by slavery. In between sat a city with open minds and open doors—a city that quickly grew to become the largest city in America and second in size only to London in the British Empire.

Today, Philadelphia is the second largest American city on the East Coast, and the social and economic nexus of a broad geographic area encompassing three states and eleven counties. A short ride across the Delaware River by ferry, bridge, or tunnel keeps the city connected to the New Jersey counties of Mercer, Burlington, Camden, Gloucester, and Salem. To the south, Philadelphia connects to New Castle County in Delaware, the most populous county in the state. Bucks, Montgomery, Chester, and Delaware Counties in Pennsylvania surround Philadelphia County to the west and north.

◀ 183

◀ As early as the eighteenth century, distinguished families from Philadelphia sought to escape the bustle of city life, and those who could afford to established estates and manors amidst the rolling hills and leafy forests of the Pennsylvania countryside. Andalusia, a stately Greek Revival estate on the banks of the Delaware River, was originally built in 1797 and used as a farmhouse by the Biddles—Philadelphia's wealthy banking family. The estate was remodeled in 1834 by Nicholas Biddle, the president of the Second Bank of the United States.

▲ Henry Lewis, a Welsh Quaker and one of the first European settlers in Haverford Township, settled the Grange Estate in Havertown in 1682. The historic buildings and eighteenth-century gardens cover nearly ten acres. On weekends from April to October, visitors can explore the grounds and get a sense of what life in the New World was like for the early settlers.

◀ The Pearl S. Buck House in Perkasie offers guided tours to the public. Built in 1835, the 60-acre homestead was owned by the first American woman to win both a Nobel and a Pulitzer Prize for literature. Visitors to Perkasie may also enjoy the town's 5,000-acre Nockamixon Park—an ideal setting for a picnic, leisurely horseback ride, and other outdoor recreation.

▲ In 1908, Henry Mercer, founder of the Mercer Museum, built and resided in Fonthill, an imposing castle-style home nestled on sixty acres of land. The castle is open to the public and provides tours through its astonishingly ornate forty-four rooms. The residence and museum, together with the Spruance Library and an annual Folk Fest on the grounds, are some of the premier attractions in Bucks County.

Within these counties, each city and town is intrinsically linked to the city of Philadelphia, whose enchanting vertical skyline, appropriately enough, soars upward in the middle of the metropolis to be seen for miles in all directions.

The effect of Philadelphia's commanding presence on many of the outlying communities is undeniably urban. Many of the towns and cities in the port area, such as Camden, New Jersey, and Wilmington, Delaware, continue to function not just as hubs of river transportation and commerce, but as key centers along the industrial backbone of the region. Despite the colossal economic significance of these communities, many are nonetheless experiencing a backward flow of the blight too often left behind in the wake of industry. Take Camden, New Jersey, for example. Like many cities throughout the highly industrialized state, Camden suffered from economic recession throughout the 1980s and early 1990s, a state of affairs further worsened by its transition from a manufacturing-based economy to a more service-oriented business community. With a healthy

economy, a strong friend in Philadelphia, and a brighter vision of the future, Camden has undergone a rebirth in recent years. The New Jersey State Aquarium, situated on Camden's waterfront directly across the Delaware River from Penn's Landing, offers visitors a world of aquatic learning and adventure. Adjacent to the aquarium is the Camden's Children's Garden, a wonderland of nature and storybook fantasy for kids. Just south of the aquarium sits the Tweeter Center at the Waterfront, a venue for performances and special events that seats up to seven thousand visitors and draws several coveted concerts and other performances to Camden every year. Two blocks east of the riverfront is the Walt Whitman House, a National Historic Landmark that gives visitors an intimate glimpse into the life of one the country's most revered poets. A little further south, the casinos and boardwalks of Atlantic City stretch out along the rolling ocean, providing Philadelphians a quick and easy escape for the day or weekend. Generations of younger Philadelphians have spent summer vacations riding roller coasters and braving haunted mansions at the amusement park piers of Wildwood while their parents basked in the sunshine and Victorian charm of Cape May.

Just a short drive north of Philadelphia yet a world removed from the urban bustle of Center City is Bucks County, a pastoral haven steeped in country charm and colonial heritage. The county seat, Doylestown, is a sterling example of historical preservation—street after street, architectural styles run the gamut from colonial to

Victorian, creating a singular snapshot of the city's rich past. The
Mercer Museum, a showcase of American industry and innovation
before mechanization, houses some fifty thousand tools representing
more than sixty trades in addition to exhibits of folk art and other
Americana. In 1908, Henry Mercer, the museum's founder, built and
resided in Fonthill, an imposing castle-style home nestled on sixty
acres of land. The castle is open to the public and provides tours
through its astonishingly ornate forty-four rooms. The James A.
Michener Art Museum is another of Doylestown's main attractions.
Named after the famous author and native of Doylestown, the museum showcases the work of many regional artists and carries on the
town's artistic legacy.

Montgomery County, which straddles Bucks County to the south
and Philadelphia County to the west, is home to Valley Forge, the
winter camp that defines the hardship, sacrifice, and devastation of the
American Revolution. Two thousand patriots died here of hunger, disease, and bitter cold during the winter of 1777-1778—more soldiers
than were killed in the battles of Brandywine and Germantown combined. The 3,600-acre Valley Forge National Historical Park is the centerpiece attraction of Valley Forge. On a clear spring or summer day,
the park's rolling green hills and flowering dogwood trees make it difficult for visitors to imagine the brutal winter that claimed so many
lives. Reminders can be found throughout the park in several statues
and monuments and in exhibits housed at the visitor's center.

▲ **Time travel is possible in the Greater Philadelphia Area. Visitors seeking some intimation with the past may explore seemingly countless estates and museums from every page in the city's history—each carefully preserved and true to its original form as possible. The Margaret R. Grundy Museum in Bristol is a sterling example of a Victorian residence, inside and out. Fine examples of luxurious European woodwork are found throughout the house.**

Just minutes away from the historical grounds of Valley Forge sits
a tremendous shrine to American commerce and capitalism—the
King of Prussia Mall. Containing nearly four hundred stores and
forty restaurants and eateries, the mall is the largest mall east of the
Mississippi and the second largest in the country. Thousands of people include the mall on their itinerary when visiting the Philadelphia
area, and thousands more make the mall a destination in itself, arriving from areas near and far.

A little farther south lies the picturesque countryside of Chester
County, considered by many visitors and residents to be without equal
in terms of charm and beauty. Chester County occupies a large swath
of the Brandywine Valley. Visitors can realign themselves with the
rhythms of nature as they amble down country roads, cross bubbling
streams on covered bridges, or bike through pristine forests and meadows of wildflowers. Industrialist Pierre S. du Pont established
Longwood Gardens in Chester County on over a thousand acres of

▲ Chadds Ford in Delaware County is home to Brandywine Battlefield, site of the largest engagement between George Washington's Continental Army and British troops, led by General William Howe. The battle nearly dealt a devastating blow to Washington's troops and led to the British occupation of Philadelphia on September 26, 1777—just two weeks after the September 11 battle.

land approximately three miles north of Kennett Square, Pennsylvania, and twelve miles north of Wilmington, Delaware. The horticultural marvel attracts more than nine hundred thousand visitors each year who arrive to explore an Eden containing forty gardens (twenty outdoor and twenty indoor greenhouse gardens), spectacular fountains, meadows, and forests. Concerts, plays, classes, educational demonstrations, and a calendar of special events make Longwood Gardens a regular destination for many area residents.

Chadds Ford in Delaware County is the home to Brandywine Battlefield, site of the largest engagement between George Washington's Continental Army and British troops, led by General William Howe. During the battle, a frontal feint on the Continental Army preceded an all-out attack on its right wing by General Charles Cornwallis' troops. Washington's men were forced to withdraw to the town of Chester. The pivotal defeat led to British occupation of Philadelphia on September 26, 1777—two weeks after the September 11 battle. Today, echoes of this chapter in American history are still present throughout the well-preserved eighteenth-century homes and villages of Delaware County.

The Winterthur Museum, Garden, and Library in nearby Winterthur, Delaware, was once the country home of Henry Francis du Pont. The estate now houses an impressive collection of early American decorative arts predating 1860. Outside, visitors can explore nearly a thousand acres of paradise, filled with native and exotic plants, ponds, woods, and meadows.

Philadelphia's neighboring communities provide a diversity of housing and lifestyle options. Many city workers who punch the clock in downtown Philadelphia drive home each evening to their

homes in the country or in one of the scores of historical villages in the area. Likewise, residents who enjoy the pulse of big city living may easily leave their downtown apartments and lofts for a getaway in the countryside, whether for a couple of weeks or just a couple of hours. Living is easy in Philadelphia even without a car. The extensive SEPTA railroad and rail transit system keeps the cities and towns of the Greater Philadelphia Area connected to the city and to each other, making the attractions, historical sites, and suburban neighborhoods easily accessible to anyone within SEPTA's reach. ℗

▲ Pennsbury Manor, a reconstruction of William Penn's country home, gives visitors a glimpse of daily life in Philadelphia during the 1600s. The original manor was in many ways a manifestation of Penn's steadfast belief in the wholesomeness of country life. Visitors will feel a sense of Quaker community and compassion as they explore the grounds, which bring to life the city founder's "greene Country Towne."

▼ After the Battle of Brandywine, General Howe's men set up camp in Germantown. On October 4, 1777, Washington launched a surprise attack on the British and Hessian troops in Germantown. Hearing the attack but confused by a blanket of heavy fog, another American detachment opened fire on its own troops, forcing a retreat. Despite the failed attack, Washington's determined offensive so soon after the defeat at Brandywine and an American victory at Saratoga convinced France to form an alliance with the Americans.

◀ (Opposite) Peddler's Village in the Bucks County town of Lahaska is a 42-acre country-style complex containing eight restaurants, more than seventy specialty shops, the Golden Plough Inn, beautifully landscaped gardens, and an entertainment center. Besides being one of the Philadelphia area's prime shopping attractions, Peddler's Village is also the location of many seasonal events and festivities, which are open to the public for free.

◀ Industrialist Pierre S. du Pont established Longwood Gardens in Chester County. The garden is a horticultural Eden containing forty gardens (twenty outdoor and twenty indoor greenhouse gardens), spectacular fountains, meadows, and forests. Concerts, plays, classes, educational demonstrations, and a calendar of special events make Longwood Gardens a regular destination for many area residents.

▼ The Brandywine River Museum in Chadds Ford showcases the works of three generations of Wyeths and a celebrated collection of illustrations, still lifes, and landscape paintings by American artists. The museum, housed in a nineteenth-century gristmill atop the river, is also home to The Brandywine Conservancy's Wildflower and Native Plant Gardens.

◀ 189

▶ In 1818, fifty years before the establishment of public schools in the area, a local community of families, mostly Mennonites, donated the labor and money to build a one-room schoolhouse in Chester County. The single-room octagonal structure also served as a Mennonite meeting house until 1835.

▶ (Opposite) The Wharton Esherick Museum in Paoli exhibits the extraordinary woodworking masterpieces of the craftsmen for whom it is named. Esherick, called the "Dean of American Craftsmen," died in 1970 at the age of 83. The unparalleled legacy of wooden artistry he left behind is open to the public.

▼ Ridley Creek State Park, situated on the southeastern-most tip of Pennsylvania, contains some of the best trails for hiking and biking anywhere as well as horse rental facilities and an equestrian trail nearly five miles long. A working farm for more than 300 years, the Park's Colonial Pennsylvania Plantation is a research and educational facility "dedicated to the preservation of knowledge about the ordinary citizen of the eighteenth century."

▶ (and Below) Built in 1758, the Peter Wentz Farmstead in Worcester Township, Pennsylvania, contains a quaint, Georgian-style farmhouse, a reconstructed barn housing farm animals that were typically raised in the eighteenth century, as well as gardens, orchards, and fields that are all tended to and harvested as they would have been in the 1700s. Though operated as a living museum of eighteenth-century farm life, the Peter Wentz Farmstead is actually a true working farm. During 1777, George Washington chose the farmstead as his headquarters while planning the Battle of Germantown.

◀ From 1722 to 1750, many Philadelphia area physicians frequently recommended to their patients a trip to the Township of Pikeland for a dip in the mineral springs. The waters of Yellow Springs, regarded as healthful and restorative, were the center of a small colonial town formed there. The cluster of historical buildings is now owned by Historic Yellow Springs, a non-profit, educational organization devoted to the town's preservation.

▼ The Gothic-Romanesque Bryn Athyn Cathedral towers over the hills of Montgomery County. Construction of the cathedral began in 1913 and continued for thirty years. The cathedral is one of the world centers of the Church of the New Jerusalem, a latter-day Christian sect based on the writing of Emmanuel Swedenborg, an eighteenth-century scientist and philosopher.

(Following page) As its named suggests, Washington Crossing Historic Park marks the site where Washington led his tattered but determined troops across the icy Delaware River and attacked the unsuspecting Hessian troops in Trenton. The historic site covers 500 acres and contains thirteen historic buildings, the 100-acre Bowman's Hill Wildflower Preserve and observation tower, and ample recreational space.

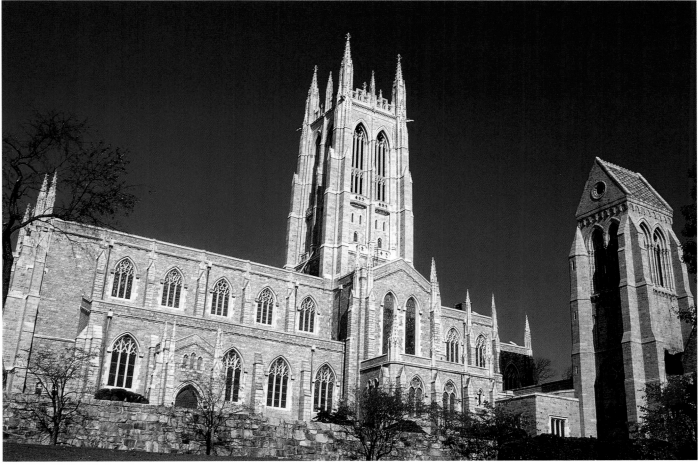

Philadelphia may be a city on the move, but there's always time for play.
No matter what season, Philadelphians of all ages enjoy a backyard
full of recreational opportunities.

The Eagles, Philadelphia's professional football team, have been enthralling crowds of reverent fans since the team's beginnings in 1933. Thanks to the city's unabashed dedication to its home team, Philadelphia's "autumn colors" are midnight green, silver, and white as much as they are the golden hues of fall. Since 1971, the Eagles have filled the 65,356-seat Veterans Stadium (affectionately referred to as "the Vet") to capacity or near capacity for every game, but starting in 2003, the team will call a new 43-acre modern stadium home. Officially to be known as Lincoln Financial Field and carrying a price tag of nearly $400 million, the new stadium will provide dramatic improvements for both the team and the sixty-six thousand fans it will seat during NFL showdowns. State-of-the-art audio and video systems, dramatically improved sightlines, extra-wide concourses, improved parking, and more restrooms, escalators, and elevators are just some of the amenities that Lincoln Financial Field will offer. How much these improvements will benefit team performance remains to be determined, yet there is no question that the new stadium will have a resounding impact on Philadelphia's economy.

NBA action riles up 76ers fans at Philadelphia's word-class First Union Center. The Sixers have called Philadelphia home since 1963, just after the Warriors left the City of Brotherly Love for San Francisco. Ever since, Philadelphians have claimed quite a few legends on the court, including Wilt Chamberlain, Charles Barkley, and Allen Iverson—each of whom has been named the NBA's Most Valuable Player (MVP).

Any 76ers home game reveals the importance of the team to the city's devoted fans, but the team's dedication to the community, while not as showy, is just as profound. The Sixers Charities is an umbrella organization for several youth-oriented charities and programs, all of which aim to improve the quality of life for children of all ages throughout the Delaware Valley. The Sixers actively promote reading to increase awareness and education; speak at schools, youth centers, and hospitals in the Philadelphia area; organize youth basketball leagues for the physical and social benefit of city children; lead fundraisers for several charities;, and take on a number of other missions too innumerable to mention.

Philadelphia has a habit of creating world firsts. It is also a city where buildings, neighborhoods, organizations, and landmarks weather the test of time to become the oldest of their kind in the country or the world. What better place, then, could be home to the oldest, continuous, one-name, one-city franchise in the world of professional sports than Philadelphia? Formed in 1883, the city's major league baseball team, The Phillies, did not begin its first season on an auspicious note. The team lost its first game to the Providence Grays and won just seventeen games out of ninety-eight that season. In spite of its gloomy start, however, the Phillies pulled through more than a century fundamentally the same, yet stronger than ever.

Like the Eagles, the Phillies will soon be leaving Veterans Stadium for a modern facility on twenty-one acres. The new Phillies

Ballpark will sport forty-three thousand seats on three levels and is slated to open in the spring of 2004 near the intersection of 10th Street and Pattison Avenue. The park will feature both aesthetic and function improvements including wide plazas, restaurants, and a panoramic view of the Philadelphia skyline beyond centerfield. In addition to imparting to the city a healthy dose of all-American fun, the Phillies are active community caretakers, donating time, money, and reputation to a spectrum of local charities, most of which are dedicated to assisting the area's children.

Every year from fall to spring, Philadelphians head to the First Union Center for fast-paced action on ice and a chance to see their NHL home team, the Philadelphia Flyers, outskate and outscore its

opponents with all the slick and rough-edged sportsmanship professional hockey can offer. For more than thirty-five years, the Flyers
have remained an active part of the Philadelphia community,
whether on or off the ice. When they're not training or competing,
Flyers players participate in youth hockey programs and make
appearances at educational events and charity fundraisers.
Philadelphia's professional American Hockey League team, the
Phantoms, also sets the ice on fire at the First Union Spectrum.

The Philadelphia Charge, one of the eight charter member teams
in the newly formed Women's United Soccer Association (WUSA), is
the city's newest professional team. Playing out of Villanova Stadium,
The Charge has garnered a following of enthusiastic fans from all

▲ **The Greater Philadelphia Area has ample world-class golf courses, both
public and private, for the golfing enthusiast. With a notably historical
ambience, Merion Golf Course and Country Club is home to one of the
oldest courses in the area.**

over the Delaware Valley, particularly made up of young women and
their families. Some of the most celebrated names in women's soccer
play for the team, and the games are an affordable and easily accessible family outing during the spring and summer evenings.

Soccer may have quite a way to go before it achieves the levels of
national popularity and enthusiasm it enjoys in Europe and Latin
America, but Philadelphia's soccer fever is running high nonetheless.

▲ **The Blue Cross River Rink at Festival Pier in Penn's Landing is an outdoor ice skating rink that offers skate rentals and skating lessons. Extended skating sessions allow skaters to enjoy the rink late into the night.**

When the women's soccer season ends, the professional indoor soccer season begins, keeping the calendar pretty much filled with soccer action year-round.

The Philadelphia Kixx, a National Professional Soccer League team, competes on Saturday nights at the First Union Spectrum beginning in October. While both The Charge and the Kixx are recent additions to Philadelphia's roster of pro sports teams, the future of professional soccer in Philadelphia appears to be bright.

In addition to all its major league sports teams, Philadelphia is home to some of the most action-packed college athletics. With nearly one hundred post-secondary schools, colleges, and universities in the Greater Philadelphia Area, the opportunities to enjoy an electrifying game of college football, baseball, basketball, hockey, soccer, and lacrosse would be overwhelming if it weren't for school allegiances. Big Five collegiate basketball is back in Philadelphia, offering hoop-crazy sports enthusiasts game upon game of fast-paced action on the court and pitting rivalries amongst The Explorers (La Salle), The Hawks (St. Joseph's), The Owls (Temple), The Penn Quakers (The University of Pennsylvania), and the Wildcats (Villanova).

The largest collegiate regatta in the United States, The Dad Vail Regatta, is an annual rowing competition held on the Schuylkill River. Every May, the regatta draws thousands of student rowers from over one hundred colleges nationwide to Philadelphia to race down the 2,000-meter, six-lane Olympic distance course. As the largest event of its kind in the U.S., the regatta draws international attention to the sport of rowing.

A new generation of sports and sports enthusiasts culminates in the annual ESPN X Games, the Olympics of action sports such as skateboarding, BMX, Moto X, inline skating, wakeboarding, street luge, and speed climbing. Philadelphia first hosted the Summer X Games VII in August 2001, with most of the event venues at the First Union Complex. The indoor and outdoor competitions at the First Union Center, along with additional events at venues in the Schuylkill River, downtown Philadelphia, and Woodward Camp, drew about 235,000 spectators. Participants compete for medals and over $1 million in prize money in a medley of wild, hair-raising competitions free for public viewing.

The Greater Philadelphia Area also offers abundant opportunities to enjoy the great outdoors. In minutes, city dwellers can leave the metro area behind without venturing beyond the city limits when they visit Fairmount Park. Spread out on 4,180 acres on the banks of the Schuylkill River, Fairmount Park is the largest landscaped park in the United States and a local paradise for Philadelphians.

▲ Although many players exclaim over the challenge of the Merion's golf course, the country club has other offerings, including lawn tennis, which is very popular in England and other countries abroad.

◀ In the nineteenth century, Philadelphia was the cricket capital of the East Coast with as many as 120 cricket clubs. While the sport continues to be played and watched by millions of fans all over the world, especially in the British Commonwealth countries, the advent of baseball diminished its popularity in the U.S. While not as common as it used to be, cricket is still enjoyed by many in the Philadelphia area. The annual Philadelphia Cricket Festival has spearheaded a local renaissance of the sport.

▲ A new generation of sports and sports enthusiasts culminates in the annual ESPN X Games, the Olympics of action sports such as skateboarding, BMX, Moto X, inline skating, wakeboarding, street luge, and speed climbing. Most of the events are in or near the First Union Complex.

Walking, jogging, and rollerblading in the peaceful wooded acres or just relaxing with a good book in one of the park's sunny meadows are activities that allow city dwellers a chance to leave the bustling streets behind and commune with the quieter side of life. The park also contains public tennis courts and picnic areas, miles of bicycle paths, hundreds of historical monuments and statues, outdoor venues and amphitheaters for musical performances, and a number of other features that make it such a vital aspect of the Philadelphia lifestyle.

A short drive northeast of Philadelphia leads to the Pocono Mountains, home to a dozen ski resorts, twice as many public golf courses, luxurious spas, and mountain lakes ideal for swimming, boating, fishing, and a slew of other water sports. Heading west from the city, Philadelphians can exit the twenty-first century and travel centuries back in time when they come upon Amish country and the rustic charm of villages in Pennsylvania's Dutch Country. Mile after mile of sandy beaches emerge with summertime fun. Whichever direction one departs Philadelphia from, one thing is certain: Philadelphians have a backyard full of seasonal recreational opportunities. ℗

◀ With nearly 100 post-secondary schools, colleges, and universities in the Greater Philadelphia Area, the countless opportunities to enjoy an electrifying athletic event might be overwhelming if it weren't for school allegiances. The Penn State Relays is just one competition that allows superior athletes to showcase their talents for the national level.

▼ The Dad Vail Regatta is the largest collegiate regatta in the United States. Every May, the regatta draws thousands of student rowers from more than 100 colleges nationwide to Philadelphia to race down the 2,000-meter, six-lane Olympic distance course on the Schuylkill River.

▲ Radnor Hunt Races in nearby Malvern, Pennsylvania, offers world-class racing and steeplechase events to the public. All proceeds from the Radnor Hunt Races go toward the Brandywine Conservatory's efforts to preserve the natural and cultural resources of Southeastern Pennsylvania and Northern Delaware.

▶ (Above) The Greater Philadelphia Area hosts scores of road races and marathons each year, including the annual Vietnam Memorial 10K run— some for cash prizes, some for charity, and some for nothing but awareness of a cause or the sheer fun of it.

▶ (Below) The First Union Liberty Classic is the only World Cup Cycling race event for women in the U.S. and the single-day women's event with the largest purse in the world. The race consists of five laps on a 14.4-mile course through Philadelphia, and includes steep climbs up the Manayunk Wall.

▲ By day, the rowing clubs at Boathouse Row ply the waters of the
Schuylkill. By night, the boathouses themselves are a fascinating sight,
each one strung with festive white lights. The boathouses were built along
the Schuylkill River from the 1860s to 1904, and, today, local rowing teams
own and use the clubhouses—a true testament to the city's love of
sculling, then as now.

▶ NBA action riles up 76ers fans at Philadelphia's word-class First Union Center, yet the 76ers are known in Philadelphia for their work off the court as well as on. Sixers Charities, Sixers Camps, the annual Beach Bash, and many other charity and community events make the 76ers players popular icons with adults and children in the area.

▼ Every year from fall to spring, Philadelphians head to the First Union Center for fast-paced action on ice and a chance to see their NHL home team, the Philadelphia Flyers, outskate and outscore their opponents with all the slick and rough-edged sportsmanship professional hockey can offer.

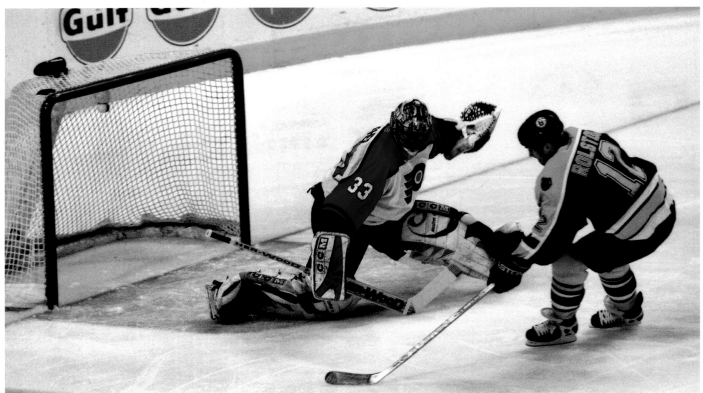

◀ The Philadelphia Kixx, a National Professional Soccer League team, competes on Saturday nights at the First Union Spectrum beginning in October. The team exhibits the moves and excitement that are rapidly increasing the sport's popularity in the U.S.

▼ Philadelphia's National Lacrosse Team, the Philadelphia Wings, are the city's top attraction for thousands of enthusiastic and supportive fans. Since the team's first game in January 1997, the Wings have entertained crowds at First Union Center when playing with home-field advantage.

▲ Win or lose, students are always eager to cheer for the Explorers during fall football games. With more than twenty athletic programs from men's baseball and golf to women's field hockey and lacrosse and everything in-between, La Salle University produces top athletes that are actively recruited by professional sports teams.

▶ The Philadelphia Eagles have been captivating crowds since the team's beginnings in 1933. Starting in 2003, NFL showdowns between the Eagles and visiting teams will take place in the new 43-acre modern stadium, officially to be known as Lincoln Financial Field.

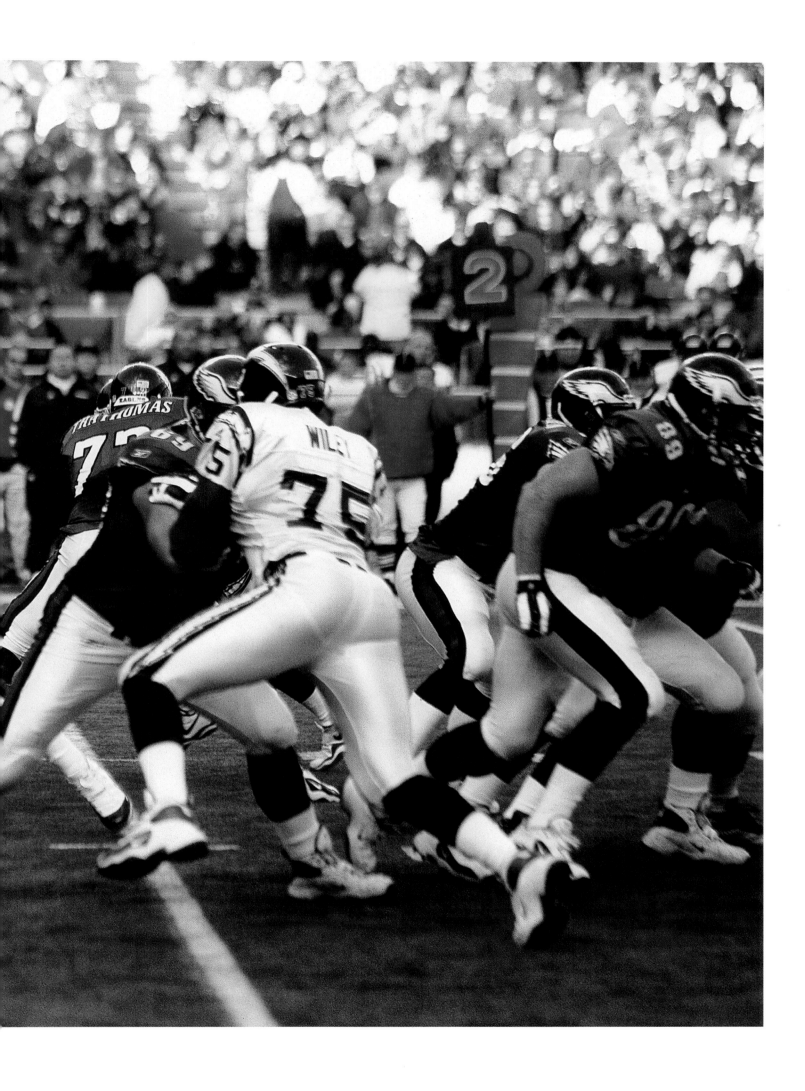

▲ Appropriately enough, Philadelphia, the city of firsts, is home to the
oldest continuously operating one-name, one-city franchise in the world of
professional sports—the Phillies. As of April 2004, Philadelphia's favorite
Major League Baseball team will play out of the new three-level, 43,000-
seat Phillies Stadium in Phillies Ballpark.

Part Two

CHAPTER TEN

Networks, Energy & Transportation

(Right) The Greater Philadelphia area's communications, energy, and transportation firms keep information, power, and products circulating throughout the Delaware Valley. Photo ©2002 John McGrail

(Previous page) The Philadelphia skyline illuminates the Delaware River at dusk. Photo ©2002 John McGrail

▶ Philadelphia International Airport

A world-class city needs a world-class airport. In Philadelphia International Airport (PHL), Philadelphia's citizens and visitors have a facility that is worthy of one of America's top destination cities. Throughout its history, PHL has served as Philadelphia's gateway to the world, hosting dignitaries ranging from Amelia Earhart and Charles Lindbergh in its formative years to world figures such as Lech Walensa and Nelson Mandela in recent years.

PHL has an undeniable economic impact on the Delaware Valley. Owned and operated by the City of Philadelphia, the airport is a self-sustaining entity that operates without the use of local tax dollars. Additionally, PHL supplies nearly $220 million in state and local taxes annually and almost $2 billion in wages to Delaware Valley residents.

During the last decade, Philadelphia has seen a steady increase in the numbers of both national and international visitors. For a large portion of Philadelphia's guests, PHL is the first impression they have of the city, and making that first experience a positive one is the force that drives the staff of Philadelphia International Airport. To accomplish this mission, PHL has initiated a number of customer service and passenger amenity programs. One key component is the Public Information Program, which is staffed 24 hours a day by helpful individuals who assist in everything from flight information and general Airport information to recommending a restaurant or hotel in the Philadelphia area.

▲ The 800,000-square-foot new International Terminal offers the latest in passenger convenience.

In addition to its customer service programs, PHL offers visitors and guests a variety of enjoyable diversions that serve to either pass the time between flights or help them get better acquainted with the city. PHL's innovative retail program features more than 100 shops and eateries that range from national name brands to regional favorites that show what Philadelphia has to offer. PHL was recently named recipient of three prestigious awards from Airports Council International-North America, including the top honor, the Richard A. Griesbach Award of Excellence for best overall retail program. PHL is also one of a handful of airports in the nation that features an Art Exhibition Program. The exhibitions program is made up of twelve rotating displays that feature fine arts, crafts, design, and photography throughout the airport and is widely acclaimed in both the airport and art communities.

As an airport that has had steady growth in passenger volume, PHL is in a position that requires continued expansion and evaluation of its infrastructure.

◀ Twenty-four million passengers pass through PHL each year.

▲ The $100 million Regional Terminal F opened in 2001.

carousels, and a state-of-the-art security system. The artwork in the Arrivals Hall in the new international terminal, created by Rob Fisher, welcomes visitors from all over the world with a larger-than-life artistic vision of the Declaration of Independence. Made up of 13 pieces of stained glass, symbolizing the original 13 colonies, and a 90-foot long wall featuring larger-than-life representations of the 56 signatures of the Declaration of Independence, the Arrivals Hall gives visitors a sense of Philadelphia's significance in the history of the United States.

Throughout, the most important aspect of PHL is not its state-of-the-art equipment, or the size and scope of its operations, but is rather the attitude that the PHL staff takes in doing their jobs. Exceeding passenger expectations, supporting its airlines in every way possible, and continuing to bring growth and opportunity to the Delaware Valley remain the goals of Philadelphia International Airport. ●

◀ 219

In the early 1990s, PHL embarked on an ambitious phase of expansion that has almost doubled the number of the airport's gates. Additions to Terminals D and E increase the size of each terminal by four gates and include expanded facilities for baggage claim and enhanced concessions. The construction of Regional Terminal F, an 185,000-square-foot facility, added 38 much-needed gates. The majority of theses gates are equipped with loading bridges specifically designed for Regional Jets, allowing commuter passengers to travel in comfort and ease.

One of the most important aspects of the airport's expansion program is the new 800,000-square-foot International Terminal. As Philadelphia continues to grow in its role as a major international access point to the East Coast, the number of foreign visitors continues to increase. The new International Terminal affords PHL the opportunity to accommodate this influx of new guests with 60 new ticket counter positions, 56 Immigration and Naturalization Service positions, 19 gates, 8 high-speed baggage

▶ PHL is located just seven miles from Center City Philadelphia.

▶ PECO, An Exelon Company

*P*ECO Energy delivers electricity to 1.52 million customers and natural gas to 442,000 customers in southeastern Pennsylvania. Based in Philadelphia, PECO and its sister utility, ComEd in the Chicago area, are subsidiaries of Exelon—one of the nation's leading energy firms and the largest energy delivery company in the United States. Exelon was created in October of 2002 when PECO Energy teamed up with Chicago-based Unicom.

The merger with Unicom was only the latest event in a history that began in 1881, almost with the birth of electricity itself. The introduction of electricity as a power source for the masses in the late nineteenth and early twentieth centuries gave birth to dozens of tiny electric companies in the Philadelphia area, among them was The Philadelphia Electric Company. The following decades brought significant consolidation that culminated in the incorporation of all the power companies as one, in what is now known today as PECO.

While known as the primary source of electricity and natural gas for its customers, allowing them to carry on at work and home, PECO also acts as a major player in the community leading civic organizations, providing employee volunteers, and making substantial donations to hundreds of not-for-profit organizations. It's a major supporter of the arts and education, specifically organizations that focus on family and children. PECO also sponsors some of the area's leading cultural institutions such as The Franklin Institute Science Museum, the Philadelphia Zoo, the Kimmel Center for the Performing Arts, Independence Seaport Museum, The Mann Music Center, and Lights of Liberty—a nightly light and sound show documenting the birth of America that takes place from Spring through Fall in the city's historical district. Additionally, PECO's president, Kenneth G. Lawrence, serves the Philadelphia region through prominent board positions including the Greater Philadelphia Chamber of Commerce and the Greater Philadelphia First Corporation.

One of PECO's most recent changes came in 1997 when Pennsylvania became one of the first states in the nation to deregulate the sale of electricity. With the advent of deregulation, PECO

▲ With automated meter reading (AMR) technology, PECO is able to remotely access usage data for customers. This translates into better customer service, timely remote home and business meter readings, more accurate billing, usage analysis, and easier account transfers. For example, since the AMR project began, PECO performance in issuing on time and accurate bills has improved to nearly 100 percent.

faced major changes in the way it did business. Prior to deregulation, PECO was a vertically integrated utility, responsible for producing, transmitting, and delivering power to its consumers. PECO now concentrates solely on the delivery of electricity and natural gas. This statewide movement toward consumer choice in power suppliers also forced additional adaptations in every aspect of the company, especially information technology, billing, information exchange with new competitive power generators and marketers, and employee training.

One of the advantages PECO has in the deregulated market is its long-term arrangement for electric power. Exelon

◀ With trained dedicated customer service representatives and state-of-the-art technology, like Twenty First Century Communications, a high volume call answering system, PECO strives to provide superior service to its customers in times of emergency and at anytime throughout the year.

▲ PECO, An Exelon Company, has been displaying community messages atop its Market Street headquarters since July 4, 1976. A Philadelphia tradition, the PECO Crown Lights consist of a total of 2,600 bulbs. The display is 38 ft. high and is 148 ft. long along the north and south side of the building and 71 ft. long along the east and west sides.

implementing new innovations, such as automated meter reading (AMR), to better satisfy its customers and shareholders. The largest deployment of an AMR system in the Unites States, PECO installed 2.1 million automated meter devices over three years, 2000-2002. This enables PECO to remotely access usage data for all electric and natural gas customers. AMR has also provided the opportunity for new residential and large business products and services including e-VALUATOR, a Web-based energy analysis tool, and Smart Returns, a voluntary load reduction reward program.

Above all, the 2,700 men and women at PECO will work to strengthen the reliability of the electric and natural gas distribution systems and maintain an infrastructure that delivers safe and reliable energy service to area consumers. They remain focused on efficient operations and customer satisfaction.

With goals firmly in place and the company stronger than ever, PECO is proud of its role as a leader in the industry and in the Greater Philadelphia community. ℗

◀ 221

Generation, one of the world's largest power producers and whole-sale marketers, gives PECO a dependable and competitively priced electric supply. PECO's distribution infrastructure, teamed with Exelon Generation's facilities, ensures that southeastern Pennsylvania's consumers have, and will continue to have, a safe, dependable supply of energy well into the future.

Although PECO remains regulated by state and federal authorities on rates, level of service, and other matters, its unregulated affiliate, Exelon Generation, participates in competitive generation markets with greater potential for growth. PECO and Exelon Generation, with its headquarters in Kennett Square, continue to be strong regional players in the Greater Philadelphia area.

On other fronts, PECO is actively investing in new technology and

▶ Thanks to extensive preventive maintenance efforts, targeted investments, more accurate estimated restoration times, and the use of new technology, PECO crews continue to work hard to keep the lights on and the natural gas flowing for customers. This hard work places the company well above the national average in the frequency of outages, when compared to other utilities.

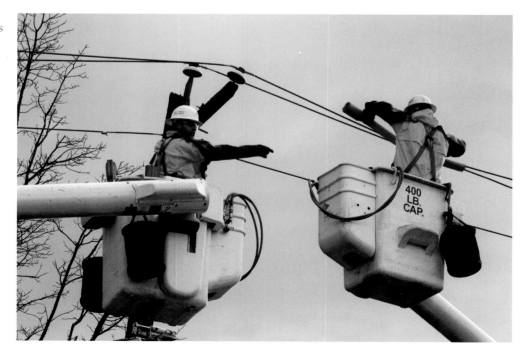

▶ Innovation Philadelphia

ℒocal Innovation, Global Realization

Philadelphia has come a long way since its days as a manufacturing hub that earned it the nickname "Workshop of the World." In the early 20th century, the city was renowned for its production of everything from locomotives and ships, to beer and Stetson hats.

Philadelphia has a rich history of innovation, which began when Benjamin Franklin recognized the potential of static electricity in a lightening bolt. In the 1890s, H. K. Mulford Company of Philadelphia became the earliest organized research program in the American pharmaceutical industry with their production of diphtheria antitoxin. GlaxoSmithKline, another Philadelphia pharmaceutical company, has recently announced its development and commercialization of AWD 12-281, leading the way in asthma research. Philadelphia revolutionized the world and introduced the computer age in 1946, when two University of Pennsylvania professors built the nation's first general-purpose computer, ENIAC. Now, Philadelphia-area companies are leading the nation and the world in healthcare innovation with products such as Robot-Assisted Microsurgery, once again making it the focus of public and private attention.

Innovation Philadelphia, established in December 2001, is a private/public partnership dedicated to increasing the region's entrepreneurial capacity and positioning Philadelphia as a leader in the global knowledge economy.

Richard A. Bendis, president and CEO of Innovation Philadelphia, works together with an esteemed collection of regional leaders representing private industry, public enterprise, nonprofit organizations, city and state government, emerging entrepreneurial companies, and civic leaders. These regional leaders are experts in life sciences, academia, information technology, emerging business law, e-commerce, industry associations, and city and state government. Representatives from the Commonwealth of Pennsylvania, the City of Philadelphia, Greater Philadelphia Chamber of Commerce, PECO, the United Negro College Fund, Morgan Lewis and Bockius LLC, and Half.com, among others, joined together as members of the Board of Directors for Innovation Philadelphia to form a truly collaborative approach to the knowledge economy in the 21st century. Innovation Philadelphia is proud to count as members of its Board: Mel Baiada, Founder and Chairman of Sengen; Lucinda Duncalfe Holt, CEO and President of Destiny; Patricia Garrison-Corbin, Chairman and CEO of P.G. Corbin & Company Inc.; Brenda D. Gavin, Managing Partner at Quaker BioVentures; Stephen M. Goodman, Partner at Morgan Lewis & Bockius LLP; Rev. William H. Gray III, President and CEO of the United Negro College Fund; Johanna Hambrose, COO and Corporate Counsel for Electronic Ink; David R. King, Consultant to Biotechnology Ventures; Joshua Kopelman, President of Half.com (a division of eBay); Kenneth G. Lawrence, President of PECO Energy Co.; Rev. Herbert H. Lusk II, Chairman of People for People; Robert McCord, President and CEO of Eastern Technology Council; Samuel

▲ **Richard A. Bendis, president and CEO of Innovation Philadelphia, and Dr. Judith Rodin, chair of the board and president of the University of Pennsylvania, are leading Innovation Philadelphia.**

J. Patterson, President and CEO of Veridyne, Inc.; Charles P. Pizzi, President of the Greater Philadelphia Chamber of Commerce; Willard G. Rouse III, Chairman and CEO of Liberty Property Trust; Secretary Samuel A. McCullough of the Pennsylvania Department of Community and Economic Development; and City of Philadelphia Mayor John Street. Led by chair Dr. Judith Rodin, President of the University of Pennsylvania; and vice-chairs, Dr. Jean-Paul Garnier, CEO of GlaxoSmithKline; and Brian L. Roberts, President of the Comcast Corporation, the Board of Directors meets regularly to decide on the best strategy to attract and assist innovators from the public, private, academic, and tech sectors. They understand the value and importance of having people work together and leveraging resources to gain a cooperative advantage.

Today, biotechnology, health-care, financial services, and knowledge and information technology companies dominate the Philadelphia economy. Small entrepreneurial firms and large corporations have made their home in the area, transforming yesterday's "Workshop of the World" into today's "Buckle on the Money Belt," referring to Philadelphia's strategic location between the private financial capital, New York City, and the public financial capital, Washington, D.C.

Among Innovation Philadelphia's first projects was the *Entrepreneurs' Guide*, a resource containing information on industry, government, academia, and nonprofit organizations involved in key economic initiatives. The 2002 *Entrepreneurs' Guide* showcases more than 160 organizations dedicated to helping entrepreneurs and businesses make industry contacts, finance their companies' growth, and achieve their ultimate goal—a thriving business in a flourishing Philadelphia economy. It ensures that entrepreneurs in the Philadelphia region are well-informed of the resources available to them. The guide's wealth of knowledge can contribute to the future success of any business.

Innovation Philadelphia will introduce a number of new projects designed to bring inventive thinkers and creative entrepreneurs to the city and keep Philadelphia's valuable assets in the region. By increasing economic stimulus investment by the city, region, and state, Innovation Philadelphia will continue, along with its partners, to provide the critical capital required for technology companies. An example is the creation of the Mid-Atlantic Angel Group, which will provide a fund of pre-seed and seed capital investments for entrepreneurs in the area.

Other examples of new investment opportunities include the Innovation Philadelphia Federal Funding Program, which supports Small Business Innovation Research (SBIR), Small Technical Transfer Research (STTR), and the Advanced Technology Program (ATP), and assists small businesses in applying for federal investments.

Researching the region's resources will help create opportunities and define the direction of the local technology economy. The findings of the biannual *Philadelphia Entrepreneurial and Innovation Index and Strategic Technology Cluster Assessment Plan* will uncover opportunities for existing companies and will attract new businesses to the region.

A key element in success is Innovation Philadelphia's contribution to accelerate the rate of commercialization of market driven technologies and supporting university research/tech transfer. Innovation Philadelphia, in partnership with the Commercialization Working Group—a consortia of regional university tech transfer offices—assists the Port of Technology and University City Science Center in the commercialization of strategic technologies from the region. This creates the foundation to develop new strategic technology research facilities, which will result in new companies, new jobs, and new investment opportunities for the region. This concentration of research

resources contributes to enhancing Philadelphia's global image as a leading knowledge region.

The University of Pennsylvania Health System is distinguished not only by its historical significance—first hospital (1751), first medical school (1765), first university teaching hospital (1874), first fully integrated academic health system (1993), and a leading recipient of funding from the National Institute of Health (2002)—but by its position as a major player on the world stage of medicine in the 21st century. To retain this reputation in anticipation of economic change, Innovation Philadelphia has begun work on the Knowledge Industry Partnership. The Partnership connects civic, business, governmental, regional community college, and higher education leaders engaged in the three pillars of this effort: attraction, engagement, and retention. For the first time, the multitude of entities functioning within each pillar have realized the necessity of vertical integration. Innovation Philadelphia will lead the retention effort by focusing on employment and internship opportunities. Job fairs, internship programs, networking groups, and local companies will be brought under the same umbrella for the first time, creating a consortium of opportunity, encouraging new graduates to stay in Philadelphia. Better coordination will enable these organizations to provide seamless services as students progress through the knowledge continuum in the Philadelphia area.

Innovation Philadelphia's future is maximizing the resources of the region, establishing new opportunities for emerging technology companies, attracting new technology companies to the region, and positioning Philadelphia as a leader in the global knowledge economy.

Innovation Philadelphia believes in strong industry, government, and university leadership promoted progress, and that progress is sustained by dynamic public and private partnerships. ℗

▶ **Philadelphia at dusk.** Photo ©2002 John McGrail

▸ Chester County Aviation

*W*hen Brian Campbell and his partner, Greg Campbell, purchased Chester County Aviation in September of 2001, they weren't starting a new business. Rather, they were taking the opportunity to grow with a company that had been a firmly established asset to the Philadelphia suburbs for nearly 40 years.

Al Sheves was entrusted with running the small airport where he would found his FBO (Fixed Base Operation) in 1962. Prior to that, Chester County Airport functioned primarily as a mail pick up point. For the next four decades, Sheves worked hard to build Chester County Aviation into a modern facility that would help to promote growth in the area. Brian Campbell, who lives in the Philadelphia Area and flies out of the Chester County Airport, was the vice-president of business development for Million Air, a national FBO Chain with several locations throughout the United States. He is now President and General Manager of Chester County Aviation.

During his time with Million Air, Campbell came to recognize many of the factors that make a successful FBO. Chester County Aviation met almost all of the criteria. For years the businesses in and around Philadelphia have been growing and expanding, a large portion of this growth is moving west along 202 corridor, into the Chester County area. Also, Chester County Airport is a quality facility with room to expand and grow. Campbell was ecstatic when Sheves agreed to sell to him. Today, Sheves is still a presence on the airfield, informally consulting Campbell and his staff, providing support and a feeling of continuity for the FBO he built.

Chester County Aviation continues its work as a full service aviation facility, providing aviation and jet fuel to aircraft. The company also provides full service maintenance, a flight school, hangars for private aircraft, and a 24-hour jet charter service.

Campbell's instincts haven't failed him or his company and he and his staff have watched their business grow. Because the airport is more convenient to the growing number of concerns in the suburbs,

▲ **Charter Aircraft.**

Chester County Aviation has witnessed a serious increase in corporate traffic to the airfield, as well as an expanded use of its charter services. While predominately serving the Philadelphia Metropolitan area, Chester County Aviation's jet charter service will pick up and deliver people almost anywhere in the country.

Today, Chester County's FBO is larger than ever before. With 12 aircraft now at its disposal for charter, as well as a combined 50,000 square-feet of hangar space, new hangars under construction, and a new terminal building, the operation continues to grow and prosper while maintaining the small-airport customer service attitude.

"Al Sheves always treated his customers like royalty, and we continue to do that today," says Brian Campbell. "We're going to continue working from the foundations that Al built here over 40 years, continuing to improve where and as we can." ℗

▼ **Chester County Aviation.** Photo ©2002 John McGrail

▶ Ben Franklin Technology Partners of Southeastern Pennsylvania

Contributing to the production of this beautiful coffee table book honoring the City of Philadelphia presents an exciting opportunity for Ben Franklin Technology Partners of Southeastern Pennsylvania. The theme of *Philadelphia: Birthplace of American Enterprise* captures the essence of our mission and coincides with the 20th Anniversary of the Ben Franklin Partnership, an initiative founded by the Commonwealth of Pennsylvania to diversify and re-create the state's economy through innovation, technology, and entrepreneurship.

Ben Franklin is building a new economic base for wealth creation in southeastern Pennsylvania by investing in technology enterprises, providing technical and business expertise and resources, and seeding regional technology initiatives to develop the infrastructure for innovation. With a focus on the entrepreneur as the key economic driver, we are the largest source of pre-seed and seed capital for emerging enterprises across all areas of science and technology. Then, we "wrap around" these businesses our comprehensive array of services and connect them to our many public and private networks in order to accelerate their growth.

For established enterprises, Ben Franklin offers risk capital for process/product development and commercialization activities. The goal—stronger companies through an improved product base and enhanced competitive ability. Our capital is coupled with customized solutions that draw from an extensive network of resources at universities, federal laboratories, and research institutions.

Since 1988, Ben Franklin Technology Partners of Southeastern Pennsylvania has seeded more than 500 companies. Our current investment portfolio of 135 companies represents more than $17 million invested in southeastern Pennsylvania. In recent years, our investments have leveraged more than $10 million annually, across a range of tech areas including IT, life sciences, communications, advanced manufacturing, and environmental.

As we grow companies, we also grow industries. From 1982 through 1992, Ben Franklin dedicated more than $20 million to strengthen research and development partnerships among universities

▲ RoseAnn B. Rosenthal, President & CEO, Ben Franklin Technology Partners of Southeastern Pennsylvania.

◀ 225

and companies in the bio/life sciences sector. These partnerships advanced scientific research in numerous areas including trauma care, chemotherapy treatment, and synthetic bone grafting. Since 1992, we have invested more than $7 million in early stage bio companies and nurtured more than 100 companies. Many of these enterprises such as Adolor, Centocor, Cephalon, and 3-D Pharmaceuticals have grown to national and international prominence.

And with the start of the new millennium, Ben Franklin launched The Nanotechnology Institute (NTI) in partnership with the Commonwealth of Pennsylvania, the University of Pennsylvania, and Drexel University. The NTI's comprehensive approach to the development and commercialization of technology emerging from bio-nano research is designed to provide an innovative platform for new regional growth.

Our 20th Anniversary presents an ideal opportunity to celebrate progress and reaffirm our commitment to promote innovation and enterprise creation through partnerships that stimulate economic growth throughout southeastern Pennsylvania. ℗

◀ The Nanotechnology Institute was created by Ben Franklin Technology Partners of Southeastern Pennsylvania, the Commonwealth of Pennsylvania, the University of Pennsylvania, and Drexel University to focus on technology emerging from bio-nano research as a platform for new regional growth.

▶ ESM Productions

*I*n a city as large as Philadelphia, few small businesses achieve success in the large multinational corporate landscape that dominates the Center City skyline. However, you do not have to look farther than 12th and Callowhill Streets to find a highly successful, small, homegrown business whose commitment to excellence and superior customer service sets them apart from the rest. ESM Productions serves a niche in the city of Philadelphia by coordinating and producing live events in addition to providing, public relations, video, and television production services, which is something no other business in the city has attempted.

ESM Productions came to fruition in 1996 with the President and founder at the helm. Initially, Scott Mirkin single-handedly ran the company out of his home, but today with a group of six employees, ESM serves an exclusive group of major corporate clients in the Philadelphia area. By providing superior customer service and dedicating himself to the needs and concerns of his clients, Scott has built a stellar reputation in the Greater Philadelphia region.

Since its inception, one of ESM's most valued clients has been the Greater Philadelphia Chamber of Commerce. ESM works with the Chamber on all of their large events and through the years they have formed a mutually beneficial relationship that continues to flourish.

While the Greater Philadelphia Chamber of Commerce is one of ESM's premiere clients, the company has also provided production and event services for other exclusive clients including the Greater Philadelphia Entrepreneur Awards for Ernst & Young, the International Maccabi Games Opening Ceremonies, the Philadelphia Orchestra's 2001 Clark Park Concert, the Commissioning of the USS Donald Cook for the United States Navy, the Republican National Convention's Lighted Boat Parade and Fireworks, and former President Bill Clinton's local appearances in 1996.

▲ Scott Mirkin, President of ESM Productions is committed to the success of the entire region.

One of the most prestigious job assignments that the company has had the good fortune of landing was the production of the President's Summit for America's Future in 1997. ESM Productions was still in its infancy when Mirkin traveled to Washington to campaign heavily for the job, knowing that an assignment of this caliber would firmly establish ESM in the marketplace. Scott's passion for the opportunity spoke volumes and he was offered the job, consequently securing ESM in its rightful place among esteemed production companies in Philadelphia.

Over the years, ESM has grown slightly and expanded its office space and payroll at a steady rate. As Scott looks toward ESM's future, he does not envision that the company will ever become a mega-corporation. He prefers a small, intimate, professional atmosphere where he and his employees can give ESM's clients their undivided personal attention. Furthermore, the small office setting allows Scott to remain personally involved in every project and uphold the hands on philosophy that distinguishes Scott as a leader in Philadelphia's business community. ℗

◀ Mirkin working with Chamber President Charles Pizzi at the 2002 Paradigm Award.

CHAPTER ELEVEN

Manufacturing
& Distribution

In the nineteenth century, Philadelphia was an industrial giant and had factories to manufacture almost every conceivable household item. Today, technology and life sciences form the nexus of the local economy, but manufacturing and distribution remain vital economic forces in the city.

Photo ©2002 John McGrail

▶ Sunoco, Inc.

For well over a century, Sunoco, Inc. has served as a leading manufacturer and retailer of petroleum and petrochemical products with over 4,100 outlets throughout the United States. Headquartered in Philadelphia, the company is one of the largest independent refiners and marketers in the country, refining approximately 730,000 barrels of crude oil a day, with interests in over 10,000 miles of petroleum and crude oil pipelines and refined product terminals.

The company's roots trace back to the late 1880s when business partners Joseph Newton Pew and Edward O. Emerson started to diversify their business - The People's Natural Gas Company in Pittsburgh. The gentlemen purchased two oil leases in 1886 in nearby Lima, Ohio. From there they acquired pipelines, storage tanks, and other leases, expanding their business to western Pennsylvania and Ohio. In 1890 they formed the Sun Oil Company of Ohio, and within a few years, acquired the Diamond Oil Company (hence the link to Sunoco's diamond-shaped logo of today). The acquisition included the company's first refinery located in Toledo and it remains in Sunoco's portfolio today. With the increase of crude oil discoveries in Spindletop, Texas, the company made another strategic move by building a refinery along a major waterway. The company chose Marcus Hook, Pennsylvania, a small town outside Philadelphia, along the Delaware River where crude oil could easily be shipped by water from Texas and then refined and sold to customers in the northeast region of the country.

For more than a century Sunoco has been known for its leadership. One notable example of this was their decision to move its

▲ Sunoco has been in business since 1886 and is proud of its reputation as a reliable supplier of quality products. This horse-drawn tank wagon from 1907 dramatically contrasts with Sunoco today.

headquarters back to the city of Philadelphia from the suburbs in the early 1990s to support the city's renaissance. The city was already home to one of Sunoco's refineries and the company's soon-to-be first chemical plant. This provided Philadelphia with job opportunities for hundreds of local residents while sending a positive message to other businesses. It demonstrated that Philadelphia is industry-friendly and open for business.

Today, Sunoco is a regional petrochemical company with a steadfast focus in the Delaware Valley. Each day about 70 percent of Sunoco's refining production occurs at its two refineries in the Philadelphia region. Sunoco also has a majority interest in a number of pipelines, including those from the Delaware River to the New York Harbor, to move product throughout the eastern portion of the country. In addition, the company has a refinery in Tulsa, Oklahoma, and chemical plants in Philadelphia and Pittsburgh, Pennsylvania; Neal, West Virginia; Haverhill, Ohio; and Pasadena and LaPorte, Texas.

◀ Sunoco is the largest U.S. East Coast refiner, with 500,000 barrels per day of crude oil processing capacity on the Delaware and Schuylkill Rivers, 730,000 overall, and annual production of approximately 275 million barrels of refined products and commodity petrochemicals.

▲ Sunoco has an integrated network of pipelines and terminals with interests in over 10,000 miles of crude oil and refined product pipelines and 35 refined product terminals.

The key to Sunoco's success and profitability has been the reliability and efficiency of its operations. Seeking sustainable, profitable growth by demanding safe and reliable operations in its business has positioned Sunoco as a leader in the marketplace. The company has made strategic acquisitions, which logically extend Sunoco's market presence.

Sunoco is proud to be headquartered in Philadelphia and understands its responsibility as an urban operator. Company resources as well as employees' personal time are given to a wide range of institutions and constituencies in the areas of Education, Health and Human Services, Arts and Culture, and Civic and Economic Development. One employee, Eck Gerner, who works in Sunoco's legal department, also serves as the Mayor of Swarthmore, a borough in the western suburbs of Philadelphia. His "second job" as mayor is an example of how Sunoco employees stay actively involved in their communities, become engaged in the life of the city and its environs, and help promote the Philadelphia Region as world-class.

Sunoco has managed to remain a successful corporation for more than a century by practicing the company's core values. To this day, Sunoco remains committed to profitable growth, positive change, enthusiastic customers, involved employees, confident shareholders, and responsible citizenship. By maintaining these values, the company will continue being respected in its industry and in the region. ℗

◀ 231

▼ Sunoco has over 4,100 retail gasoline outlets (including 650 convenience stores) and retail sales of almost 4.0 billion gallons of gasoline and $500 million of merchandise sales per year.

▸United Parcel Service

*U*nited Parcel Service is a company that has reinvented itself to meet the changing needs of the business community, and positioned itself to handle all three flows of commerce—goods, information, and funds. As a leader in the transportation industry, UPS has discovered that the flow of information about packages—enabled by technology and the Internet—is nearly as important as moving the packages themselves. The establishment of UPS Capital Corporation is enabling UPS to handle the movement of funds.

A History of Service

Beginning in 1907, the concept was simple—deliver messages and parcels to customers, emphasizing courtesy, reliability, and service. By the early 1950s, UPS had perfected the small package delivery business and decided to compete directly with the U.S. Postal Service for common carrier rights to deliver packages between any address, for any customer—residential or business. In 1987, UPS became the first package delivery company to service every address in the United States. Domestic success bred international opportunity, and today, UPS has developed an integrated network that can meet customer needs on the ground, through the air, and across the ocean.

The Philadelphia Experience

Since establishing its roots at 22nd and Walnut Streets in 1938, UPS now operates eight facilities in the Delaware Valley. These include district headquarters in South Philadelphia, regional headquarters at International Plaza, and a 212-acre airport facility at Philadelphia International Airport.

More than 9,200 employees service the Greater Philadelphia region. Maintaining a fleet of over 1,300 delivery vehicles and 343 trailers, Metro Philadelphia service providers pick up and deliver roughly 500,000 packages daily. The airport facility processes an average of 305,000 packages daily, with 32 flights—including destinations such as Hamilton, Montreal, Cologne, and Paris.

▲ UPS has positioned itself to move all three flows of commerce—goods, information, and funds.

UPS Online

UPS moves approximately six percent of the U.S. gross domestic product across more than 200 countries and territories around the world by offering an unmatched array of traditional and electronic commerce services that puts the world at your fingertips.

Utilizing a multi-billion dollar technology investment, UPS connects buyers and sellers worldwide through e-commerce. The company can provide superior time-definite worldwide delivery options, programs to quickly process information, and services to speed the flow of funds.

UPS Online is an integral part of the global supply chain. It allows customers to access the UPS network for customized reports and shipment information. This Web-based application includes many services for our customers. Of the 13.6 million packages UPS ships every day, about 11 million come from customers who are electronically connected to UPS. ℗

◀ UPS has developed an integrated network of services that can meet customer needs on the ground, through the air, and across the ocean.

▸ Zitners Fine Confections

While there are several thousand businesses based in the Philadelphia area, few elicit the type of fond memories of a carefree youth like Zitners Fine Confections. Its trademark Bunny on its boxes is a tradition at stores throughout the area. In fact, there are few people in the city who aren't familiar with the products that Zitners produces. The popular candy company has been tantalizing taste buds since the 1920s when Sam and Annie Zitner began selling the chocolates they made in their home near Kensington and Allegheny Avenues. As the years went by, the demand for these scrumptious candies grew. The company was passed down to Sam and Annie's nephews who relocated the business to its current home, a 120,000-square-foot factory in the Hunting Park West section of Philadelphia. In 1990, the family sold the business to the husband and wife team of Sid Rosenblatt and Christine Murphy who have been operating it ever since.

Without a doubt, it's the company's line of Easter products that has solidified Zitners' reputation as one of the best regional candy companies in the nation. Available in several different flavors, including Butter Cream, Coconut, Peanut Butter, Marshmallow, and the company's own Butter Krak, Zitners Easter candies have become as much a part of the Philadelphia Easter tradition as Easter egg hunts and jelly beans.

And while the Easter eggs are the primary product that Zitners has become famous for, the company manufacturers a large array of other delectable confections that have pleased both young and old throughout the years. For corporate gifts, the company ships thousands of tins containing another Philadelphia favorite—pretzels—covered in caramel, then chocolate, and then nuts. Producing everything from freshly dipped caramel apples to gourmet chocolate pretzels and boxed chocolates, the company manufactures rich and creamy treats

▲ **Pretzels are covered in chocolate and then decorated with colorful toppings. The pretzels move down the tables to be lifted and packed at the back of the drying tunnel. Remember Lucy and Ethel?**
Photo ©2002 John McGrail

to please every sweet tooth in the region. The people at Zitners take pride in using only the freshest and highest quality ingredients.

At 17th and Allegheny Avenue since 1965, the company has seen the neighborhood transform. Chris and Sid have seen real progress made recently in restoring their Allegheny West/Hunting Park neighborhood. A collaboration of City officials from the mayor's office, the Commerce Department, the Law Department, city council, and representatives of state agencies working together with the Allegheny West Foundation have changed the look of Allegheny Avenue.

Generally regarded as making one of the most loved and respected products to come from Philadelphia, Zitners has managed to not only bring smiles to the faces of young and old alike with its assortment of chocolate treats, but it also values the history and traditions that keep this city and its neighborhoods working. And that's something we can all smile about. ℗

◀ **Zitners products include more than 50 varieties of chocolate covered pretzels used for corporate gift programs or sold in specialty candy stores. Caramel apples are made in fall and sold through grocery stores and convenience stores. Zitners is best known for chocolate covered Easter eggs, large and small, in several varieties. These are sold in grocery stores, drug stores, convenience stores, and specialty candy stores throughout the region.** Photo ©2002 John McGrail

▸ Rohm and Haas

*R*ohm and Haas Company, headquartered at Sixth and Market Streets in Philadelphia, was founded in 1909 by two young men with one product and a dream.

Dr. Otto Rohm, a chemist in Darmstadt, Germany, had created a chemical called Oropon, designed to aid in the tanning of animal hide for leather production. Otto Haas, financial genius and Dr. Rohm's trusted friend, sensed the need for such a product in the United States. Mr. Haas came to America and, after establishing Philadelphia as the company's home, built the first U.S. manufacturing plant in Bristol, Pennsylvania, in 1917. From that humble beginning, Rohm and Haas Company now operates more than 100 manufacturing and research facilities in 25 countries around the globe. The company employs 17,000 men and women in locations in North America, Europe, Latin America, and Asia.

Rohm and Haas Company manufactures intermediate chemicals, which means that most Rohm and Haas products are not visible to consumers. So, while you won't find its name on many retail shelves, Rohm and Haas products are found in almost everything we touch. Whether it's the electronic materials that make up a PC, cellphone, or pager; the cosmetics or shampoos that keep our skin and hair clean and healthy; the paints that decorate the walls of our homes and offices; or the packaging in which you buy your frozen vegetables, Rohm and Haas is there.

The company attributes its success to a number of factors, including a rigorous dedication to consistent production of high quality, high value products that customers expect and deserve. A talented, motivated, and creative workforce continues to raise the bar for technological capabilities, improving existing products while searching for new and innovative applications and ideas. Rohm and Haas values both internal and external relationships, extending and receiving support from communities like Philadelphia that host the manufacturing and research facilities.

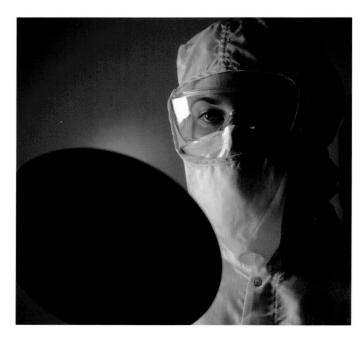

▲ Ultra-high purity products from Rohm and Haas provide the enabling technology needed to make today's state-of-the-art integrated circuits.

In addition to superb technologies, excellent talent, and financial success, Rohm and Haas Company is dedicated to its responsibilities as an involved and committed community member. The William Penn Foundation, one of Philadelphia's largest private philanthropic organizations, has the Haas family as its roots. John Haas, son of company founder Otto Haas, is a former chairman of the United Way of Southeastern Pennsylvania and still plays a major role in that charity's activities. Following the example and tradition of the Haas family, company executives and employees are involved in a variety of organizations, volunteering both time and financial support.

Rohm and Haas Company has been honored for its global efforts to enhance environmental awareness and its responsible stewardship of the earth's resources. The company received the World Environmental Excellence Award, and two Presidential Green Chemistry Awards for the environmental friendliness of various products and continuing efforts to assist in preservation of the environment.

For nearly 100 years, Rohm and Haas Company has built its reputation on delivering quality products, upholding ideals of honesty and integrity in its business practices, involving the company in community activities, and the ethical management of its resources. Continued pursuit of these goals remains the cornerstone of this Philadelphia institution. ℗

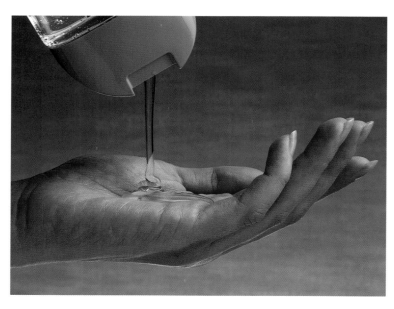

◀ Purity also is essential for everyday products. Rohm and Haas chemistry keep shampoos, toiletries, and other personal care products free from contamination.

▶ Delaware Valley Industrial Resource Center (DVIRC)

*T*he Delaware Valley Industrial Resource Center (DVIRC) is part of a statewide network of organizations dedicated to helping the Commonwealth's small- and mid-sized manufacturers improve their competitiveness. Each of the program's seven centers act as a private, not-for-profit economic development corporation, supported by the Commonwealth, and are managed by private industry. Established in 1988 by the Pennsylvania Department of Commerce, and sponsored by the Greater Philadelphia Chamber of Commerce, the Philadelphia Industrial Development Corporation, and the University City Science Center, the DVIRC is singularly concerned with the operations and business performance of manufacturers in the five counties that make up Southeast Pennsylvania.

Since it was founded, the DVIRC has evolved into a vigorous economic development organization, which has developed and expanded its services to encompass almost every aspect of a manufacturing business—from strategic planning, staffing, production engineering, financial programs, to the latest in operational methodologies. The Center also manages network groups. The DVIRC can find ways of providing peer input for CEO's, offers programs in marketing, IT, and product development, as well as state-of-the-art educational facilities with programs in all areas of World Class Manufacturing.

Since 1995, the DVIRC also has been part of the National Institute for Standards and Technology's (NIST) Manufacturing Extension Partnership, a federal program that provides funding for the support of small- and medium-sized manufacturers. As is the case with State support, this Federal support takes the form of a multi-year performance based contract.

Being the only organization of its kind in the region, the DVIRC has been able to use its position to develop regional initiatives to support broader economic development efforts and cultivate productive working relationships with a broad array of institutions and organizations. The DVIRC has managed to maintain its commitment to its target audience, while continuously working to expand its programs and services in order to respond directly to the needs of its clients, as well as evolving those offerings to provide manufacturers a holistic approach to project engagement and productivity improvement.

The DVIRC has received numerous testimonials from customers on the quality of their services and the role they have played in the success of clients, but this doesn't mean that the company intends to slow down. Executives feel that the DVIRC is just beginning to scratch the surface of finding potential ways of helping their clients, and will continue to expand the organization's services based on developing customer needs. The Delaware Valley Industrial Resource Center, with the help of its partner groups will continue to address the major issues that confront small- and mid-sized manufacturing interests, aid current residents of the five county area, make the region more attractive to potential businesses, and help the economy of Southeastern Pennsylvania remain healthy. ℗

◀ 235

◀ **DVIRC Headquarters,**
2905 Southampton Road,
Philadelphia, Pennsylvania.

CHAPTER TWELVE

Business & Finance

Philadelphia's vast intellectual resources and its strategic location on the Eastern Seaboard lure companies of all types to the area. A multitude of businesses find that Philadelphia possesses the perfect business climate.

Photo ©2002 John McGrail

▶ Beneficial Savings Bank

*P*hiladelphia is a city steeped in history, with a rich tradition of independence. One of the city's most treasured commercial traditions is embodied in Beneficial Mutual Savings Bank, a truly independent financial services company with a rich history of its own.

From its humble beginnings in the mid 19th century as safekeeper of the meager savings of hopeful immigrants to the city of Philadelphia, Beneficial has evolved into a full-service financial company. With more than $2 billion in assets and over 30 offices throughout the metropolitan area, the Bank remains dedicated to helping its customers achieve their financial goals.

Between 1846 and 1851, a devastating potato famine resulted in a great wave of emigration from Ireland. During the 1850s, it is estimated that over 100,000 Irish citizens per year escaped that poverty-stricken nation. Unrest and revolution in central Europe added many thousands more to the vast throng who sought refuge in the United States. As a major port city, Philadelphia was one of the chief points of entry for those seeking a new life in America.

This sudden and extraordinary increase in the city's population made labor plentiful and cheap. The immigrants were not only hard working, but thrifty. As their earnings began to accumulate, they needed a secure place to deposit their savings. At the time, the major commercial banks were not designed to serve working men and women, but instead, catered to the wealthy businessmen who were their primary backers. In order to qualify for a bank account, customers were required to provide formal identification records, along with personal referrals from established bank members.

Without a bank at their disposal, many of these new citizens turned to another established organization that was always glad to welcome them, the Catholic Church. It was not uncommon at this time to find parish priests filling the role of banker for the new members of their congregations. As balances began to build, priests became concerned about security, and so did John Neumann, the Bishop of Philadelphia.

▲ **Corporate headquarters at 6th and Walnut Streets.**

A far-sighted and extremely intelligent man, Bishop Neumann spoke eight languages; was a pioneer of the Parochial School System in America; and, in 1977, was canonized as a Saint by the Catholic Church. Bishop Neumann saw the risks in the patchwork financial system his parishes were operating, and began investigating ways to address the issue.

While Bishop Neumann's inspiration was the catalyst behind the founding of what would become Beneficial Savings Bank, it took the vision and dedication of a group of businessmen—members of the Board of Managers of St. Joseph's Hospital—to get things started. They began meeting among themselves in February 1853, and on April 20, 1853, The Beneficial Saving Fund Society of Philadelphia was incorporated.

◀ *The Historical Society of Pennsylvania, Immigrant Station, Philadelphia,* from *American Line, Philadelphia, Queenstown, Liverpool,* accession #Wd*.199 vol. 3.

▲ Saint John Neumann, bishop of Philadelphia, 1852-1860.

proof chest" at a cost of $175 in 1854. Until 1859, Bank officers served without compensation, but in that year, the board decided to pay a salary of $500 per year to the President and $300 to the Treasurer.

In December 1860, one month after Abraham Lincoln was elected President of the United States, the Bank purchased the property at the southwest corner of Twelfth and Chestnut Streets for the sum of $38,000. For more than 140 years, this location served as Beneficial's corporate headquarters.

The Civil War provided the first true test of stability for the fledgling Institution. Closer to the Mason-Dixon Line than any other large northern city, Philadelphia witnessed the steady flow of troops to southern battlefields and the sad return of thousands of wounded. A short distance to the west of the city, General Lee massed his armies at Gettysburg, and tensions in Philadelphia rose. Heavy withdrawals, numerous bankruptcies and bank failures, and the imposition of a three percent tax on interest on deposits challenged the Bank's management. Through it all, the Bank was successful in satisfying every demand made by depositors, and emerged from the crisis with its public confidence intact.

In addition to the War between the States, Beneficial Savings Bank has endured through other military conflicts. During World

The purpose of the newly formed organization, along with the genesis of its name, was spelled out in the preamble to its Charter: "Whereas, experience has demonstrated the beneficial results to the industrious and careful, of having a place of investment for their earnings..."

The founding board structured Beneficial as a mutual company, and it remains mutual today. Unlike public companies, whose main focus is to maximize the wealth of their shareholder-owners, Beneficial's management is primarily accountable to its customers, the neighborhoods and communities it serves, and its employees. As the Bank celebrates its 150th anniversary, the mutual charter retains its value by affording Beneficial the flexibility to focus on providing excellent customer service, and investing in the people and businesses that make up its community.

A review of the Bank's early records indicates that 166 accounts were opened before the name of the first American-born depositor appeared. These same records reveal that the Bank's founders were concerned with security, as they authorized the purchase of a "fire and theft-

SOUTH-WEST CORNER OF TWELFTH AND CHESTNUT STS.

▶ Beneficial's first headquarters.

War I, the Bank supported the war effort by investing in Liberty Bonds and promoting their sale to its customers and employees. Similarly, during the Second World War, Beneficial not only made its offices available for the sale of Government Bonds to the public and its employees, but also subscribed heavily to each Bond drive for its own portfolio. During both wars, the Bank made provisions for any member of its personnel who entered the armed forces. In addition to providing full insurance and pension benefits, the Bank's board approved monthly payments of the employee's salary to his or her family for the duration of the employee's military service.

Beneficial's commitment to the American community remains evident today. In the wake of the tragic terrorist attacks in 2001, the Bank helped its customers and employees manifest their concern for the victims, and their generosity, by facilitating the collection of thousands of dollars in donations to the relief effort, and then matching those donations from its own reserves.

Even greater risks to banking companies emanated from the financial crises that have gripped the U.S. during Beneficial's long history.

▲ **Sale of Liberty Bonds.**

From the Panic of 1873 which touched off a six-year period of economic decline, to the Great Depression, beginning with the stock market crash of 1929, Beneficial's financial strength and conservative management allowed the Bank to retain the utmost confidence of the public.

Perhaps the Bank's most challenging period occurred in the late 1970s and early 1980s, when the rapid pace of financial deregulation coincided with a period of rampant inflation in the U.S. economy. Once deregulated, interest rates rose sharply, increasing the cost of short-term deposits, while long-term asset yields remained fixed. Paying 15 percent to 20 percent for deposits, while earning 8.5 percent on loans was clearly a losing proposition. And like many other financial institutions at the time, Beneficial suffered significant losses.

In spite of its vulnerability to what would become known as the Thrift Crisis, Beneficial Savings Bank did have several

◀ **The lobby of 12th and Chestnut Streets office, completed in 1918.**

advantages. The first was a strong capital position, and enough liquid assets to continue operating despite its losses. The second was a board and management team that possessed both the capability of seeing past the immediate danger and the vision to recognize what steps needed to be taken in order to weather the storm. Perhaps the most important advantage was Beneficial's structure as a mutual savings bank, which allowed it to minimize the importance of quarterly profit and focus on its long-term survival.

Instead of reaching for speculative investments to increase income, the Bank's management saw the need to restructure the composition of its assets so that they more closely matched the characteristics of its deposit liabilities. Thus began a measured shift in investment from a sole focus on long-term fixed rate mortgages, to more market sensitive assets such as adjustable rate mortgages and shorter-term consumer loans and commercial loans. In doing so, Beneficial Savings Bank not only avoided disaster, but found new ways to prosper by meeting the more diverse needs of its customers. While many other institutions were forced to close their doors, or succumb to acquisition by larger banks, Beneficial Savings Bank was able to survive the storm and maintain its independence, and now finds itself in a stronger position than ever before.

Even before the Great Depression, Philadelphia's growth in area and population challenged the Bank's management to keep pace. In 1924, the first neighborhood office was opened in the Kensington section of the city. This historic event was followed just four years later, with the opening of an office in South Philadelphia. As evidence of the Bank's stability and commitment to its customers, both of these offices are still operating in their original buildings as

▲ Jim Connor, vice president and community development officer, and Sister Ellen Marvel, C.S.R. at the Dreuding Center/Project Rainbow, a facility of transitional housing for homeless women and children. Volunteers from Beneficial assisted in the construction of the playground.

◀ 241

◀ Beneficial's modern office in Eddystone, Pennsylvania.

Beneficial celebrates its sesquicentennial in 2003. While the Bank remains a vital part of these neighborhoods, its expansion has continued. Today, Beneficial serves neighborhoods throughout the city of Philadelphia, and in the surrounding areas including Bucks, Delaware, Montgomery, and Chester Counties in Pennsylvania, and in Burlington County, New Jersey.

Beneficial's geographic expansion is matched by the extent of its product diversification. Throughout its history, the Bank has worked to keep pace with the ever-changing needs of its customers. From its early focus on passbook savings accounts as the sole deposit vehicle, Beneficial has steadily increased its offerings to include savings certificates, money market accounts, and checking products. Recently, the Bank has further expanded its offerings of savings and investment products to include mutual funds, annuities, and general securities. Many of these products can now be provided in tax-advantaged plans designed to help customers meet their retirement needs and the demands of college education.

In addition to providing residential mortgages, Beneficial now can finance just about any of its customers' needs. Auto and marine loans, home-equity and student loans, as well as loans to help finance businesses, are now important components of the Bank's asset mix.

A hallmark of Beneficial's rich history is its contribution to the enrichment of the neighborhoods and communities it serves. One of its better-known programs was designed to help instill the merits of saving in young children, while providing the beginnings of financial education. Under the School Savings Program, instituted in 1927, Beneficial employees visited local schools to offer basic financial education, and provide banking services by taking deposits right

▲ Christy DeLuca, senior staff auditor, reads to a first-grade student as part of the Philadelphia Reads Program.

at the school. An updated version of this program, the Student Saver Account, continues to this day. Both programs have allowed children to start a savings account of their own, giving them a chance to handle their own funds, and build sound, money-saving habits at an early age.

The most visible element of Beneficial's community commitment is its people. A Volunteer Support Group has been established at the Bank to organize and coordinate the varied volunteer and charitable activities in which Beneficial employees are involved. One of this group's most successful efforts to date also involves education. The Philadelphia Reads Program pairs individual students

◀ School Savings Department, formed October 1927.

▲ Branch manager Connie Flanagan and Tom Highsmith of Consumer
Credit review a customer loan application.

from a local school with employee mentors who meet on a weekly
basis to work on reading skills. In addition, the Bank has expanded
its efforts to increase the financial literacy of consumers throughout
the area, and is involved in a number of initiatives to
support affordable housing in all of the neighborhoods
and communities it serves.

In the 150 years since its founding, the Bank's management and employees have worked hard to fulfill the
vision of Saint John Neumann and the founding board
by providing sound, trustworthy financial services to the
citizens of Philadelphia and its suburbs, and steadfastly
maintaining the Bank's financial strength and independence in the face of significant industry consolidation.

With such a rich history of service and independence, it seems only fitting that Beneficial's newly relocated headquarters is situated next door to the most
enduring symbols of historic Philadelphia,
Independence Hall and the Liberty Bell.

The men and women of Beneficial Mutual Savings
Bank celebrate this history, and look forward to providing their neighbors in and around Philadelphia with
another 150 years of sound financial products, and the
excellent service its customers have come to expect. ℗

▶ View from executive conference room.

▶ The Graham Company

*T*he Graham Company has been one of the Philadelphia area's best-kept secrets for more than fifty years. As a specialist in Property and Casualty Insurance Consulting and Brokerage services, Graham insures major landmarks and industries in the Philadelphia area and around the world—including The Benjamin Franklin and Walt Whitman Bridges, Philadelphia International Airport, Packer Avenue Marine Terminal, and The Coca-Cola Bottling Company.

William A. Graham, III founded the company in 1950 as a small insurance agency serving the needs of individuals and small businesses in the Philadelphia community. William A. Graham, IV became the sole owner of the firm in 1972 and transformed The Graham Company into one of the fifty largest insurance brokers in the nation. He has grown the business from 6 employees with revenues of $300,000, to a team of 160 employees and premiums of more than $200,000,000. The company remains privately held today, while providing a full spectrum of Property and Casualty Products and Surety Bonds for an elite client base.

Maintaining an exclusive focus on Property and Casualty Insurance for businesses with complex insurance requirements in high-risk industries allows The Graham Company to gain a deeper understanding of the risks associated with each client's operations and design tailor-made insurance programs to best meet the needs of these clients.

By keeping an exclusive client roster, Graham ensures its clients receive the most personalized service and attention in the industry. While most top-tier insurance firms of similar size and ranking typically service 2,000 to 4,000 clients, The Graham Company only services 200 clients. Once clients experience the Graham difference, they simply don't leave. Graham's 98 percent client retention is the highest in the industry. Clients are well-managed, financially strong companies where the principals have a vested interest in the quality and value of their Property & Casualty Insurance Programs.

"Our reputation is reflected in the company we keep," says William A. Graham, IV, CEO of The Graham Company. "We develop close, long-term relationships with our clients, and we have a strong understanding of our clients' businesses and challenges."

The Graham Company prides itself on being a pioneer in the insurance industry and is constantly raising the bar for success. Its Outsourced Risk Management Model℠ has been recognized as an industry blueprint for effectively managing complex business risks in today's ever-changing market. Graham's Model is driven by continuous strategy and service delivered on a daily basis throughout the year. Maintaining regular contact with clients enables the Graham team to better understand the needs of its clients, work through continual loss development analysis, and deliver superior coverage with "no surprises."

And while Graham's model is innovative, it's the unique blend of talented, driven people that sets Graham apart. The Graham team consists of attorneys, engineers, technology specialists, military

▲ **Offices of The Graham Company.** Photo ©2002 John McGrail

officers, naval aviators, CPAs, and CPCUs. With proven track records in select industries, these professionals bring a strong understanding and creativity to their clients' business challenges. Graham employees are required to go through more than three years of technical training—*more than eight times the industry standard.*

"From the very beginning, we've always recognized that, if you attract, recruit, and train the very best people, you'll have a great organization," says Graham.

Graham's clients are the ones who ultimately benefit from that talented mix of highly trained professionals. Unlike other brokers who may assign one or two people to an account, The Graham Company assigns a dedicated service team to each client while offering a variety of in-house services. Those services include an in-house safety department, an in-house claims management department staffed by 25 people and an attorney, and an account management unit that handles all of the day-to-day servicing activities required by each client.

The Graham Company has one of the largest in-house claims departments of any firm of its size. Claims consultants work closely

244 ▶

for innovative ways to improve the capabilities it can deliver for its clients. In 1994, The Graham Company formed a strategic alliance with Globex International, Inc. to provide clients with foreign facilities and exposures with a continuum of risk management services and representation around the world. The Globex network of international brokers is located in more than 90 foreign countries, including Russia and most nations in Eastern Europe. Graham's multinational growth companies primarily include manufacturing sector clients who import, export, manufacture, and warehouse their goods around the world.

The Graham Company has established an international reputation as a first-class insurance broker through top-notch client service and its ability to develop creative and innovative risk management and insurance strategies. But the rest of the world is just getting a glimpse of what Graham has provided Philadelphia for half a century—broad coverage, superior service, piece of mind, and a true business partnership.

◀ 245

▲ **Bill Graham, CEO, and Mike Tiagwad, President.** Photo ©2002 John McGrail

with insurance companies to make sure clients claims are handled promptly and fairly. The company's in-house safety capabilities help clients impact one of the most critical areas of insurance costs—losses. Graham's safety services include the development of formal safety programs, review of existing programs and procedures, on-site field observations, in-house safety training, and accident investigation.

As The Graham Company continues to grow, it is always looking

▶ **The Graham Company's Board of Directors. Standing left to right: Ken Ewell, Mike Tiagwad, Harry Johnson, Tony McIntyre, Mike Mitchell. Seated left to right: Lucille Carey, Bill Graham, Margaret Jones.**

Photo ©2002 John McGrail

▸ McDonald's East Division

*I*t was in 1954 that Ray Kroc, a milkshake machine salesman, met the McDonald brothers, owners of a very successful hamburger stand in San Bernadino, California. The brothers were in the process of looking to expand their fast growing business. Recognizing the potential in this concept, Kroc became the exclusive franchising agent for McDonald's restaurants. He opened the doors to the prototype McDonald's restaurant on April 15, 1955 in Des Plaines, Illinois, an event that has had a significant historical impact on business over the past half century.

Since its inception, McDonald's has established itself as the world's largest quick service restaurant (QSR) business. The brand was built on a foundation of QSC&V (Quality, Service, Cleanliness, and Value)—the pillars upon which the company continues to operate. Now with approximately 30,000 community-based restaurants operating in 121 different countries, McDonald's is one of the most recognized and respected brands in the world. McDonald's employs one million individuals worldwide and provides high quality food to over 45 million people across the globe on a daily basis.

When the company first began serving customers in the 1950s, the McDonald's menu consisted of eleven items, highlighted by hamburgers, cheeseburgers, its now world-famous french fries, beverages, and milkshakes. Always a trailblazer in the QSR industry, McDonald's added a host of popular food items to its menu over nearly five decades. The Big Mac, the Quarter Pounder, Chicken McNuggets, the Filet-O-Fish, fresh-tossed salads, the Egg McMuffin, and bagel sandwiches were just a few of the food innovations that set McDonald's apart from the field. In fact, the latter two helped lead to the introduction and popularity of breakfast menus in quick service restaurants. Recent concepts introduced as part of the company's New Tastes Menu—such as Triple Thick Milkshakes and Chicken Flatbread sandwiches—have continued this rich tradition of food innovation.

But food isn't the only innovation that has put McDonald's on the map. The company has also been responsible for a number of

▲ **Rosa and Freddie Rosado in their McDonald's at Broad and Arch Streets, Philadelphia.** Photo ©2002 John McGrail

revolutionary service advancements that have proven critical to the success of quick service restaurants and other businesses. This includes concepts like the Happy Meal for children and Extra Value Meals for adults, both of which simplified and expedited the ordering/service process for customers in a hurry. McDonald's also revolutionized drive-thru service beginning in 1975, which has dramatically changed the way people order food and decide where to dine—car or home. In addition, the introduction of Playlands for children in 1971 enhanced the dining experience for kids. And of course Ronald McDonald has established himself as the most recognized spokesperson in the world, beloved by children and adults alike.

◀ **Chris Gabriel at his McDonald's in Warwick, Pennsylvania.** Photo ©2002 John McGrail

▲ **John Dawkins, III at his McDonald's at Broad and Carpenter Streets, Philadelphia.** Photo ©2002 John McGrail

In 1999, McDonald's East Division office opened in Philadelphia, relocating from its former Oak Brook, Illinois headquarters. The city of Philadelphia has proven to be an ideal choice for this office as McDonald's seeks to meet the needs of its 5,000 restaurants located from Pittsburgh to Maine and down to Florida. The city's thriving business community, access to all major modes of transportation, and central location along the east coast have proven beneficial to the company and its restaurants.

McDonald's also has a tremendous economic impact within the regions it serves. For example in the Philadelphia Region, which includes eastern Pennsylvania, southern New Jersey and south/central New York State, the company employs more than 25,000 people of diverse backgrounds in nearly 600 restaurants. And more than $300 million in goods and services are purchased, much of it through local suppliers who also create thousands of jobs. In fact, in a recent two-year period, McDonald's invested over $1 billion in the greater-Philadelphia marketplace alone when one factored in development, labor costs, taxes, purchasing, advertising, and donations to worthy causes.

Approximately 85 percent of the restaurants in the East Division are run by independent owner/operators, men and women who live and work in the communities served by their restaurants. McDonald's franchisees have a rich tradition of supporting the communities in which they

▶ **Mark Heinz at his McDonald's in Marlton, New Jersey.** Photo ©2002 John McGrail

do business, and this is evidenced among the 130 entrepreneurs that run restaurants in the Philadelphia Region. This reflects Ray Kroc's belief that, "We have an obligation to give something back to the communities that give us so much."

This focus on supporting those in need is perhaps best exemplified by the outstanding contributions made to society by Ronald McDonald House Charities (RMHC). By creating, finding, and supporting programs that directly improve the health and well being of children, Ronald McDonald House Charities is working to better the lives of children and their families around the world.

In fact, the very first Ronald McDonald House was opened in Philadelphia on October 15, 1974. In the 28 years since it's founding, RMHC has grown to include 216 Ronald McDonald Houses worldwide. The Ronald McDonald House program now stands as one of the most respected charities in the world, and has provided a comforting and caring environment for approximately three million family members since its inception. The newest RMHC program features a Ronald McDonald Care Mobile, one of which is located in Philadelphia. This state-of-the-art mobile unit provides needy children with direct access to cost-effective medical and dental care.

No matter what their taste preferences, McDonald's customers can continue to expect wholesome foods, great service, and good value, all in a clean and welcoming environment. The company will also continue its rich tradition of giving back to the communities it serves. ℗

▶ First Union/Wachovia

irst Union is proud of its banking legacy in the greater Philadelphia region, a legacy of leadership and community commitment that began with the establishment of the Bank of North America in 1781 and continues to this day. It is a heritage that will continue building as Wachovia.

Today, First Union is the leading retail and commercial bank on the East Coast and the nation's fifth largest full-service retail broker dealer. The bank is the nation's third largest commercial lender and has relationships with one third of the businesses in its East Coast footprint.

First Union is also the premier financial services company in the Philadelphia region, leading the market in both retail and commercial relationships. Its success has come from helping individuals, businesses, organizations, and communities prosper and grow—growth that over the years has contributed significantly to the economic, civic, and cultural vitality of the region.

First Union has created a new kind of financial services company to meet the needs of this broad and diverse customer base—one with customer-driven products, services, and delivery channels designed to combine the best aspects of a traditional bank, an investment bank, and an asset management company.

Its retail banking franchise provides customized deposit and lending products, comprehensive commercial lending and commercial real estate solutions, and integrated investment products and services. The institution operates the region's largest branch delivery system that is fully integrated with telephone and Internet banking services and the nation's fifth largest ATM network. Convenience, customer service, and state-of-the-art products and services are the hallmark of First Union's retail banking franchise.

As one of the largest wealth managers in the United States, First Union provides financial advice, planning, and integrated wealth

▲ **First Union has a strong commitment to community involvement, led by the spirit of its employees. They volunteer their time and talent to support many organizations in the Philadelphia region, such as the March of Dimes WalkAmerica these employees are preparing to participate in.**

management services through business lines that include private banking, personal trust, investment advisory services, charitable services, financial planning, insurance, and executive services.

First Union has one of the nation's largest asset management and retail brokerage firms, with a complete line of investment products that includes the third largest bank provider of insurance annuities as well as corporate and institutional trust services to institutional and retail investors.

For large corporate and institutional clients, the bank offers a range of fixed income and equity products, asset securitization, and strategic advisory and cash management services.

First Union is dedicated to helping lead development and progress in the Philadelphia region. The focus of its community efforts lies in two key areas: strengthening neighborhoods and improving education. Through corporate contributions, loans, investments, and employee volunteerism, First Union does more than enhance the quality of life for others; it sets examples of industry leadership and community excellence.

Its civic efforts focus on building strong, vibrant neighborhoods across the Philadelphia region, working with hundreds of

◀ **First Union has a long history of supporting events and institutions that define Philadelphia, like the USPRO Championship, a world-class cycling event.** Photo by Jonathan Devich

248 ▶

▲ Reading First is First Union's ongoing early childhood literacy program and signature volunteer initiative. Each year, employees like Bob Reid, State CEO for Pennsylvania and Delaware, and Rosie Saez, Atlantic Region community development manager, read to thousands of students in class rooms across the region.

community-based partners throughout its markets. By improving the quality and availability of affordable housing, promoting small business growth, and devising innovative capital solutions to assist in the revitalization of neighborhoods and promote economic development, First Union has played a vital role in the urban renaissance that Philadelphia has experienced over the past several years.

The bank's innovative Education First program has reached millions of children since its origin in 1989. Education initiatives include encouraging employees to volunteer in local schools, matching financial contributions to educational institutions, and providing educational tools to parents of small children. Its "Time Away from Work for Community Service" policy allows each employee four hours of paid time off each month to volunteer in schools or other volunteer programs. Reading First, First Union's signature volunteer initiative, promotes early childhood literacy. Each year, bank employees volunteer once a week for 30 weeks, reading to thousands of students in classrooms across the region.

First Union has a long history of supporting events and institutions that define the Philadelphia region. Recognizing that a vibrant civic

▶ Pamela L. Frey, Regional President of Greater Philadelphia and Delaware, is responsible for all commercial, small business, and retail operations in the region, including over 200 financial centers.

and cultural life contributes to the economic vitality of the region, the bank was an early and strong supporter of the Avenue of the Arts as well as the Regional Performing Arts Center. First Union is also proud to be the naming sponsor for the First Union Complex (to be renamed the Wachovia Complex) home to the Philadelphia Flyers and the Philadelphia 76'ers, as well as the site of the 2000 NCAA Women's Final Four and the Republican National Convention. The company was also a critical factor in bringing world-class cycling to the region in the First Union USPRO Championship, where the best professional cyclists, nationally and internationally, compete.

More than anything else, it is the people of First Union who have created the company's success by working toward the success of their customers and their communities. First Union's people have made a truly significant investment in time, talent, and energy to make the company's impact on this region meaningful and beneficial. The bank is as confident today as at its beginning in 1781 that this ongoing interaction between its people, its customers, and its communities will expand opportunities and enhance growth for the greater Philadelphia region.

In September of 2001, First Union and Wachovia joined to form Wachovia Corporation, with local First Union offices transitioning to the Wachovia name by 2003. ℗

▸ Advanta

*A*dvanta's story is uniquely Philadelphian. Following in the footsteps of Philadelphia entrepreneurs like Benjamin Franklin and Matthew Carey, a forward thinking individual started with little and succeeded in the creation of his vision through hard work and determination.

In the early 1950s, Philadelphia schoolteacher Jack Alter noticed that his fellow teachers had difficulty securing loans. Traditional banks looked askance at teachers who were paid just nine or ten months of the year and made no accommodation for those whose workday did not allow for visits to a bank during banking hours. Alter, on the other hand, saw individuals with good credit and prudent spending habits whose needs were not being served. In 1951, with $30 in seed money and little else but his vision, Alter set out to find ways to provide the teachers of Philadelphia with the loans they needed, founding the company that would one day become Advanta from his spare bedroom. Over the next 50 years, Advanta pioneered many of the marketing techniques now common in the financial services industry today, including remote lending, direct mail, and affinity and relationship marketing, and today is one of the leading commercial credit card issuers in the nation.

One of the keys to Advanta's sustained success has been the company's ability to innovate with the times. Under the leadership of Jack Alter and later his son Dennis, Advanta grew and adapted, expanding its client base and branching out into new and different types of financial services. In 1982 Advanta began issuing credit

▲ In 1951, former Philadelphia schoolteacher Jack Alter founded an innovative financial services company to meet the needs of his fellow schoolteachers, whose unique needs were often overlooked by traditional lenders.

cards nationwide, building one of the largest consumer credit card portfolios in the U.S. over the subsequent 15 years. When the company ultimately exited the consumer credit card business in a transaction valued at $1.3 billion, it returned approximately $850 million to its shareholders via a tender offer. Advanta now brings its 50 plus years of financial services expertise and customer service excellence to the rapidly growing small business market. It is an exciting market and one that enables Advanta to fund and grow the dreams of a new generation of entrepreneurs like Jack Alter.

Although Advanta's client base now extends throughout the country, the Philadelphia area remains home to the Alter family and headquarters to Advanta Corp. Says Dennis Alter, Chairman and CEO of Advanta, "The nature of Philadelphia is one of a small city grown large. In spite of its size and scale, there is a sense of community

◀ Advanta President Bill Rosoff and Chairman Dennis Alter, both Philadelphia natives, are proud to work with the 850+ talented Advantans located primarily in the Greater Philadelphia region and Draper, Utah.

graduates to transitioning professionals. For 37 years, this event has been one of the Chamber's most successful contributions to the economic viability of the region.

Procurement, Services, and Support

Offering convenience, cost-effectiveness, and value are the cornerstones of the Chamber's commitment to its members. Accordingly, they are the foundation of what makes Chamber membership effective for business. Whether a company has one employee or thousands, the Chamber works to help save them time and money by offering group discounts and below-market buying plans.

Among the benefits and discounted plans are low-cost health, dental, vision, life and disability insurance, plus 401K savings and retirement plans that help member companies improve hiring and retention of their workforce. Members can even call the Chamber personnel for one-on-one consultations with friendly, familiar representatives who will act on their behalf with the insurance providers.

In addition to savings on healthcare benefits and services, membership offers other valuable features as well. The Chamber's partnership with Office Depot tenders savings of up to 60% on office supplies and products—and through other negotiated deals— reduced premiums on UPS delivery services, long distance, Internet, and voice and data telecommunications.

Marketing & Exposure

In times when marketing and exposure are the breadth of business success, perhaps the greatest advantage of Chamber involvement is that it can be used to directly influence industry position, recognition, and accountability of member companies. On the flipside of the collective influence of 6,000 companies are useful marketing opportunities, such as event sponsorships and partnerships, which can produce substantial investment returns. Companies may capitalize on networking opportunities with a diverse group of executives and business professionals, generate enhanced exposure, and impact their public image. Altogether, the Chamber hosts over one hundred business/community-oriented programs each year.

For the young and newly graduated, the Chamber's Young Professionals Network (YPN) hosts enlightening and entertaining activities in the region. Events are planned to keep these young professionals informed about the marketplace, encourage networking, and guide them toward success in future leadership roles.

The Chamber At Work

Resolute in its mission to stay one step ahead of the marketplace, the Greater Philadelphia Chamber of Commerce is committed to offering programs, services, and exclusive benefits to keep its membership involved. The On the Move® Campaign has been a key instrument in this endeavor. This 12-week, fundraising effort enables the Chamber to continue the important task of business development by

raising funds for future programs, partnerships, and initiatives. Conversely, the campaign benefits member companies that become involved through increased exposure and networking.

Uniting the Arts and Business communities is another GPCC initiative. The Chamber views arts and culture as an economic engine for the region. The Chamber's Arts & Business Council of Greater Philadelphia provides professional development and leadership programs in the arts for businesses and its employees. Programs such as Business Volunteers for the Arts, Business On Board, and Business On-Call offer opportunities for business professionals to leverage their expertise and resources through board services, management consulting, and general volunteer services to experience the richness of the region's arts and cultural community.

Working to expand the region's profile, the Chamber encourages global business affiliations through international programs where members meet business people and American consuls from around the world. Attendees gain insight on foreign business protocol and take advantage of special networking opportunities. The Chamber is directly associated with international Chambers from around the world, including the British, Italian, Chilean, Hispanic, Japanese, and Israeli Chambers.

For every Chamber business member, there is a range of packaged resources that serve every agenda. From employee development series, forums and symposia to business roundtables, networking events, and industry-specific programs. Topics clarify new market trends, focus on best business practices, and offer tips for increasing efficiency.

In brief, there is no area of business in which the Greater Philadelphia Chamber of Commerce is not concerned or involved. From arts to business, local to international, manufacturing to technology, the Chamber staff and membership is dedicated to ensuring a prosperous region where people are happy and business is booming.

Simply put—Get involved. Get results.

To find out more about the Greater Philadelphia Chamber of Commerce, visit www.philachamber.com or call (215) 545-1234. ℗

▶ The TASA Group

*W*hen a dispute results in litigation and experienced experts are needed to advise, investigate, or possibly testify about technical aspects of the situation—or when a business needs a consultant's insight—there is a high probability that The TASA Group will be asked to provide the experts. The Blue Bell firm has earned a solid national and international reputation as the one-stop source for virtually any kind of professional expertise essential for litigation, consulting, and alternative dispute resolution. For more than 46 years, they have referred countless experts and consultants for tens of thousands of high profile and everyday matters.

Known as North America's Largest And Most Experienced Expert Referral Service®, The TASA Group has built a select, constantly-expanding proprietary network, with thousands of experts and consultants in more than 9,000 categories. The firm can readily refer specialists in fields as disparate as accident analysis, biotechnology, cardiology, manufacturing, and risk assessment. They are neutral and their services are equally available to plaintiff or defense, and for every business need.

The TASA Group is a classic "Philadelphia boys make good" story. In 1956, two friends, Edwin H. Sherman and Jay L. Rosen, both graduates of Temple University with degrees in psychology, were looking for a way to utilize their skills and experience. They formed a partnership that tested and placed job applicants and screened others for job promotions. In the course of this work, they referred a recently retired Naval officer to a local Admiralty lawyer who, as it turned out, needed an expert for an accident case. The officer helped win the case, leading Sherman and Rosen to realize that there was an unmet need for a direct, central source of experts and consultants to serve the legal and business sectors.

▲ Worldwide Headquarters, Blue Bell, Pennsylvania.

Clients include some 200,000 law and insurance firms—from "the top 100" to sole practitioners—as well as businesses, and government agencies.

Crucial to The TASA Group's reputation and success is its emphasis on customized referrals and personal service. Clients who call or inquire online can speak immediately with experienced staff who are familiar with the experts in the requested location. Referrals are most often completed within 24 hours, saving clients many hours of search time.

The company's largest and best-known division is TASA—concerned primarily with expert referrals for potential litigation. Other divisions include TASAmed, for medical and health care referrals; TASconsulting, which refers consultants for primarily short-term, non-litigious projects; and TASL, which serves clients in the UK and Europe.

A unique service corporation, The TASA Group pioneered the expert referral concept and remains its leader. While there are some small referral firms limited to narrow fields like engineering or accounting, The TASA Group is comprehensive and global, meeting clients' needs around the world. ℗

◀ Top (left to right): Suzanne Olita, Executive Vice President; Michael Ardron, Controller; Carol Stein, Vice President. Bottom (left to right): Carol Sherman, Co-CEO; Edwin H. Sherman, Co-Chairman of the Board; Jay L. Rosen, Co-Chairman of the Board; Lee Faden, Co-CEO. Photo ©2002 John McGrail

▶ U.S. Trust

U.S. Trust was established in 1853 with a unique mission. As one of the nation's first investment management and trust companies, its duty was to help preserve and enhance the wealth of affluent individuals and families. Today their mission remains the same. The company believes that few firms can match their ability to provide the comprehensive range of sophisticated services the affluent require—investment management and consulting; fiduciary services; financial, tax, and estate planning; and private banking—as well as the depth of expertise necessary to help address the complex financial issues they face. All of these services are integrated, and each is customized to address a client's unique situation and delivered with an emphasis on building long-term, personal relationships.

Many families have seen their assets grow with U.S. Trust for generations. Others—such as corporate executives, professionals, and entrepreneurs—are building their families' wealth. U.S. Trust believes that the key to longevity and the success of client relationships is their heritage of performance, integrity, and quality. The company focuses on understanding the needs and concerns of each client and other members of the client's family. At every level of its organization, the company employs experienced, knowledgeable professionals whose breadth and depth of expertise is matched only by their commitment to helping clients realize their goals.

U.S. Trust believes that a combination of resources and experience makes them uniquely suited to meet the special wealth management needs of their clients. Although the services the company offers may often be complex in nature, they aim to make the financial lives of their clients simpler.

As part of its continuing national expansion, U.S. Trust opened an office in Wayne, Pennsylvania in 1999. This full-service office on the Main Line of Philadelphia allows the company to better serve the wealth management needs of its current and prospective clients throughout eastern Pennsylvania. U.S. Trust's presence in Wayne

▲ Senior executives from U.S. Trust's Pennsylvania office: (left to right) Douglas H. Pyle, managing director and chief investment officer; Howard E.N. Wilson, president and chief executive officer; and Barry C. Hamilton, senior vice president and head of private banking.

enables it to become more involved in the community where its clients live and work. As a firm, U.S. Trust strives to be a vital force in the communities where it does business. In addition to providing financial support, the company encourages its employees to be actively involved in local community organizations.

U.S. Trust's office in Pennsylvania is located at 100 West Lancaster Avenue in Wayne.

◀ U.S. Trust established a presence in Pennsylvania with the opening of its Wayne office in 1999.

▸ Commerce Bank

*A*s Philadelphia is the birthplace of America and of American enterprise, so too does the spirit of American enterprise continue alive and well at Commerce Bank. Beginning with its founding in 1973, it has embodied an entrepreneurial vision and a markedly non-traditional and unique retail marketing strategy.

Founder, Chairman, and President Vernon W. Hill II began Commerce Bank that year with one branch and eight employees in nearby Marlton, New Jersey. The Bank has grown to more than 200 branches in four states (Pennsylvania, New Jersey, Delaware, and New York) with a goal of more than 375 branches and over $25 billion in assets in the next five years. Commerce Bank maintains corporate headquarters just across the river in Cherry Hill, New Jersey. In recent years, Commerce has broadened its portfolio of services by establishing two subsidiaries, one of which—Commerce National Insurance Services, among the nation's largest insurance brokerage firms—is also located in Cherry Hill.

Philadelphia is home not only to Commerce Bank's Pennsylvania Regional Headquarters but also to the headquarters of the Bank's

▲ The Commerce Bank prototype branch is an inviting, airy structure, with office space surrounded by glass walls that provide a warm and naturally lit environment. All Commerce branches feature a wall mural of a historical photo of a local community landmark.

▲ At the front line of Commerce's unique retail marketing strategy are its employees, all of whom deliver "WOW! The Customer" service excellence. Left, wearing the trademark Commerce vest, is Cami Caputi, Branch Teller Service Manager; right, is Branch Manager Jill Ross.

other subsidiary, Commerce Capital Markets, the largest public finance firm in both Pennsylvania and New Jersey. Both are located at 20th & Market Streets. Pennsylvania continues as a vital market for Commerce Bank. Commerce's presence in eastern Pennsylvania continues to grow at a pace matching the Bank's overall growth throughout its four-state footprint.

From its inception Commerce Bank—through the leadership and vision of Vernon Hill—has developed a unique and highly successful retail model, incorporating the best practices of the nation's leading consumer-focused retailing companies. As *America's Most Convenient Bank*, Commerce looks different, thinks different, and provides a truly different banking experience.

Among Commerce's hallmark convenient services are: seven-day branch banking; Internet banking and stock trading at the award-winning commerceonline.com; and the Penny Arcades, free coin-counting machines located in the lobby of every one of Commerce's branch offices.

A firm commitment to active involvement in the local community is another important element of the Commerce philosophy. The Bank established the Commerce Corporate Fund in 1988. Since the Fund's inception, Commerce has contributed more than $20 million to help improve the quality of life of people living in the communities served by the Bank. ❷

▸ United Bank of Philadelphia

*U*nited Bancshares, Inc. is an African American controlled and managed bank holding company for United Bank of Philadelphia (the "Bank"), a commercial bank chartered in 1992 by the Commonwealth of Pennsylvania, Department of Banking and is a member of the Federal Reserve System. The Bank provides full service community banking in Philadelphia's neighborhoods that have traditionally been underserved by commercial banks.

The Bank's corporate offices are located at 300 North Third Street. The Bank has four financial service centers strategically located in natural markets in Philadelphia specifically, Center City, West, Northwest, and North. Comprehensive deposit and loan services are provided at each location with wealth management services launched in the Fall of 2002.

In addition, the Bank was certified by the United States Department of Treasury as a Community Development Financial Institution. This designation was a direct result of the Bank's consistent efforts in providing services to the low- to moderate-income areas in its communities and has been distinguished with five consecutive *outstanding* ratings in Community Reinvestment by the Federal Reserve Bank.

The Bank takes its role as a community development institution very seriously and works to heighten its presence as a catalyst for wealth creation and economic development in low- and moderate-income, underserved, and emerging markets. Every attempt is made to provide innovative financing through partnerships, programs, and loans. The majority of the Bank's commercial loans are categorized as small business loans and loans to religious organizations.

The Bank's strategic focus includes maintaining key alliances with other banks, small businesses, and institutions to achieve common goals in this urban market by fostering economic and community stabilization and revitalization. With the leadership of a dynamic and diverse board of directors and a focused management

▲ Under the leadership of United's President and CEO Evelyn F. Smalls, the Bank continues to offer a full array of loan and deposit products. United Wealth Management Services was introduced in the Fall of 2002.
Photography by Michael R. Husik

team, the Bank will continue to grow and enhance its presence in the financial services arena in the Greater Philadelphia region.

New Horizons

United Bank of Philadelphia dares to make a difference. As a community development bank, it is poised to work within the communities to ensure that basic banking products and services are available. The Bank will continue to be accessible and innovative. United Bank believes that the inner city, urban markets are ripe for business opportunities and growth. The Bank's leadership team recognizes and is acquainted with the challenges that go with serving these urban communities. United Bank is positioned to participate in concert with partners sharing similar visions in the transformation of untapped and unexplored economic resources from the potential to the profitable. ℗

◀ A diverse management team with a commitment to relationship banking, profitability, and community reinvestment.
Photography by Michael R. Husik

▶ Lincoln Financial Group

$\mathcal{L}$incoln Financial Group is one of the nation's leading providers of wealth accumulation and protection products, financial planning and investment advisory services for the affluent and retirement markets. The corporation holds a prominent position among financial services companies due primarily to its strategic focus, excellent customer service, risk management expertise, and broad range of sophisticated financial products.

LFG was founded in 1905 in Fort Wayne, Indiana, during a time when the insurance industry was highly suspect, under Congressional investigation, and scorned by the popular press. The original founders were a group of bankers, attorneys, wholesalers, hoteliers, manufacturers, physicians, and brokers. In order to separate them from the stigma that was attached to the industry, the founders of the company sought to associate themselves with the good name and reputation of Abraham Lincoln. Seeing the potential and believing in the good intentions of the company, Robert Todd Lincoln, the son of the famous president, granted the company permission to use the Lincoln name and thus the Lincoln National Life Insurance Company was born.

Lincoln has changed significantly since its foundation, having moved away from the role of a multi-line insurer to a focused financial services company. In addition to life insurance, LFG now provides annuities, managed accounts, mutual funds, retirement

▲ **Jon A. Boscia, Chairman and Chief Executive Officer of Lincoln Financial Group.**

plans, 529 college savings plans, institutional investment management, and financial and estate planning services. In 1998, Jon Boscia became president and CEO and then chairman in 2001 of LFG, since then, the changes have been numerous and significant. In 1999, the corporate headquarters was moved to Philadelphia in order to take advantage of the city's central location between New York City and Washington, DC., as well as its accessibility to the rest of the northeastern United States. The move has helped to reinvigorate LFG's business and maintain its position as a leader in the industry.

LFG sets itself apart from the competition with a deep understanding of estate planning, income management, and wealth protection. It has worked hard to develop strategic partnerships with other financial services companies, thus turning potential competitors into partners.

Lincoln Financial Group exists to satisfy the multiple financial needs of affluent individuals and small businesses. In so doing, LFG creates superior value for shareholders, offers quality products and services to customers, provides satisfying jobs for employees, and is a responsible citizen in the communities in which it operates. LFG seeks to live up to the reputation of Abraham Lincoln, and with its statement of values, LFG reaffirms that "its name indicates its character." ●

◀ **Lincoln Financial Group's Corporate Headquarters located in Philadelphia, Pennsylvania.**

CHAPTER THIRTEEN

Professions

The Greater Philadelphia area contains a vast network of qualified financial and legal professionals that make doing business in the city possible. Whatever the type of business, every kind of professional resource needed to operate effectively is available. Photo ©2002 John McGrail

▸ Public Financial Management

*P*ublic Financial Management, Inc. (PFM) was founded in 1975 on the principle of providing sound independent financial advice to state and local governments. PFM has become the nation's leading municipal financial and investment advisory firm headquartered in Philadelphia with offices throughout the United States. The company is owned by its Managing Directors and operates like a partnership with one goal in mind: to provide the highest quality advice to clients so they are able to raise, invest, and manage the resources they need in the most cost-effective manner possible.

PFM has always been in the forefront of new ideas on how to structure debt, how to manage federal restrictions on the investment of proceeds, what investors look for in the market, and the formation and execution of capital plans. The firm's very culture is designed to explore these ideas and push them to the limits of their effectiveness. PFM employs over 230 professionals nationwide. This talented group of men and women, many of whom hold experience in government and a variety of other professions, provide a broad perspective and an understanding of the unique pressures that often weigh on clients.

From the time employees come to work at PFM, they are trained to understand and appreciate that their job is to help bring added

▲ Since 1975, PFM has grown to over 230 employees in 20 offices nation-wide. PFM serves its clientele by creating project teams comprised of experts in specific financing techniques, governmental businesses, and geographic regions. Pictured are the Project Managers in our Philadelphia headquarters: (left to right, back row) Dean Kaplan, Pamela Forbes, Scott Quehl, Michael Nadol, Wendy Deats, Nancy Winkler, David Scott, and Napoleon Nelson, (left to right, front row) Bernard Cummings, Steve Boyle, John White (CEO), Benjamin Rayer, and Barbara Bisgaier.
Photo ©2002 John McGrail

value to servicing the financial needs of the firm's clients—the public, the taxpayers, the ratepayers, and their elected and appointed representatives of America's state and local governments.

PFM has a comprehensive orientation that focuses on three areas: transaction management related to debt issuance, provision of investment advice and portfolio management for bond proceeds and working capital, and strategic municipal consulting related to operating and capital budgets. While most financial advisors only manage debt transactions, PFM offers its clients a horizontally integrated array of services designed to meet *all* of their financial needs.

PFM's only business is providing financial, investment, and consulting advice to its clients. Involved in the capital markets on a daily basis, the firm offers clients professional resources equal to any investment bank. However, PFM does not trade or underwrite securities. While an underwriting firm must meet the needs of both buyer and seller of securities, PFM has no such inherent conflicts, focusing solely on the interests of the municipal client.

As a financial advisor, PFM engages in capital planning, revenue forecasting and evaluation, resource allocation, debt management,

◀ As Financial Advisor to the City of Philadelphia, PFM led the effort to develop, research, analyze, and write the City's comprehensive Strategic Plan to meet requirements of a state oversight board. This ongoing project results in annual updates that refine and quantify the financial impact of the City's management initiatives. PFM's work has resulted in several credit upgrades for Philadelphia. Photo ©2002 John McGrail

▲ PFM was retained in 1992 to develop and implement the financing plan for SEPTA's capital program. SEPTA's plans to finance rail cars, light rail vehicles, and the purchase of a new building were realized with the assistance of PFM and their many talents and services. Chuck Matthews of PFM, working with Faye Moore of SEPTA, is presently assisting on a second long-term capital financing for its rail program.
Photo ©2002 John McGrail

policy development, and debt transaction management—including structuring, documentation, and execution. PFM delivers an unmatched depth and breadth of experience and expertise, helping clients to resolve the myriad of technical and financial concerns they routinely confront during the capital formation process. PFM's national reputation and consistent growth, from $5 billion in managed debt transactions in 1986 to $25.1 billion in 2001, reflect the clients' recognition of PFM's capabilities and the value it provides.

As an investment manager, PFM brings a complete spectrum of services to the business of money management. The company manages both state-oriented investment pools and individual client portfolios designed to earn competitive yields while maximizing safety and liquidity. Services include timely, market-driven portfolio management, portfolio design, state-of-the-art accounting, and arbitrage rebate

▶ Lou Verdelli of PFM at the Chester Water Authority, a PFM client since 1987. Recently, PFM implemented a bond refinancing program that reduced the Authority's debt service payments by $675,000. PFM has also brought the latest financial technology to the Authority. PFM completed four bond issues since 1999 by selling the Authority's bonds on the Internet in an auction format. Photo ©2002 John McGrail

calculation services. Client assets under PFM's management have increased from $1 billion in 1986 to well over $13 billion today.

As a strategic consultant, PFM brings its clients the most effective capital and operating budget advice available enjoying a proven track record in performance management, benchmarking, revenue enhancement, and privatization. Since 1993, PFM has helped clients eliminate billions of dollars of projected budget deficits without increasing taxes or reducing services.

Since the opening of its corporate headquarters in Philadelphia in 1975 and with the additions of offices in Harrisburg and Pittsburgh, PFM has developed vast client relationships throughout Pennsylvania that range from statewide organizations to small local communities and school districts. While Philadelphia is the location of the largest of PFM's offices, and Harrisburg is the home of PFM's Municipalities and School Districts and Money Management Groups, the firm maintains 18 other offices throughout the United States.

The City of Philadelphia currently represents PFM's largest financial advisory client. The City has several governmental authorities and quasi-governmental, non-profit corporations—collectively the "authorities"—that provide services and issue debt. As financial advisor to the City and authorities, PFM has the task of assisting the City to reduce its cost of government without compromising services or further infringing on its tax base. Philadelphia's size and economic condition necessitate a broad scope of services to address concerns that reach beyond the issuance of debt. PFM provides a number of daily and long-term services to comprehensively address the economic condition of the City and the operation of government.

PFM has led the Philadelphia's effort to develop comprehensive financial plans. These plans have been designed to change city operations and provide practical steps and measurement tools for implementing change. The immediate goals of Philadelphia's Five-Year Plans were to solve its cash crisis and to cure the structural deficit of $248 million. PFM helped Philadelphia achieve this during the mid-1990s.

With the return to fiscal health, the City and its various enterprises (the water department, the municipal gas works, and the airport) have once again been able to access the credit markets. PFM has served as financial advisor for each of Philadelphia's transactions since 1992, bringing new ideas to bear while working on these and other projects, including the competitive purchase of refunding escrow securities, the development of a productivity bank, the establishment of a master lease financing program, and the implementation of a tax lien securitization sale.

PFM has developed a number of computerized financial models and analytic tools to assist clients in their management and decision-making processes. PFM also maintains substantial disclosure documents and debt structuring models on its computer system, updating and revising them as required. PFM is available on a daily basis to advise public officials on small and large financial matters that occur in the normal course of business.

PFM is also responsible for the investment of its clients' refunding escrows, their debt service reserve funds, and often their operating cash. PFM is often asked to undertake the arbitrage compliance responsibility for clients and does so through its comprehensive monitoring, tracking, and calculation effort.

Over its 25-year history, PFM has built a solid presence in the municipal marketplace, having been involved in financing programs totaling more than $249 billion. In 2001 alone, PFM advised on over 500 bond transactions with a total volume of over $25 billion, surpassing all competitors and earning recognition by Securities Data Corporation as the number one financial advisor in the nation.

The financial advisory business has long grown past the point where the financial advisor merely reviews and critiques the work of other members of the financing team. PFM was one of the first to

▲ **Scott Quehl and Pete Nissen stand with an original statue from The Benjamin Franklin Bridge, which is managed by the Delaware River Port Authority (DRPA). PFM has been retained by the DRPA since 1995 to advise on its financing program. As a general financial consultant, PFM reviewed DRPA's investment strategies and financing opportunities. PFM developed the financing plan that allowed DRPA to fund its capital program. PFM also assisted in structuring a financial package to provide incentives for shipbuilding in the Port Zone.** Photo ©2002 John McGrail

broaden their role and become more like that of the senior investment banker. The firm believes in its responsibility to bring each client new ideas, save them money, and help them plan for the future. To fulfill this obligation, PFM has developed the most sophisticated technical and analytical resources in the business.

PFM uses innovative ideas and structures as tools to help clients realize their objectives, not simply as a means of doing deals.

◀ **Led by Barbara Bisgaier, PFM has served as Financial Advisor to the Philadelphia International Airport since 1992. PFM has worked on three major bond issues, upgraded the airport's credit rating, and worked with the airport on the development and implementation of a plan of finance that is essential to the airport's future expansion.**

Photo ©2002 John McGrail

▲ John White, Barbara Bisgaier, and PFM served as Financial Advisors to the City of Philadelphia in connection with the development and implementation of a financing plan for the construction of a new football stadium and practice facility for the Philadelphia Eagles, a new baseball stadium for the Philadelphia Phillies, and the demolition of Veterans Stadium.

Photo ©2002 John McGrail

Innovation for its own sake has little value and may be risky, but as part of a carefully crafted plan that reduces costs, increases revenues, or maximizes future flexibility, innovative financing techniques can add significant value and make the infeasible achievable.

The men and women at PFM have developed and assisted clients in implementing hundreds of innovative financing techniques, each one tailored to the objectives and constraints of that particular entity. While many innovations involve debt transactions, PFM has also succeeded in assisting clients in such things as privatization and the development of long-term strategic plans.

PFM completed the first competitive advance refunding and variable rate bond issues, assisted clients with asset sales and securitizations

▶ Dean Kaplan of PFM at the Philadelphia Water Department, a longstanding PFM client. Together they have successfully implemented the largest Automatic Meter Reading (AMR) project in the U.S. water industry. As a result, the utility has experienced a significant improvement in customer service while achieving net present value benefits.

Photo ©2002 John McGrail

of tax liens, pension fund contributions, and other assets or revenue streams as a means of managing cash flow and increasing net income. PFM is the nation's leader in using the Internet to help clients lower their cost of capital by obtaining broader distribution for their debt and has competitively bid over 250 sales using the Internet. PFM has extensively analyzed and managed the competitive and negotiated placement of many derivative securities, but only after ensuring that all risks were understood and appropriately managed and that contract terms were written to protect each client's interests. The firm has managed a host of synthetic advance refunding techniques to allow clients to guarantee debt service savings from outstanding high coupon bonds that, under federal tax law, cannot be advance refunded. PFM has integrated the management of assets and liabilities to minimize interest rate risks, cash flow variances, and other risks through techniques such as forward rate agreements, interest rate swaps, and commodity price swaps.

Today, no other firm can match PFM's level of experience or record of innovation in the field of municipal finance on the state and local level in both the capital creation and investment management sides of the business. PFM offers a comprehensive range of financial planning, debt management, and investment management services from a staff of expertly trained and uniquely qualified professionals.

The people at PFM are in the financial and investment advisory business because they believe their clients deserve effective, informed representation when they bring their debt to the market, invest their funds, and manage their operating and capital budgets. PFM is a financial and investment advisory company only. The entire structure of the firm is designed to provide the most professional financial advice available to its clients. ☻

◀ 265

▶ ACE INA

*S*ixteen years after the Continental Congress adopted the Declaration of Independence, a group of merchants and other prominent citizens, sitting in the same room in Independence Hall, organized the first U.S.-based marine insurance company. Its first policies, written in 1792, insured the hull of the ship "America" and the goods it carried from Philadelphia to Ireland.

By removing the financial risk from the dangers of ocean commerce, the company, Insurance Company of North America, now part of the ACE INA group of companies, helped the young U.S. shipping business flourish. To this day, ACE INA is in the business of managing risk. While other companies try to shed volatility from unforeseen events, ACE INA accumulates, diversifies, and manages volatile risks in a way that provides security to its clients. Facing a landscape of increased peril, businesses large and small turn to ACE INA because it brings together unparalleled expertise in managing risks and a stable capital base to draw on should a loss occur. As a profitable and sound insurance company, ACE INA has the resources to tailor solutions for a wide range of customer needs.

The ACE Family

Headquartered at Two Liberty Place, ACE INA is the largest component of the ACE Group of Companies, one of the world's largest and most innovative providers of property and casualty insurance, reinsurance, and financial services. With $37 billion in assets and more than 8,000 employees worldwide, ACE is a widely diversified global financial services firm capable of meeting clients' needs in virtually every sector of the property and casualty insurance industry and in every major market around the globe. It provides risk-related products and services to a broad range of local and multinational corporations. Trading on the New York Stock Exchange as ACE, the group's stock is part of the Standard & Poor's 500 index.

Just as the founders of INA did more than 200 years ago, the ACE Group consistently breaks through established barriers to develop new products and new markets. INA was the first insurance company to underwrite business in China in 1897, and 105 years later, in 2002, ACE forged a historic alliance with a leading Chinese insurer. As China opens its doors to world trade, ACE's strategic investment in Huatai Insurance Company of China represents the first time that a foreign insurer has been allowed to own such a large share of a Chinese insurance company. For ACE, the venture represents tremendous opportunities for growth. It provides ACE a platform to offer its products and services to a huge population in the world's fastest growing insurance market.

Though its historical roots run deep, ACE INA is keenly oriented toward the future. Its nearly 2,000 employees in the Delaware Valley strive each day to further enhance the company's reputation for crafting innovative, creative solutions for every challenge, from health insurance for consumers in Latin America to highly specialized insurance for the aerospace industry.

▲ Susan Rivera serves as president, ACE INA Holdings, Inc.

The ACE INA holding company oversees operations that span the globe. Almost two-thirds of ACE Group's $10.2 billion in premium revenue are generated in North America by businesses that are part of Philadelphia-based ACE INA. Its largest unit, ACE USA, offers sophisticated property, casualty, marine, accident and health, and financial and risk-management products and services to corporate and consumer clients. ACE INA's other units are, ACE Financial Solutions, ACE INA Consumer Solutions Group, ACE Canada, ACE Global Accident & Health, ACE Europe, ACE Latin America, ACE Far East, and ACE Asia Pacific.

Filling the Void in Critical Times

Throughout its history, ACE has been able to step in at critical times and fill voids in the marketplace. On September 11, 2001, that legacy withstood its greatest test. Even as the insurance industry grieved the loss of so many colleagues, clients, and business partners, these unprecedented events quickly made clear the tremendous challenges to the business environment.

This was the insurance industry's largest aggregate loss in history. The result was a significant reduction in its capacity to accept risk. At the same time, business leaders were alerted to the need for adequate coverage, and consequently, the demand for comprehensive insurance solutions surged. While other insurers were withdrawing from important markets, ACE continued to provide critical forms of coverage. The company also stepped up to add lines that were in especially strong demand.

Before the terrorist attacks on the World Trade Center, the Pentagon, and in Pennsylvania, the risk of terrorism had been viewed as minor. But in the new environment, businesses were hard-pressed to find coverage to protect themselves against losses resulting from terrorist attacks. As the industry worked with lawmakers to develop a solution, ACE USA began providing insurance against terrorism to U.S. and Canadian commercial property customers in vulnerable industries. The company focused on sectors that faced a high degree of risk, including utilities, financial institutions, real-estate firms, manufacturers, the entertainment industry, and telecommunications companies.

The energy industry presents another striking example of ACE INA's ability to meet the needs of clients in turbulent times. In 1998, ACE USA developed the first insurance product to protect against the price risks in the deregulated power industry. A year later, it launched a second-generation product to protect against simultaneous unplanned outages among multiple power units of a large utility. The policy provides a safety net by paying the difference between the market price for replacement power during an outage and an agreed upon price level. As the deregulated industry evolved, ACE USA responded with more novel products and services. One product delivers power to utilities during an outage, while another cushions a utility against the earnings shock that could result from the long-term loss of a power-generating unit.

"Our innovation and creativity got us to where we are today," said Susan Rivera, president of ACE INA Holdings Inc. "It is our ability to continue to meet the evolving needs of our clients and business partners that sets us apart from our competition."

Sharp Pencil, Entrepreneurial Spirit

ACE INA is constantly evolving and exploring new markets and new products. ACE expects to become a player in the life insurance arena and the volatile business of environmental risk. It recently staked a claim in

the world of employee benefits with its acquisition of YouDecide. YouDecide provides corporate employees with an employer-sponsored platform for learning about and buying insurance and financial products online or by phone.

At the other end of the business spectrum, ACE Financial Solutions provides companies with creative financial risk management and risk-financing products. These sophisticated products help clients manage risks associated with credit exposures, asset valuation and financing, and other complex financial exposures.

ACE INA's growth is driven by a unique combination of entrepreneurial spirit, intellectual firepower, and a sharp pencil. An insurance company is only as good as its ability to pay claims. That requires a strong capital base, disciplined underwriting, accurate pricing, astute investing, and overall good financial management. These are the hallmarks of ACE INA, achievements made possible by a professional staff that possesses a breadth and depth of expertise built on a foundation of knowledge and sound experience.

"Insurance is a business that relies upon many people to deliver the final product," Rivera said. "It is our people, their working together, our integrity, and our personal relationships that drive our success."

◀ 267

▶ **Orginal insurance documents and advertising material dating back to the early 1800s. Insurance Company of North America is the oldest stock fire and marine company in North America and is now a proud member of the ACE Group of insurance companies.**
Photos courtesy of ACE Archives, American Philosophical Society, CIGNA Museum and Art Collection

Good for Business, Good for Philadelphia

The dedication of ACE INA and its employees extends well beyond the business and its clients into the wider community. Through its philanthropic arm, ACE INA lends support to worthwhile educational and community organizations and cultural institutions. The ACE INA Foundation is actively involved in programs concerning youth, education, and the arts.

ACE INA employees in Philadelphia and field offices around the United States raised almost $200,000 for the 2001 United Way Campaign, and the Foundation's 50 percent match raised the total contribution to almost $300,000. ACE INA also encourages employees to donate their time and money to other charitable organizations by providing financial rewards to the causes they support through the Foundation's Matching Gifts and Gift of Time programs.

Among the region's many worthwhile organizations that benefit from the ACE INA Foundation are the Philadelphia Museum of Art, Philadelphia Academies, Inc., Meals on Wheels, Need in Deed, and Philadelphia Cares.

ACE INA also lends support to the Police Memorial PAL Center's Adopt-a-Center Initiative. This allows the Philadelphia-based center to provide free after-school programs to more than 200 children between the ages of 6 and 19, many of whom are economically disadvantaged.

ACE INA Foundation's support also enables the center to expand its after-school curriculum, maintain existing general operation, and continue with its mission of "Cops Helping Kids."

In its work with Philadelphia Academies, ACE INA assists in the development of a variety of education and work-related activities with the Business Academy at William Penn High School. Philadelphia Academies, one of the nation's largest school-to-career programs, serves more than 7,000 public high school students in Philadelphia.

ACE INA also makes a strong contribution to the culture and beauty of Philadelphia. ACE INA joined forces with the Center City District and the Avenue of the Arts in their initiative to revitalize and decorate North Broad Street with 44 brightly colored banners designed by elementary and high school students.

The ACE INA Foundation provides ongoing support to the Philadelphia Museum of Art through participation in its Corporate Partners program and support of the historic Philadelphia treasure known as Mt. Pleasant in Fairmount Park. The company's connection to Mt. Pleasant is long lasting. INA insured Mt. Pleasant in 1796.

▼ **ACE INA strives to make a positive impact in the communities where its employees live and work. The ACE INA Foundation donates both time and money to Delaware Valley educational and community organizations.**

Many ACE INA employees contribute their own time serving on boards and doing the critical work required to keep nonprofits running smoothly. Dominic Frederico, the ACE INA chairman and chief executive officer, is a member of the Pennsylvania Business Roundtable and is an executive board member of the Philadelphia Chamber of Commerce.

Looking Ahead

ACE INA's historical roots in Philadelphia keep the company grounded in solid business fundamentals even as it branches out with new products and in new directions.

In addition to terrorism coverage and innovative offerings for the power industry, ACE INA has recently introduced new products in the areas of accident and health insurance, medical professional liability insurance, consumer solutions, excess commercial liability insurance, and excess workers compensation.

"We are always looking for new avenues of growth," Frederico said. "We work hard everyday to keep moving ahead and seizing the valuable opportunities that present themselves."

Even before INA wrote the first policies issued in the United States for ships and their cargo, the insurance business had been a numbers-oriented statistical business. In recent years, it has become even more so. ACE takes advantage of the most sophisticated tools and the brightest professional staff to better understand its risks, accurately price its products, and evaluate the probability of the "unthinkable" happening.

"As insurance gets more complicated, the strongest insurance companies will propel forward," Rivera said. "But the fundamental values that it takes to be successful will remain the same. It is critical for us to know our customers, understand their problems, and provide innovative solutions and outstanding service. The market remembers and values companies that can assist them in the time of need. ACE strives to continue this legacy."

▲ Dominic Frederico serves as chairman and chief executive officer of ACE INA Holdings, Inc.

ACE INA, ACE USA, ACE Financial Solutions, ACE INA Consumer Solutions Group, ACE Canada, ACE Global Accident & Health, ACE Europe, ACE Latin America, ACE Far East and ACE Asia Pacific are trade names used to describe certain of the subsidiaries or operating divisions of the ACE Group of Companies. The ACE Group of Companies is headed by ACE Limited (NYSE: ACE) and provides insurance and reinsurance products and services for a diverse group of clients around the world. Additional information can be found at www.ace-ina.com. ℗

▶ ACE INA employees support the area's Philadelphia Cares Day volunteer activities, where they cleaned and painted the exterior of a local public high school and refurbished the school library.

◀ 269

▶ Doyle Consulting Group, Inc.

*D*oyle Consulting Group, Inc. provides employee benefit consulting and brokerage insurance services to employers both regional and national in scope. Tracing its roots to the late 1950s, Doyle Consulting Group has evolved into the premier consulting firm with a strong client base that is made up of some of the most successful industry leaders.

Today, firmly established as an innovator in service delivery with a reputation of integrity that any company would be proud of, Doyle Consulting's services encompass just about every facet of benefit delivery, administration, design, organization, budgeting, forecasting, and funding. It provides employers with the concept and development of any narration of benefit plan, whether it be a medical program that includes PPO's, HMO options, dental, prescription drugs, life or a disability policy, and 401K, as well as voluntary benefits, and any area of retirement planning.

In today's world, all employers share a need for excellent employees, arguably, the most important factor in running a successful company. Doyle Consulting recognizes and addresses this fact on two different but equally important levels. Over the years, Doyle Consulting has worked hard to make itself an integral part of the employee compensation evaluation process for its clients. The company prides itself on developing programs that are not only budget sensitive and cost effective, but are also able to provide exceptional benefits for the employees. Such programs not only allow employers to keep top quality personnel on board, but also allow them to recruit high quality people during times of expansion.

Doyle Consulting recognizes that a superior workforce is necessary, not only for its clients, but for its own success as well. To that end, Doyle Consulting constantly searches for ways to improve its abilities to recruit and keep the very best professionals in the industry.

▲ **Francis L. Doyle, III, Chairman and CEO of Doyle Consulting Group, has led the company into its sixth decade of providing top quality benefits consulting services to a select group of regional and national clients.**
Photo ©2002 John McGrail

The company achieves this by affording its employees a combination of enhanced compensation and a high-energy work environment that offers unmatched career development possibilities. Doyle Consulting hires only the best and pays them to achieve. This company outlook proves itself through an almost non-existent employee turnover rate, which has, in turn, led to an equally impressive client retention rate.

As with almost every type of business, Doyle Consulting has had to deal with constant change in its industry. One of these changes can be seen in a willingness and an ability of employers to provide for the diverse benefit needs of their employees and dependents. While this is beneficial to both employee and employer, in terms of employee

◀ **Frank Doyle and his management team have built a sterling reputation as a leader in the employee benefits consultancy and insurance brokerage by utilizing state-of-the-art technology to create top-notch solutions for its clients.**
Photo ©2002 John McGrail

▲ **Doyle Consulting Group's Chairman and CEO, Frank Doyle, with Sandra Cornelius, President of Elwyn, Inc., on-site at Elwyn with one of its clients, representative of Doyle's commitment to community involvement. Elwyn is one of the nation's oldest and largest human services organizations serving people with special needs.** Photo ©2002 John McGrail

consistent demands of the clients that seek out the services of Doyle Consulting. Knowledge is the key to staying ahead of the game in benefits consulting. Clients want to know what the future holds, the newest trends in benefit provisions, and they want to be assured that their needs are going to be addressed in whatever program they choose. Doyle Consulting realizes that it is necessary to provide reliable, consistent, and timely information to its clients, in order to allow them to concentrate on operating their business.

The future of Doyle Consulting is promising. Since its formation, the company has shown a consistent record of high growth. The complexity of factors such as continued escalation of health care costs has shown the need for firms to grow and adapt. Doyle Consulting's utilization of the newest information systems and software, combined with a highly knowledgeable staff, has given it the ability to accept challenges and generate solutions for its client companies on a long term basis.

"The major hallmark of our success has always been that we have not only gotten some of the largest employers in our target market, but we have also maintained those relationships over a long period of time," says Francis L. Doyle, III, Chairman and CEO of Doyle Consulting Group, Inc. "The best barometer of success for any company is in the long term associations it develops.

"We will continue to exceed our client's expectations only by the virtue of our ability to deliver an innovative approach, exceptional service, and execution of their objectives." ℗

 ◀ 271

satisfaction and productivity, it continually challenges a company's capacity to stay within budget.

Another sign of industry evolution can be seen in how much better informed and more knowledgeable employees are in terms of the value of employee benefit programs. Both factors have made it necessary for companies to seek out fresh, innovative ways to provide the benefits that their staff members need and deserve, in ways that will conserve company resources.

What has remained the same since its foundation is the

▶ **Doyle Consulting Group's broker network team in front of the company's headquarters at One Commerce Square in center city Philadelphia. Doyle prides itself on attracting and retaining top talent in the industry.**
Photo ©2002 John McGrail

▸ Wolf, Block, Schorr and Solis-Cohen LLP

𝒯n 1903 Morris Wolf, a graduate of the University of Pennsylvania Law School asked Horace Stern, a young professor at the same school, to be his partner in a new law firm. Although the two men had never met before, each saw characteristics in the other that he respected. From this seemingly spur of the moment beginning, came Wolf, Block, Schorr and Solis-Cohen LLP. For over a century WolfBlock has strived to establish itself as a leader in the business, legal, and public communities in the Mid-Atlantic region. Today, with seven offices throughout the East Coast, WolfBlock has more than 250 lawyers working in 18 practice groups. These groups range from litigation to employment law, from personal planning and tax law to information technology and consumer law, from intellectual property to venture capital counseling and international transactions.

WolfBlock takes great pride in its role as a leader among Philadelphia area law firms. Over the years WolfBlock has evolved into a dynamic firm that values innovation and excellence in everything it does. Their seasoned attorneys have in-depth experience in a wide range of industries and practice areas, and know what steps to take to keep each client ahead of the competition.

Today's legal system is one of constant change—remaining current and anticipating potential issues are vital components to any firm's success. WolfBlock makes it a priority to bring a keen awareness of changes across all industries, as well as a vigorous sense of purpose to each project. The effective and efficient achievement of the clients' objectives is the sole focus of WolfBlock attorneys, whether it be structuring complex business transactions, leading high-stakes litigation, guiding strategic corporate planning, or designing comprehensive tax strategies. Their problem solving approach begins with a thorough understanding of the clients' needs and objectives and then tailoring a solution to achieve the clients' ultimate goals.

One of the many attributes that distinguishes WolfBlock from its competition is that the firm understands and encourages the individuality of each of its attorneys. This appreciation of the diversity and uniqueness each attorney brings to the table provides the firm with an invaluable resource—open-minded staff members with the ability to think "outside the box." Each attorney willingly offers his or her own distinct interpretation in open interaction with colleagues, giving each client extraordinary consideration, and creative and fresh solutions.

The professionals at WolfBlock are highly skilled at proactively creating real-world solutions for the needs of every client. They take the initiative in providing alternative forms of legal counsel, offering innovative suggestions and occasional business opportunities to clients, and upholding and expanding the dynamic spirit of the firm's founder, Morris Wolf.

While WolfBlock has long been recognized as a leader in the legal industry, the firm is equally committed to remaining a valued

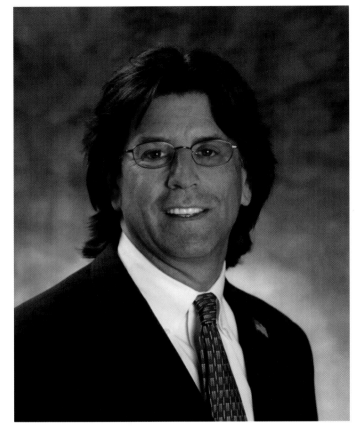

▲ **Mark L. Alderman, Chairman.**

corporate citizen. Each year the firm makes substantial monetary contributions to many of the area's non-profit organizations that promote the values upon which WolfBlock was founded. The attorneys themselves make a tremendous impact by contributing thousands of hours annually to providing pro bono legal services, and serving in volunteer and leadership roles in various local and national organizations.

To further enhance and support the communities in which its staff works and lives, firm members have been directly involved in governmental elections on a local, state, and national level and have served as advisors to elected officials in the resulting transitional periods. WolfBlock attorneys have held positions in the public sector also. They have served on the Philadelphia City Council; as members of the municipal, state, and federal bench; and as professors at law schools. Among their ranks are former members of the U.S. Attorney's Office, the Environmental Protection Agency, the Securities and Exchange Commission, a former ABA Chairman, and a member of the U.S. Postal Board of Governors. Other notable alumni served as the Commissioner of Internal Revenue and as the U.S. Ambassador to Switzerland. Many of the attorneys hold leadership positions in local, state, and national bar associations. Founding member Horace Stern was on the bench for 37 years, eventually becoming Chief Justice of Pennsylvania, before returning to the firm in 1957.

▲ **The Wolf Institute.**

Complementing WolfBlock's legal offerings are its ancillary services provided through The Wolf Institute, a division of WolfBlock, and WolfBlock Government Relations, a wholly owned subsidiary. Employee management and executive training courses are offered at The Wolf Institute. WolfBlock Government Relations is dedicated to promoting effective government relations and lobbying services for clients.

The attorneys and staff of WolfBlock have made delivering optimum results for each client a hallmark of the firm's existence. The reason behind the firm's success is a combination of several ingredients. First, the commitment to be available 24 hours a day, seven days a week to every client, regardless of whether they are a large national company, a small family-owned business, or a single individual; second, a relentless dedication to producing exceptional results; and finally, a comprehensive approach to addressing the clients' concerns. Continuing to provide exemplary service is key to the ongoing development of this strong regional firm and what will make WolfBlock the partner of choice for the Mid-Atlantic region for another 100 years. Ⓟ

▶ **Reception area at WolfBlock's Philadelphia office.**

▶ Duane Morris LLP

*N*ot An Art Gallery

Or is it? One wouldn't know when first coming upon the halls of the 43rd floor of One Liberty Place in Philadelphia. The walls are peppered with original works of art done by "self-taught" artists whose lives are as diverse as their works. The atmosphere is one of creativity and individuality, and the people encountered, reflections of the diligence and originality of the walls of artwork.

A Cultured Background

But Duane Morris LLP is not an art gallery. It is, however, one of Philadelphia's largest, most prominent law firms, with offices throughout the United States and in Europe. With a firm history that spans almost a century, Duane Morris boasts a robust client base and a track record of success. Founded in 1904 by Russell Duane, Roland Morris, and Stevens Heckscher, the firm was built around the principles of creativity, diligence, and success—principles found in the attorneys and staff who work in the firm today.

Law and Art

Duane Morris does, however, appreciate a connection between Philadelphia's rich art culture and its history as a center of law— a connection not realized by many other local institutions. As a full-service law firm headquartered in Philadelphia, Duane Morris represents a wide range of clients in every field of practice in law. With this experience comes the understanding that law *is* like art; seen differently by different people, constantly changing, and in many instances open to interpretation.

A Century of Growth; Growth Going Forward

Like many early Philadelphia businesses and institutions, Duane Morris was founded in the Quaker tradition, which is reflected in

▲ "Three Blue Eyed Horses" by William L. Hawkins.

the current firm culture. Duane Morris has found its longevity in its ability to evolve and reshape itself throughout its near century-long history. Like an artist at an easel, Duane Morris' attorneys and leaders have worked for nearly a century to refine the firm into the perfect piece of art—or the consummate law firm.

With 18 offices across the United States, Duane Morris is recognized by the Am Law 100, a preeminent survey of the 100 largest law firms in the nation. The Philadelphia office alone employs more than 500 attorneys and staff, and since 1998 the firm has more than doubled in both size and revenue. When the firm opened its London office in 2000, Duane Morris further expanded its international client base.

In recent years, Duane Morris has also developed several affiliate organizations in order to expand its capabilities and service offering to clients and others. These companies include Wescott Financial Advisory Group LLC, a money management firm; and Public Affairs Management LLC, providing government relations and lobbying services; and Wescott Strategic Management LLC, a business advisory firm to financially distressed companies.

◀ "Yaekle Building" by William L. Hawkins.

▲ "Assembleage" by Simon Sparrow.

Extending the Duane Morris Culture Outward

As representatives of a city so rich in culture and diversity, Duane Morris attorneys understand that the artwork on the firm walls is only the beginning. Duane Morris attorneys and staff are visible throughout the city in numerous civic positions and participate in various community organizations.

The firm supports educational programs such as *Philadelphia Reads*, an initiative of the Office of the Mayor of Philadelphia that works to ensure that all children read well and independently by the end of third grade. Duane Morris participates by inviting elementary school children into their offices once a week, reading with them and exposing them to a productive, professional culture.

Lawyers at Duane Morris participate in *Philadelphia Futures*, a non-profit organization based in Philadelphia that helps economically disadvantaged Philadelphia teenagers to excel in their studies and prepare for college and careers. Other Duane Morris attorneys participate

in the *Support Center for Child Advocacy* and the *Peoples Emergency Center*, a comprehensive social service agency for homeless women, teenagers, and their children.

Duane Morris attorneys also participate in *The Committee of Seventy*, a not-for-profit, nonpartisan political watchdog organization dedicated to advancing good government for the city of Philadelphia and its surrounding communities, and *Philadelphia Cares*, a group that addresses social, educational, and environmental needs throughout the community. Additionally, a member of the Duane Morris team recently subsidized the art department of a local Philadelphia high school, and the firm itself is a Corporate Partner with the world-renowned Philadelphia Museum of Art.

Not an Art Gallery—but a Steadfast Patron of the Arts

Today, Duane Morris continues to work diligently to expand the firm's presence in the United States and in Europe. The firm also continues to value and revere the Quaker principles on which Duane Morris was founded, and works to instill these principles in lawyers throughout the firm.

Although Duane Morris is not an art gallery, the firm will continue work to support local and national artists by displaying their artwork throughout the firm's 19 offices and by continuing to support arts in the Philadelphia area and elsewhere. ℗

◀ 275

▼ "Family Band" by Jon Serl.

▸ Greater Philadelphia Venture Group

For many years, Philadelphia was viewed as a mere Amtrak stop between New York and Washington, D.C. In 1984, a dedicated group of venture capitalists and related service providers joined together to change this perception and to open the eyes of investors to the advantages of doing business in Greater Philadelphia. Their vision resulted in the creation of the Greater Philadelphia Venture Group (GPVG), an affiliate of the Greater Philadelphia Chamber of Commerce. Since its inception, the GPVG has dedicated itself to foster the creation and growth of the private equity and entrepreneurial environment through a series of educational and networking events.

Along with the rest of the United States, the mid-Atlantic region experienced a major economic upswing in the 1990s. In 1991, the total venture capital investments in the mid-Atlantic region exceeded $256 million. By 2000, that number had increased 50-fold to a staggering $12.7 billion, helping to push the five state area into the forefront of the American markets. This surge of economic activity culminated in two consecutive years of venture capital investments topping $1 billion in 1999 and 2000. The GPVG takes pride in its part of that economic boom, helping to account for more than $4.7 billion in investments in the Greater Philadelphia region.

As a result of this vitality, the mid-Atlantic region is a net importer of investments, meaning that the flow of venture capital dollars into the region consistently exceeds the flow of dollars going out. This has provided the GPVG with an opportunity to network with an elite group of investors, and gives those investors the ability to network with their business peers. There are over 50 venture

▲ Press debrief by Mayor John Street at the 2001 Mid-Atlantic Venture Conference held October 15, 16 & 17. The venture conference featured more than 75 companies seeking venture funding from our audience of Venture capitalists and investors.

capital firms currently active in the Greater Philadelphia region, 41 of which are headquartered here. These companies currently boast an estimated $10 billion in assets under management. More than half of these companies didn't exist in 1995 and have risen to prominence in a relatively short time. The support that these funds provide to the GPVG has helped the organization bring recognition to the community and help continue the financial growth that the area currently enjoys.

The GPVG employs four full-time employees and is led by an active board of directors made up of 25 industry leaders.

The GPVG sponsors a number of programs that offer major opportunities for companies to increase their contacts through luncheons, receptions, and various other networking events. The GPVG is also extremely proud of *GPVG Venture Institute*—an undertaking that is

◀ Lobby outside of the presentation arena of the 2001 Mid-Atlantic Venture Conference, which includes the literature table and the GPVG information help desk.

and acknowledges significant growth in sales, impact upon the market, and value. *The Raymond Rafferty Entrepreneurial Excellence Award* is recognition of an individual who has founded one or more successful venture-backed companies and influenced a specific industry with revolutionary ideas. *The Blair Thompson Lifetime Venture Award* is given for a direct, major, and successful role in furthering the venture interests of the region by promoting or strengthening the area's venture capital base, as well as innovatively enhancing the venture process. The list of recipients of each of these awards is a "Who's Who" of area businesses.

Over the past two decades, the GPVG has seen steady development of its networking relationships and has enjoyed continued growth in membership and attendance at its events. The organization carries on in its attempts to encourage further activity and the unwavering commitments of its venture capitalists. The GPVG is also a major supporter of tax reform, and supports state and city initiatives that promote further economic development for Greater Philadelphia.

The GPVG is the premier organization in the Greater Philadelphia community that networks the investment industry. While economic development is strong within the Greater Philadelphia area and Pennsylvania as a whole, there remains room for expansion and improvement. The GPVG intends to be a part of that growth and development, expanding its staff and increasing its visibility on a national level. The Greater Philadelphia Venture Group has a strong reputation as a great vehicle for industry leaders to learn about the current trends and to network in order to find new opportunities. ℗

◀ 2 7 7

▲ **Attendees enjoy the luncheon program at the 2001 Mid-Atlantic Venture Conference.**

designed to provide attorneys, accountants, venture capitalists, and entrepreneurs with a better understanding of the critical issues the young companies must deal with in their attempts to grow. The workshop format gives young entrepreneurs the opportunity to solidify their financing fundamentals through exploration of the various matters that affect them and the financial community as a whole. Attorneys, accountants, venture capitalists, and entrepreneurs can earn valuable CLE/CPE credits.

The GPVG also sponsors their Annual Awards Luncheon where they recognizes local businesses for their contributions to this industry. *The Entrepreneur of the Year Award* is given for recent entrepreneurial success in the development of venture-backed business

◀ **The GPVG board of directors includes industry leaders that play a critical role in the Philadelphia venture community. Bottom row (left to right): F. Newberg, L. Fry, R. Blumenthal, J. Brown, G. Schaafsma, S. Carney, G. Rieger, T. Collison, J. Costello, R. Pace, S. Nissenbaum. Middle row (left to right): C. Jones, T. Fratis, K. Griffith Gryga, E. Harper. Top row (left to right): M. Dipiano, W. Molloie, M. Hollin, J. Millar, S. Neff, M. Celano, G. Smith, B. Luehrs, R. Jaffe, and A. Kaplan.**

▶ Janney Montgomery Scott LLC

𝒫 hiladelphia-based Janney Montgomery Scott LLC (JMS) is a full-service securities brokerage and financial services firm that traces its history back to 1832 when Thomas Watson bought the second seat on the New York Stock Exchange. Since its distinguished beginning, JMS has remained a prominent financial name in the Philadelphia community and has established roots throughout the eastern United States.

Today, JMS employs nearly 1,000 financial consultants, serving more than 350,000 customers nationwide through over 70 full-service investment offices along the East Coast. In addition to a strong and growing capital base, JMS has the extensive resources of its parent company, The Penn Mutual Life Insurance Company, which is another Delaware Valley-based institution. Founded in 1847, Penn Mutual is one of the 15 largest mutual insurance companies in the nation, with over $10 billion in assets.

With a staff of experienced professionals in research, asset management, corporate and municipal finance, and retail and institutional sales, JMS offers a full line of diversified investment services to assist clients in attaining their long-term financial goals. Few investment and financial services firms can offer the level of one-on-one personal service and insight on which Janney Montgomery Scott has built its reputation.

From retirement planning to estate planning, and money management to insurance, JMS financial consultants are supported by Janney's many product and service departments in their efforts to help each client meet his or her individual investment objectives, with maximum efficiency and minimum cost. In addition, Janney Montgomery Scott's Financial Planning Department is composed of highly skilled professionals who can work with Janney financial consultants in performing a more detailed analysis of a client's financial situation to develop a customized investment program that can reduce taxes and increase wealth.

Janney's award-winning team of research analysts functions as a primary resource for investors by providing original and objective information on local, regional, and national companies. Composed of individuals widely recognized for their specialized knowledge of such fields as technology, basic industries, and financial institutions, this expert staff has been successful in offering objective and sound market coverage.

Furthermore, the Investment Banking division of JMS, which includes both Corporate Finance and Public Finance, complements and supports the complete array of services available to Janney's retail, institutional, and

"Through our focus upon and dedication to the individual client, we have developed a tradition of trust and service excellence, always committed to the highest ethical standards."

—**James W. Wolitarsky,**
President and Chief
Executive Officer

corporate clients. The Janney Montgomery Scott Investment Banking group is committed to providing investment banking services to middle market companies, as well as municipal and not-for-profit clients throughout the United States. This experienced team assists clients with merger and acquisition advisory services, equity underwriting, private placements, consulting, and special studies.

Still, Janney recognizes that the opportunity to serve lies in more than just providing sound financial advice. That is why the JMS team members and the offices they represent take pride in being part of the communities that trust them. Throughout its branch system, JMS routinely sponsors local sports teams, donates to area hospitals, and contributes to a variety of charitable events. This focused, firm-wide team effort enables the JMS professionals to provide outstanding service to both their clients and the surrounding communities.

For 170 years, Janney Montgomery Scott has successfully served the needs of investors. JMS is committed to continuing this tradition of excellence. ℗

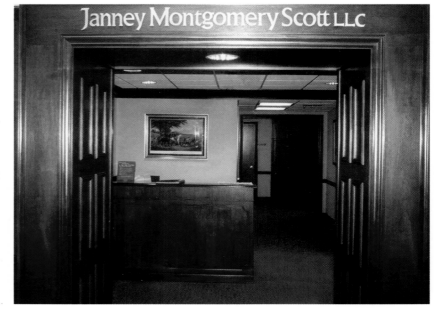

▶ **Janney Montgomery Scott is the largest Pennsylvania-based NYSE regional firm. Its Philadelphia headquarters serves as the nucleus of operations for 70 JMS offices that service clients throughout the country.**

▸ Lexicomm International Ltd.

$\mathscr{I}$n 1987, frustrated by huge costs and mediocre results from the largest translation company at that time, Cigna Corporation turned to one of its own international management consultants to address its need for translation of documents and videos for its overseas offices. Nancy E. Smoler spoke six languages and had just returned from nine months in Europe and Asia, reviewing the company's subsidiary operations. In addition to being multilingual, Ms. Smoler brought the perspective of an insurance professional to the project. She knew what questions to ask, as well as the appropriate insurance and financial terminology for the target audiences. Her translations were so well received overseas that the demand for international communications exploded. She soon established Lexicomm International Ltd. to handle the translation needs of Cigna and others.

For many years, Lexicomm's strongest support came from Cigna, which represented more than 80 percent of the fledgling company's business. Lexicomm expanded and diversified and now specializes in translation, localization, and multimedia production for life sciences, biotechnology, specialty chemicals, finance, law, engineering, and manufacturing. Insurance remains a strength, though it is now a smaller part of total revenue.

Lexicomm has emerged as one of the region's premier global communications and consulting firms, providing foreign language translation for all media, Web site localization, quality assurance consulting, and international document development. Currently employing a small full-time staff, Lexicomm uses the skills of hundreds of independent translators, editors, and proofreaders representing 45 languages and at least a dozen scientific, business, and technical specialties. Drawing on a talent pool of nearly 200 professional multilingual actors, Lexicomm produces the highest quality audio, video, and multimedia with lip-sync and voiceover.

"Use of the best production staff, talent, and translators is essential to our commitment to meet our client's needs and exceed their

▲ Nancy E. Smoler, President.

◂ 279

expectations. We are entrusted to adapt a vast range of general, technical, legal, scientific, and corporate content into materials for global audiences. Our staff and colleagues must perform at the highest levels," said Ms. Smoler.

While Lexicomm serves companies around the globe, 70 percent of its clients are from the Greater Philadelphia Region. This customer base has been built primarily through satisfied patrons within the same or related industries. One of the earliest players in multimedia translation, Lexicomm has found that Philadelphia is an ideal business location with rich language and production resources. Lexicomm's future is promising. Client demand for traditional and digital communications continues to grow. The company continues to maintain high quality and personalized service while doubling in size over the last few years.

Having established itself as a leader in a relatively new field, Lexicomm holds itself to the highest standards to remain there. ℗

◂ Lexicomm has emerged as one of the region's premier global communications and consulting firms, providing foreign language translation for all media.

▶ American International Group

*W*ith a presence in virtually ever major market on the globe and ties in many countries that stretch back more than half a century, American International Group has long been recognized as one of the worlds premier providers of General Insurance and Life Insurance to commercial, institutional, and individual customers through a variety of distribution channels in approximately 130 countries and jurisdictions throughout the world. With more than 81,000 employees worldwide, 200 of which are located right here in Philadelphia, AIG has established itself as one of the world leaders in its field.

In addition to its already well established position in the world of insurance, AIG has also been steadily growing in two other key business areas—Financial Services and Retirement Savings & Asset Management. AIG's financial services businesses currently include aircraft leasing, financial products, trading and market making, and consumer finance. The company's retirement savings interests is one of the largest in the United States and is a leader in asset management for the individual and institutional markets, with specialized investment management capabilities in equities, fixed income, alternative investments, and real estate.

Today, the demand for property and casualty insurance is at an all time high, yet many have found that the insurance industry's capacity for meeting these demands is limited. This has given rise to what has been referred to as a "flight to quality," meaning that many consumers are seeking to purchase insurance from only the strongest companies that they know they can count on. Because of its reputation for financial strength, stability, and its capacity to respond effectively to each client's needs, AIG has become the go-to company for many of these customers, in Philadelphia and throughout the world. This solid financial condition has won AIG the recognition from the most demanding principal ratings services around.

In addition to the proud history of participating in relief efforts following natural disasters such as flood, earthquake, and hurricane,

▲ Under the leadership of Laurie A. Tribuiani, Regional Vice President of the AIG Mid-Atlantic Region, AIG continues to be one of the leading insurance offices in Philadelphia

many AIG companies are heavily involved in ongoing humanitarian programs that aim to fight poverty and help eradicate disease on a regional, national, or global level. On a more local level, AIG Philadelphia employees raise funds, offer support for, and participate on the boards of numerous charitable and community-based outreach programs, thus helping to strengthen their community.

While it remains a global franchise with interests and contacts throughout the world, American International Group still manages to retain a heart and mind that are rooted in the communities it serves, focusing on each individual client. ℗

◀ George Stratts, General Manager, Eastern Risk Specialists, reviews a new proposal for the City of Philadelphia Neighborhood Transformation Initiative Construction Wrap-Up Project with Alexis Goulard, National Accounts AVP and Chris Gallagher, Commercial Accounts AVP.

CHAPTER FOURTEEN

Health Care

As the birthplace of American medicine, Philadelphia is appropriately

postured to lead the world in the medical technologies of the future.

Photo ©2002 John McGrail

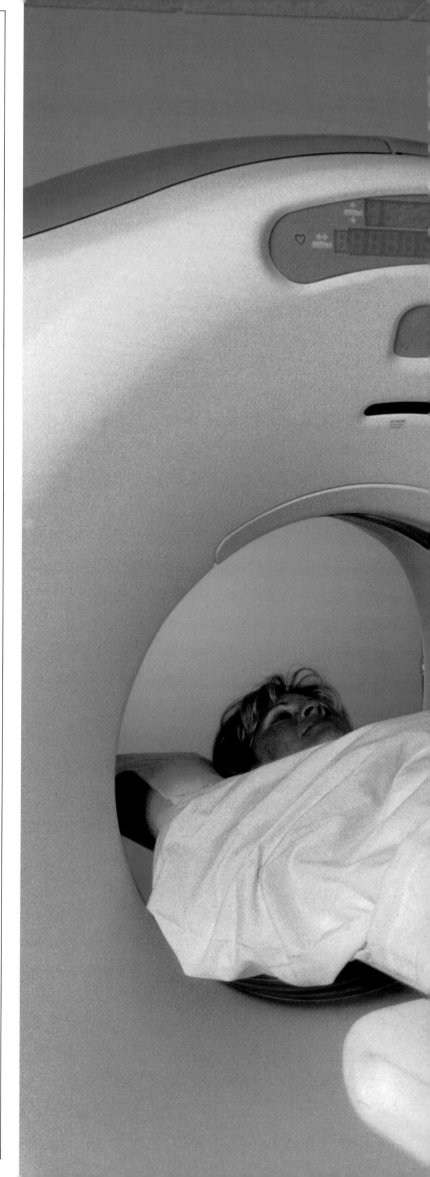

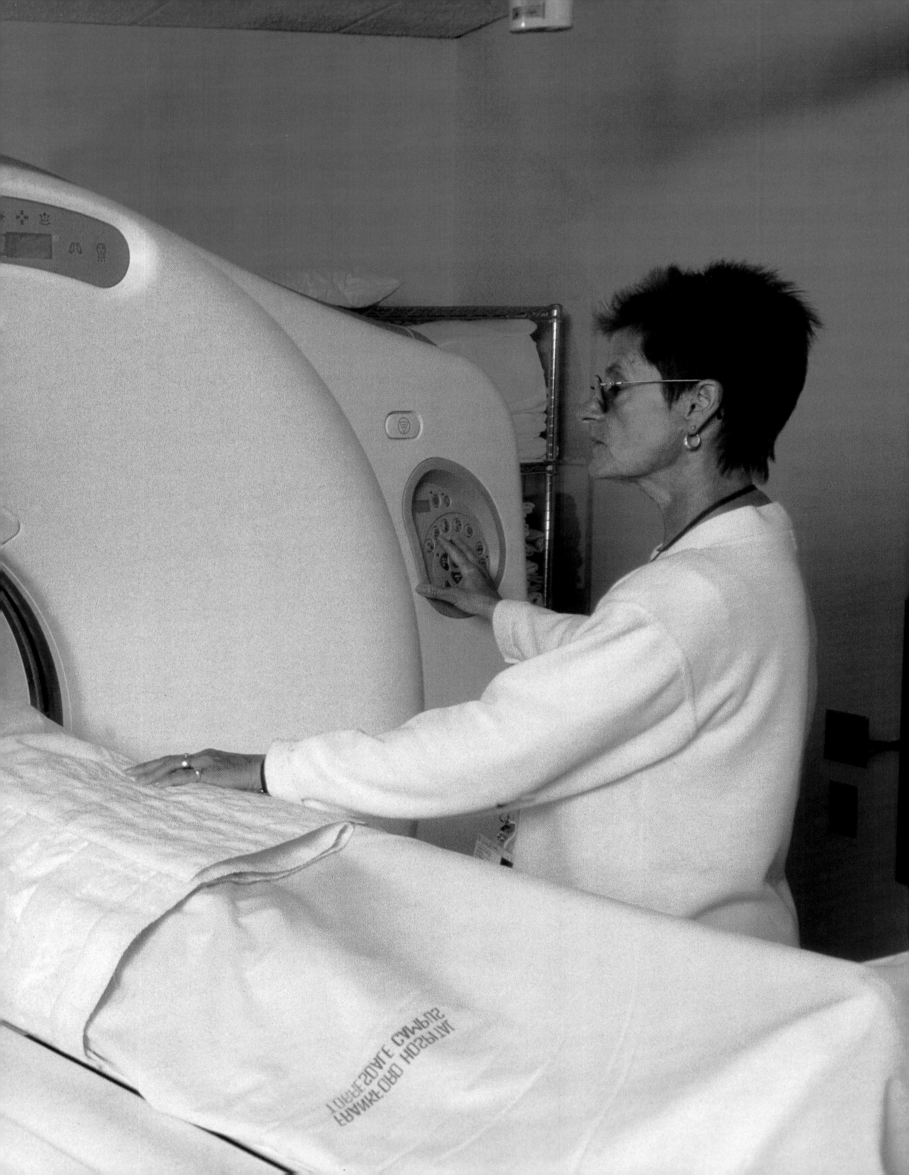

▸ The Children's Hospital of Philadelphia

- Thanks to fetal surgery to repair spina bifida while still in the womb, a 3-year-old from Connecticut can now walk, run, and talk like other toddlers.

- Born in Missouri with a rare condition called congenital hyperinsulinism, an infant undergoes a unique insulin test along with a surgical cure that leaves him risk-free for diabetes.

- A 12-year-old from New Jersey with liver disease is managed successfully for nearly a decade until a liver transplant offers renewed hope for the future.

- Diagnosed with a heart defect in utero, a baby in West Philadelphia is carefully monitored for months, with cardiac surgery performed successfully soon after her birth.

Although their stories are different, each child has found similar hope at The Children's Hospital of Philadelphia.

Founded in 1855 as the nation's first pediatric hospital, The Children's Hospital of Philadelphia has maintained a pioneering spirit throughout its long and distinguished history. Credited with nearly 150 years of innovative medicine and breakthrough research, Children's Hospital is a premier pediatric healthcare provider for children and families living in this region and far beyond.

Change and transformation are key to Children's Hospital's success. In the past 15 years alone, Children's Hospital has grown from a single hospital, exclusively focused on inpatient care, to an integrated pediatric healthcare network with more than 40 locations throughout southeastern Pennsylvania, Delaware, and southern New Jersey. Today, Children's Hospital is a wide-ranging, integrated system that is capable of treating children from before birth through young adulthood—from routine to rare, from primary to emergency care, from subspecialty and intensive care to rehabilitation and home care.

▲ Recognized and respected internationally for its leadership in clinical expertise, research excellence, and quality education, Children's Hospital continues to push the boundaries of medicine and seek discoveries that will profoundly influence the health of children across the globe.
Photo by Paul Crane

▼ Children's Hospital is a world-class hospital that operates an integrated pediatric healthcare network with more than 40 locations throughout southeastern Pennsylvania, Delaware and southern New Jersey. To accommodate the rapid growth of its clinical and research enterprise, Children's Hospital has proactively embarked on a major, state-of-the-art facilities expansion program that will double the size of its Main Campus (architectural rendering shown) and extend its facilities further into the community.

▲ Children's Hospital has long been a magnet for clinical innovation, with physicians, nurses, and healthcare professionals working together across multiple disciplines to develop groundbreaking treatments and cutting edge techniques. The Fetal Heart Program (team shown) is the largest of its kind in the nation, attracting patients from across the United States.

Photo by Stromberg/Gunther Photography

Children's Hospital's network includes Specialty Care Centers, Ambulatory Surgery Centers, Primary Care Centers, CHOP Connection inpatient units at community hospitals, and Kids First Pediatric and Adolescent Practices. All are part of Children's Hospital's ongoing effort to bring its renowned medical expertise directly to the community.

Progress, however, does not end there. To accommodate the rapid growth of its clinical and research enterprise, Children's Hospital has proactively embarked on a major facilities expansion program that will double the size of its Main Campus and extend its facilities further into the community.

Children's Hospital continually seeks to evolve and change. From its rich history of medical and research "firsts" to current innovations involving gene therapy, molecular research, and fetal surgery,

▶ From its pioneering history of medical and research "firsts" to current innovations involving gene therapy, molecular research, and fetal surgery (shown, including inset), Children's Hospital offers a far-reaching vision that heralds great promise for the future of pediatric healthcare.

Photo by Paul Crane

Children's Hospital offers a far-reaching vision that heralds great promise for the future of pediatric healthcare.

This promise is based on a historic foundation. Among many achievements, Children's Hospital is known for establishing the first formal medical training for pediatrics and for creating the first neonatal surgical and intensive pediatric care units in the United States. Physicians and scientists at Children's Hospital are credited with numerous clinical and research innovations, from the first use of a balloon catheter technique to cure certain heart defects to the development of vaccines for rubella, mumps, influenza, and rotavirus.

Children's Hospital has long been a magnet for clinical innovation. Today, medical staff and healthcare professionals from 36 clinical specialties and 51 specialized programs work together across multiple disciplines, pushing the boundaries of medicine to develop groundbreaking treatments and cutting edge techniques.

Premier programs include the full range of pediatric subspecialties, from adolescent medicine to urology. Rated as one of the top two pediatric hospitals in the country for more than a decade by *U.S. News & World Report,* Children's Hospital continues to set the standard for excellence in pediatric healthcare.

The Center for Fetal Diagnosis and Treatment™, for example, is at the forefront of research and clinical practice in the emerging field of fetology—the treatment of infants before they are born. The Cardiac Center at Children's Hospital is internationally recognized as having among the best outcomes in the world. Thanks to a unique acute insulin response test developed by endocrinologists here, Children's Hospital is the only place in North America where pediatric surgeons can perform specialized surgery to successfully cure patients with focal lesions of congenital hyperinsulinism.

◀ 285

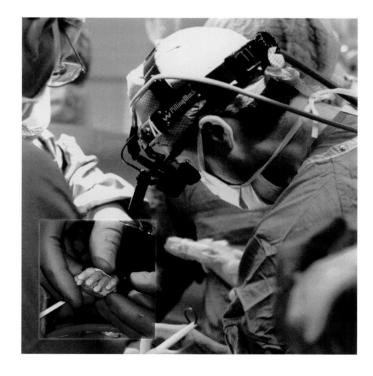

In addition, the Fetal Heart Program at Children's Hospital is the largest of its kind in the nation, attracting patients from across the country. Children's Hospital's transplantation programs are nationally recognized, with experts providing multidisciplinary evaluation, treatment, and follow-up care for children with heart, lung, heart/lung, liver, and kidney disease. A pioneer in pediatric oncology, Children's Hospital is nationally recognized for its follow-up program on long-term effects.

Children's Hospital has established numerous multidisciplinary centers that unite experts from various disciplines to provide integrated care for complex conditions. The Center for Childhood Communication, Sleep Disorders Center, and Sports Medicine and Performance Center are just three among many Children's Hospital centers that combine the expertise of specialists to provide comprehensive care to patients and their families.

In addition to integrated care, Children's Hospital has been a leader in establishing a national model of compassionate, family-centered care. Children's Hospital has been a pioneer in promoting this philosophy, which recognizes patients and family members as key partners in the healing process.

Located in the Hospital's Main Building, the Connelly Resource Center for Families is an attractive complex that provides space for information, support, and other services for families, including sleep rooms, a family library, and teaching area for families. Children's Hospital has also opened ambulatory care family resource centers at several outpatient locations in its network.

In addition to clinical innovation, Children's Hospital has a rich history of research excellence, generating new knowledge on a continual basis. Investigators at Children's Hospital conduct cutting edge research, from gene therapy to stem cell research, from molecular biology to developmental studies.

Children's Hospital has one of the largest and most prestigious pediatric research programs in the world. Growth of the research enterprise has been extraordinary. Currently, Children's Hospital has

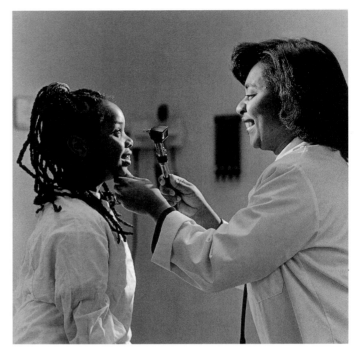

▲ Recognizing that most children are healthy, Children's Hospital has created several Primary Care Centers and opened numerous Kids First pediatric and adolescent practices that seek to protect the health and well-being of children through preventive, primary care, such as vaccinations and annual check-ups. Photo by Stromberg/Gunther Photography

the second largest NIH-sponsored research program among pediatric hospitals, with several hundred major research programs underway.

Children's Hospital is one of the few institutions nationwide with the resources and intellectual environment capable of supporting a world-class pediatric research enterprise. To support individual researchers—whether they're working in a laboratory, clinic, or office—Children's Hospital provides a rich combination of state-of-the-art facilities, integrated services, and opportunities for collaboration among investigators of diverse disciplines.

Over the next five years, Children's Hospital will double its research enterprise to build the largest pediatric program in the world for basic science and clinical research. The goal: to have daily clinical impact by more rapidly transforming knowledge gained through scientific discovery into valuable treatments, products, and services.

Discovering scientific explanations to treat and cure pediatric disease is an exploration that engages the hearts and minds of physicians,

◀ Children's Hospital brings its medical and surgical expertise directly into the community by building Specialty Care Centers and Ambulatory Surgery Centers that provide the full spectrum of outpatient pediatric specialty services. Children can receive sophisticated treatments, including outpatient chemotherapy (shown), in a convenient, quality setting located close to home—enabling families to miss fewer hours of work and school. Photo by Bill Cramer

▲ Children's Hospital has one of the largest and most prestigious pediatric research programs in the world, attracting the best and brightest minds in pediatric medicine and research. Nationally renowned physician-researchers seek to have daily clinical impact by rapidly transforming new knowledge gained through scientific discovery into valuable treatments, products, and services. Photo by Paul Crane

scientists, research technologists, laboratory technicians, and clinical study coordinators at Children's Hospital. Children's Hospital continues to attract and retain the best and brightest minds in pediatric medicine and research, recruiting nationally renowned physician scientists at a greater rate than any other pediatric institution in the United States.

Further, Children's Hospital enjoys an academic association with the University of Pennsylvania, a leading university and medical center, creating additional opportunities for basic and clinical research collaboration.

A teaching center of choice, Children's Hospital plays an important role in educating and mentoring the pediatric healthcare leaders of tomorrow. Each year, Children's Hospital trains thousands of pediatricians, pediatric specialists, nurses, scientists, and other healthcare professionals for positions in academic medicine, research, and community practice around the world.

Key education programs include LEND (Leadership Education for Neurodevelopmental Disabilities), which provides annual funding to train fellows in the field of developmental disabilities. Further, Children's Hospital is one of only six institutions nationwide to receive a major grant from The Dyson Foundation to support its innovative

▶ Children's Hospital is a pioneer in promoting family-centered care—a philosophy that recognizes patients and family members as key partners in the healing process. The Connelly Resource Center for Families is a national model that provides space for information, support, and resources, including sleep rooms, a family library, and learning center. Nurse educators train family members in procedures ranging from CPR to tube feeding, while child life specialists conduct medical play to help allay the fears of pediatric patients (shown). Photo by Elena Bouvier

residency program. The goal is to build on existing programs (which include home visits, school presentations, and a clinic for homeless children) by giving residents the skills and knowledge to become effective advocates for children and families.

Children's Hospital also hosts numerous continuing medical education courses and conferences that attract pediatricians and pediatric specialists around the world. These conferences play in important role in fulfilling Children's Hospital's educational mission to advance pediatric healthcare worldwide.

Physicians and scientists from Children's Hospital travel around the globe to spread their knowledge and expertise. For example, as part of the American Austrian Foundation, Children's Hospital sends pediatric specialists to Austria each year to provide weeklong training and education to pediatricians from Eastern Europe. Children's Hospital has also established relationships with pediatric institutions around the world, from England to Israel and from China to Chile.

Children's Hospital offers a voice for children at home and around the world, with advocacy intricately woven into the fabric of the institution's mission. Children's Hospital recently established a Vaccine Education Center, which offers fact-based, scientific information to educate healthcare professionals and the general public, and is an active participant in Reach Out and Read, a national pediatric literacy program that seeks to educate families in understanding that a healthy childhood includes reading books.

Working in collaboration with State Farm Mutual Automobile Insurance Company, Children's Hospital created the Partners for Child Passenger Safety, a program that offers the nation's first and most comprehensive, peer-reviewed research investigation of how and why children are injured or killed in vehicle crashes.

Dedicated to a noble mission, Children's Hospital continues to serve as a beacon of hope for children and families living in this region and around the world. By demonstrating a pioneering spirit, by pushing the boundaries of medicine, and by endlessly seeking new discoveries, Children's Hospital will continue to grow and transform itself in an ongoing quest to meet the healthcare needs of children and families today and far into the future. ℗

◀ 287

▶ Jefferson Health System

*I*t All Begins with the Human Touch

Although every community throughout the Delaware Valley served by the Jefferson Health System member hospitals is unique, all share a common and very human need—the desire for excellent health care and skilled, compassionate professionals to deliver it.

At Jefferson Health System, our mission, accomplished through our members, is: to improve the quality of life by offering comprehensive, cost-effective, state-of-the-art healthcare services; to be actively involved in education in clinical practice; and to encourage research related to the advancement of healthcare delivery.

Part of our commitment to improving the quality of life for patients means providing health care in an ethical manner. Our dedication to excellence and integrity is embodied in the Jefferson Heath System Code of Conduct, which provides the guidance and pathways to ensure that we conduct ourselves appropriately and honorably at all times.

Likewise, Jefferson Health System member institutions have been accredited by the Joint Commission on Accreditation of Healthcare Organizations (JCAHO), a healthcare standards setting and accrediting body. Our healthcare professionals are dedicated to the highest quality and safest patient care.

Equally important is bringing the empathy, respect, and hope every patient deserves—a bridge to remembering that at Jefferson Health System member hospitals, it all begins with the human touch.

Full Range of Care Options

Founded in 1995, the nonprofit Jefferson Health System is the largest health system in the Delaware Valley. A partnership of healthcare institutions with a history of hundreds of years of excellent patient care and similar objectives and philosophies, that brings together the region's premier healthcare institutions. We continue to

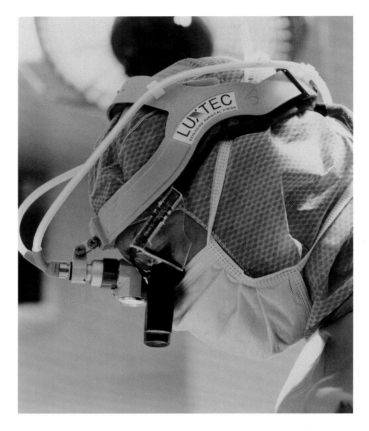

▲ Physicians on staff at Jefferson Health System's member hospitals perform leading-edge procedures, such as "beating heart" bypass surgery, which shorten patients' hospital stay and recovery time.

honor the community roots of our individual institutions. This heritage of sensitivity in delivering care is what distinguishes our health system:

- **Albert Einstein Healthcare Network**—including Albert Einstein Medical Center, Germantown Community Health Services, MossRehab, Willowcrest (a center for sub-acute care), Willow Terrace at Germantown (a long-term care facility), Belmont Behavioral Health, a number of outpatient and satellite locations, and Einstein Neighborhood Healthcare (a primary care network)
- **Frankford Hospitals**—includes the Frankford, Torresdale and Bucks campuses (community teaching hospitals), three additional outpatient sites, and Frankford Health Care Network Physician Services
- **Magee Rehabilitation**—including Magee Rehabilitation Hospital, Magee Riverfront Outpatient Center, and Magee-MossRehab at Voorhees
- **Main Line Health**—including Bryn Mawr Hospital, Lankenau Hospital, Paoli Memorial Hospital, Bryn Mawr Rehab, Mid-County

◀ Operating room nurses at Jefferson Health System member hospitals provide comfort to patients as well as expert clinical assistance to surgeons.

▲ There's nothing more inspiring than a new life coming into the world, and technicians on staff at Jefferson Health System member hospitals' nurseries look after each new arrival with tender, loving care.

Senior Services, Wayne Center, and Lankenau Institute for Medical Research

• **Thomas Jefferson University Hospitals**—including Thomas Jefferson University Hospital Center City, Jefferson Hospital for Neuroscience, Methodist Division, Ford Road, and Jefferson HealthCARE-Voorhees

These institutions joined the Jefferson Health System while maintaining their identities. Each hospital brought its own strengths to the network, supporting each member and benefiting each community. Our expertise is used in prevention and routine care, as well as in the more sophisticated treatment options provided in our institutions. Most important to this effort, we work collaboratively. This enables each institution in the system to craft delivery systems focused on individual community needs.

Likewise, by joining together the healthcare expertise and resources of our members, Jefferson Health System is able to provide unparalleled care to more people and to keep many critical and needed services close to home. Joining community hospitals with teaching hospitals is the best of both worlds because it provides more patients with several clinical and healthcare options.

The Jefferson Health System also has alliance relationships with Riddle Memorial Hospital, Underwood

▶ Infants born with medical problems or prematurely at Jefferson Health System member hospitals are treated in the hospitals' Neonatal Intensive Care Units, which regularly receive letters and photographs from grateful parents of infant patients who benefited from this specialized care.

Memorial Hospital, Pottstown Memorial Hospital, Christiana Care Health System, and AtlantiCARE.

The Jefferson Health System uses business-planning models to anticipate the changes to healthcare financing, in order to adjust and investigate opportunities for operational efficiencies so that we can continue to meet the demands of our community for healthcare.

The Jefferson Health System members combined have over $2 billion in revenue, 20,200 full-time employees, 3,100 staffed beds, and more than 4,000 medical staff members. The hospitals are major employers, community resources, and education centers. All the members benefit from the extraordinarily high quality educational institutions in the region, which prepare an exceptional workforce and outstanding healthcare professionals, who have joined our ranks.

At the Jefferson Health System, we continually look for ways to touch the lives of the people in our community. Our members take great pride in reaching out to the community. For example, Women's Health Source information and educational resources have brought a real "human touch" to the communities they serve. Also, the health centers serving Asian patients are staffed by professionals fluent in the patient population's language and understand their culture.

The Jefferson Health System recognizes that healthcare delivery systems must pay attention to the entire patient and his or her family, not just his or her acute care needs. Toward this goal, we provide a broad spectrum of health-related services from smoking cessation and health screenings to parenting classes. In addition, our members comprise one of the largest providers of home care in the region. And in the system's innovative Congregational Nurse Program, full-time nurses are employed by religious congregations throughout the Delaware Valley to oversee the health care of their older adults. It is the only service of its kind in the area.

◀ 289

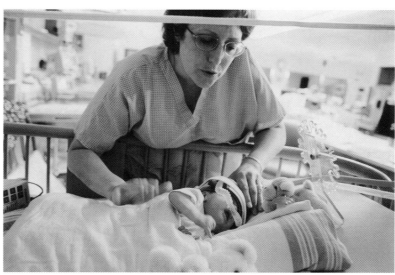

Leaders within the system are well known and respected in the region for their civic involvement. They take leadership roles to resolve significant issues through local, city, and state government, educational affiliations, national and local hospital associations, as well as charitable organizations working in our communities. Likewise, to address tort reform and skyrocketing medical malpractice insurance rates, which threaten community members' access to health care in Pennsylvania, physicians on staff at our member hospitals formed their own political action committee.

Drawing upon our wealth of healthcare expertise and resources, from acute care hospitals, physical rehabilitation facilities, and research capabilities, to a network of primary care and specialist physicians, outpatient facilities, and home health services, the Jefferson Health System members can take care of every member of the family at each stage in life. We offer a full range of care options, from sophisticated nurseries for the most fragile pre-term infants to long-term care facilities for aging adults, from the latest cancer and heart care treatment to treatment for colds and immunizations for children.

The typical patient hospitalized at a Jefferson Health System member hospital will start with a primary care physician, who will, if necessary refer him or her to a specialist. The patient may require medical tests, procedures, or surgery or need sub-acute care, rehabilitation, home care, or long-term care. Jefferson Health System members can meet all of these needs within the comprehensive, sophisticated set of clinical programs and services, which define our System as a market leader.

Jefferson Health System members also provide the prevention, wellness, and screening programs important in maintaining the health of every family member. Our member hospitals are community resources and education centers. They take pride in the quality of healthcare and service initiatives they undertake for community members of every age.

Through their academic affiliations with Thomas Jefferson University, our member hospitals bring research breakthroughs to bedside care expeditiously. Patients choosing our system for care

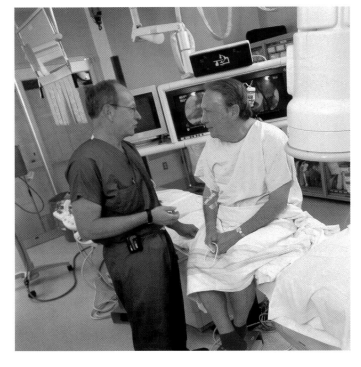

▲ **Sophisticated minimally invasive procedures available at Jefferson Health System member hospitals return patients to health with minimal discomfort.**

benefit from these leading-edge therapies. Because our members are strategically located, the Jefferson Health System's quality healthcare services are available to a broad geographic area.

Focus on Patient Care

The primary focus of the physicians on staff at each Jefferson Health System member hospital is on the patient. Our philosophy of patient-focused care is what attracts both world-renowned physicians and those with exceptional promise to our institutions, and it's what keeps them there. We seek and attract physicians who value the time they spend one-on-one with each of their patients, talking and forming relationships, and who take special care to ensure that patients and their families understand their treatment options and are involved in the process of choosing the option that's right for them.

◀ **Annual Opening Exercises at Jefferson Medical College, the academic affiliate of Jefferson Health System, include the White Coat Ceremony, during which first-year students receive a gift of white coats from the Jefferson Medical College Alumni Association and learn their symbolic significance.**

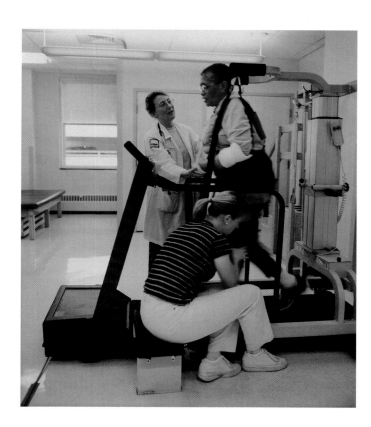

▲ Expertly supervised therapy at member rehabilitation facilities within the Jefferson Health System enables patients to regain fundamental skills such as walking.

Recognized for Excellence

U.S.News & World Report annually rates various Jefferson Health System member hospitals among "America's Best Hospitals." Among those specialties for which one or more of our member hospitals have been praised are cancer, cardiology/cardiothoracic surgery, geriatrics, gynecology, orthopedics, rehabilitation medicine, rheumatology, and urology. Some of our institutions are also listed in Solucient's 100 Top Hospitals for excellence in cardiovascular care, patient care, teaching, management, stroke care, and ICUs. The member hospitals are fully accredited by the Joint Commission of Healthcare Organizations—several with commendation. *Philadelphia Magazine* and *Main Line Today's* annual "Top Docs" appraisals always include numerous physicians on staff at Jefferson Health System member hospitals. In addition, our member institutions, physicians, and nurses have been recognized for excellence by many other local and national publications and organizations, including AARP.

Affiliations

Many of the institutions that make up the Jefferson Health System have a strong, historical commitment to training and educating

▶ Bedside nurses at Jefferson Health System member hospitals are attentive, thorough, and compassionate.

medical and nursing school students, graduate and practicing physicians and nurses, and other healthcare professionals.

Taking advantage of system-wide purchasing and contracting with insurers enables Jefferson Health System to deliver superior quality care to the greatest number of patients cost effectively, as well.

Innovations in Patient Care

Jefferson Health System members benefit from its approaches in clinical research. From its combined facilities, the System has a greater number of patients who are candidates for investigation protocols. Joint research studies and additional research sites enable our researchers to find answers quickly—frequently resulting in advancements in patient care.

Through the Jefferson Health System member hospitals, physicians and their patients benefit from the breakthrough therapies and treatments. The System has established a large patient population for clinical trials of innovative therapies to improve care. Combined member resources make the Jefferson Health System a market leader in acute care, behavioral health, rehabilitation, home health, and senior services. Patient care innovations by Jefferson Health System member hospitals are featured frequently in the local and national media.

◀ 291

In Conclusion

The Jefferson Health System is proud of the clinically sophisticated and humane health care each member institution provides its respective community. It is this excellence and sensitivity—the human touch—which sets Jefferson Health System apart and keeps in place the high regard its communities have for the member institutions, their dedicated physicians and employees, and the entire System. ℗

▶ University of Pennsylvania Health System

The University of Pennsylvania Health System (UPHS) was created in 1993, yet its history in health care dates back to the founding of our nation. Beginning with medical lectures in the fall of 1765, the University of Pennsylvania's School of Medicine became the first medical school in the thirteen American colonies. In 1874, the Hospital at the University of Pennsylvania (HUP) was established as the nation's first teaching hospital. Today UPHS is a full-service, academic health system that combines teaching, research, and clinical care, embracing both its rich history and dynamic future.

During the 1990s, UPHS acquired Pennsylvania Hospital, Presbyterian Medical Center, and Phoenixville Hospital, as well as about 70 different primary-care facilities throughout the Delaware Valley. Currently, 13,000 employees serve UPHS throughout the region, and some 1,200 highly qualified physicians offer expertise in a host of medical subspecialties. UPHS takes pride in its four acute-care facilities, which enable the health system to meet patient needs in almost any circumstance.

As the health system's flagship facility, HUP is at the center of Penn's academic and teaching programs. HUP is recognized as having one of the finest trauma centers in the country. It is one of the largest hospitals in the U.S. in terms of capacity and number of patients treated each year, and its general excellence has earned it an annual spot in *U.S. News & World Report's* Honor Roll of Hospitals. Pennsylvania Hospital is well known for its large obstetrics and orthopedic programs. Presbyterian Medical Center is nationally recognized for its cardiac services and cardiothoracic services.

UPHS credits the city of Philadelphia for playing an important role in its success. Both the city and the healthcare industry have traditionally enjoyed a mutually beneficial relationship. With six different schools of medicine, the city has long been a magnet for both graduate and undergraduate students who wish to continue their education in a wide array of health fields. Penn's School of Medicine

▲ **Hospital of the University of Pennsylvania.**

is recognized as one of the top medical schools in the U.S. Moreover, it also ranks second in the nation in receiving National Institutes of Health funding for medical research. Such recognition enables UPHS to select its students from among the most gifted in the country. Many of these students choose to remain in the Delaware Valley upon graduation, helping to maintain a large number of highly skilled physicians in the area.

In addition, UPHS is a major supporter of the United Way. Each of Penn's hospitals is active in numerous charitable organizations, and employees and executives participate in various civic boards, programs, and activities throughout Philadelphia and the Delaware Valley. UPHS employees are active in organizations such as the University City District and the Urban Hospital Consortium.

Currently there are no plans to increase the number of UPHS operations. There is, however, a continuing need to update and expand existing facilities. Upcoming projects for the health system

▼ **Phoenixville Hospital.**

▲ **Presbyterian Medical Center.**

have helped us through a few very difficult years. All of us in the University of Pennsylvania Health System understand that excellence in patient care, research, and education depends on maintaining a sound financial foundation," Martin continued.

Medical research has always been a rapidly evolving area of study, and these are especially exciting times to be involved in academic medicine. Penn's School of Medicine has been recognized repeatedly, and its researchers have been responsible for several recent breakthroughs that have potential applications to patient care and health improvement.

One study—at Penn and nine other sites—involves a treatment for Type 1 Diabetes, the most serious form of this disease. After harvesting healthy islet cells from the pancreas of a donated cadaver, the surgeons inject them into the patient's liver. After a single infusion, there is generally a substantial decrease in insulin need; after a second infusion, the first four patients in the Penn study have become insulin-free. This promising treatment is still in the experimental stage.

Another recent study has produced very encouraging results to treat genetic blindness. Sight was restored in three dogs that suffered from Leber Congenital Amaurosis (LCA), the first time that congenital blindness had been reversed in an animal larger than a mouse. LCA is a severe form of retinal degeneration that, in humans, renders infants permanently blind. Working collaboratively with scientists from two other universities, Penn researchers injected a recombinant adeno-associated virus (AAD) into the area between the photoreceptors and the retinal pigment epithelium of the dogs. The AAD carried a missing Vitamin A-like compound to the mutated gene. This gene therapy protocol could have comparable benefits for humans.

UPHS researchers have also determined that a molecule in a person's urine may provide a way to identify Alzheimer's Disease in patients. A urine test that provides a simple, painless, and noninvasive way of discovering the early forms of AD would be a great leap forward for researchers and doctors. Such a test would allow for

include: adding buildings at campus locations, rebuilding the entire emergency room at Presbyterian Hospital, and constructing a new ambulatory surgery center at the Phoenixville Hospital.

UPHS is continuously faced with new challenges. In recent years, there have been major changes in how private medical insurance companies and federal programs like Medicare and Medicaid compensate hospitals. Like other hospitals, UPHS must care for an aging population, and acquiring and implementing new medical technology is expensive. These changes, however, do nothing to dampen the outlook of UPHS's team members; instead, they encourage innovation.

"The University of Pennsylvania Health System continuously faces new challenges in the areas of technology, resource allocation, and payment issues. These challenges do nothing to dampen the outlook of UPHS's team members. Instead, they encourage innovation," Robert D. Martin, Ph.D., CEO of UPHS, said.

"We feel that the hard work, dedication, and resolve of the scores of men and women in our organization

▶ **Pennsylvania Hospital.**

earlier diagnosis and a more complete and accurate charting of the disease, and it would likely contribute to better courses of treatment.

Penn researchers also developed a promising new technique to cure atrial fibrillation that preserves the heart's electrical circuitry and eliminates the need for a pacemaker or medication. Traditional procedures for arrhythmia require the delivery of an electrical charge that permanently blocks the electrical impulse from the atria to the heart's lower ventricles and require the permanent implant of a pacemaker. UPHS researchers are working to identify and target the triggers for such fibrillation on the pulmonary veins. Once identified, a catheter-based ablation procedure isolates the abnormal fibers without affecting the electrical connection between the heart's atria and lower ventricles. This promises to be an effective

▲ **Providing excellence in patient care and quality.**

and relatively uncomplicated technique—one that may eliminate the need for pacemakers and drugs in the future.

Researchers have also won a small victory in the fields of HIV and cancer research. Taking a self-donated transfusion of pure CD4 T-cells from the patient, the researchers rework the cells and reintroduce them in large amounts into HIV-positive volunteers. The result is that the volunteers became more resistant to infection. This research could also prove important in the control of chronic viral infections and cancers that affect the immune system.

The University of Pennsylvania School of Medicine is also working to make the link between several cardiovascular complications resulting from high blood pressure and Chronic Renal Insufficiency, a disease that affects the kidneys and often requires dialysis or transplants. Along with six other universities, Penn will track 3,000 CRI sufferers throughout the country. In addition to being one of the clinical centers awarded funding, Penn will also take the lead role as the project's data-coordinating center. Penn will be in charge of organizing the scientific conduct of the study, analyzing the data, and disseminating any findings the study produces.

In the field of rehabilitation medicine, a new Penn procedure uses nucleoplasty radio-wave injections for some spine problems. The injections are less traumatic and less invasive than open-spine surgery and may prove to be a more permanent treatment than drugs and steroids. Radio-wave energy is released into the damaged spinal disc through the tip of a narrow pen-shaped transmitter, which is

◀ **Penn Medicine at Limerick.**

▲ Improving the lives of patients everyday.

Because physicians direct 80 to 90 percent of all healthcare expenses, Penn's health system developed the Clinical Effectiveness and Quality Improvement Program. The CEQI program for clinical utilization and management is led and monitored by physicians. One of the first responsibilities for each clinical department was to identify opportunities for reducing costs, but departmental teams were also successful in improving care. A team from neurosurgery, for example, was able to reduce the length of stay for craniotomy cases from 8.9 days to 5.4 days. The CEQI Program has also developed an on-line Safety Bulletin page and has sponsored a medication safety fair.

A related initiative in the last few years has been the UPHS Quality Awards. Entries are judged on the basis of organizational impact, demonstration of a sustained impact, innovation, and collaboration. Two winning projects, from Pennsylvania Hospital, involved accelerated cash collections for bills and greater awareness of pain management services and resources. In the latter case, the pain scale is utilized and documented more consistently in all areas, and patient satisfaction scores have risen as a result.

The mission of UPHS is to remain a world-leading institution in the interrelated areas of patient care, education, and research. This goal can only be achieved through the integration of its School of Medicine and its health services, and by having and retaining a world-class faculty and staff who strive for excellence, innovation, quality, and professionalism. ℗

◀ 295

about the size of the diameter of pencil lead. Instead of cutting, freezing, or burning, like other currently used procedures, nucleoplasty targets problem tissue and gently dissolves it with low-temperature ionized gas. The procedure eliminates excess tissue within the spinal disc, relieving the pressure on disc walls that causes herniations and irritates surrounding nerve roots.

One of the new high-technology machines at the Hospital of the University of Pennsylvania is a positron emission tomography (PET) scanner that was specially designed by a professor in the radiology department. The scanner is dedicated to imaging studies that track the patterns of brain activity related to addiction. It operates at a significantly higher level than standard clinical scanners, having a spatial resolution of 3.7 millimeters instead of the conventional 5.5 millimeters.

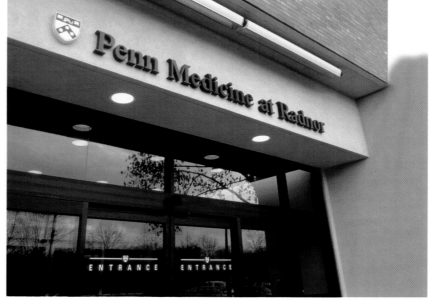

▶ Penn Medicine at Radnor.

▸ NovaCare Rehabilitation

ℰvery day, the team at NovaCare Rehabilitation has the opportunity to work with a wide variety of patients ranging from a senior citizen who had knee replacement surgery, an adult who suffers from arthritis, an individual who was injured on the job, or a college or high school athlete who is recovering from a sports-related mishap. All of these patients are individuals with different needs, emotions, levels of functionality, and rehabilitation goals. NovaCare Rehabilitation works hard to relate to its patients, answer their questions, address their concerns, and help motivate them to achieve their rehabilitation goals. Simply put, the goal at NovaCare Rehabilitation is to make a positive difference everyday for its patients and referring customers through excellence in clinical care and customer service.

NovaCare Rehabilitation takes pride in its status as a nationally prominent, locally driven provider of outpatient physical rehabilitation. The company offers a wide range of preventative, rehabilitative, and performance-enhancing programs and services that maximize functionality and promote well-being in patients of all ages and abilities. These include: physical therapy, hand therapy, work injury prevention and management, occupational health services, low back rehabilitation, sports performance and athletic training services, aquatic therapy, wellness/fitness programs, and other core and specialized services. And throughout the country, NovaCare Rehabilitation effectively partners with its key referring customers—physicians, employers, payers, case managers, and athletic directors—to provide them with the following benefits: excellence in clinical care and customer service; proven clinical outcomes; a national presence with a local market focus; convenient hours and locations; timely and effective communication; managed care and contracting expertise; and proven network building and management.

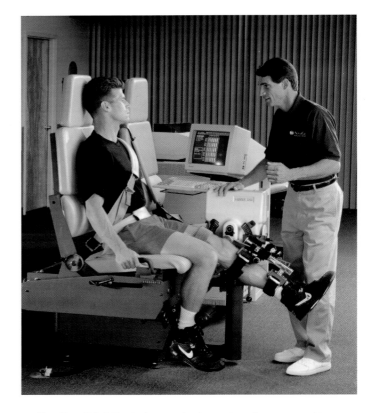

▲ NovaCare Rehabilitation's expertise in sports performance enables athletes to return to optimal performance quickly and safely.

Although NovaCare Rehabilitation has more than 500 centers in more than 30 states, the company doesn't think of itself as "national." Instead, NovaCare Rehabilitation is focused on the specific needs and concerns of each local community that it serves. Local market leaders are committed to developing the programs, services, locations, and/or processes that best address the needs of each local community.

In 1999, NovaCare Rehabilitation was purchased by, and is a division of Select Medical Corporation. As part of the Select Medical organization, the mission of NovaCare Rehabilitation is to ensure high-quality health care and cost-effective outcomes by providing outpatient rehabilitation services to those served, while providing a positive work environment for staff, and a reasonable return to its shareholders. The company's division headquarters are situated in suburban Philadelphia, which is also one of NovaCare's largest and most important markets. The company maintains a presence of several dozen conveniently located NovaCare

◀ NovaCare WorkStrategies™ Program Specialists work with employees to identify worker postures, positioning, motions, and habits that directly relate to musculoskeletal disorders to decrease the potential for injury in the workplace.

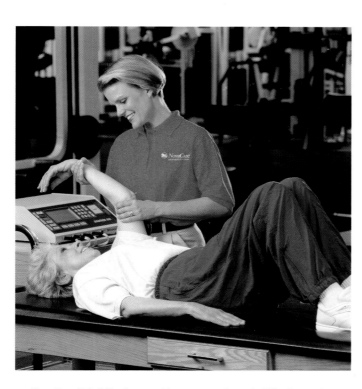

▲ NovaCare Rehabilitation provides preventative, rehabilitative, and performance-enhancing programs and services that maximize functionality and promote well-being in patients of various ages and abilities.

Rehabilitation centers, maintains a close relationship with the Chamber of Commerce and area employers, serves as the official rehabilitation provider to several of the city's professional sports teams, and partners with many area colleges, universities, and high schools.

NovaCare Rehabilitation also acted as a partner with the Philadelphia Eagles to build The NovaCare Complex, a 108,000 square-foot, state-of-the-art complex designed by architect Michael Graves. Situated in South Philadelphia, The NovaCare Complex is the official headquarters for the Philadelphia Eagles and boasts three 100-yard, natural grass practice fields; a 70-yard indoor practice facility; the largest and most comprehensive weight room within the NFL; a 3,500-square-foot training room; and an all-digital, state-of-the-art auditorium with nearly 200 seats. Within the Complex is a NovaCare Rehabilitation outpatient center, which is open to the public and provides the Philadelphia community with a broad range of quality rehabilitation programs and services close to home or work.

Part of being a good corporate citizen comes in making contributions to the community and helping to build a better place for everyone to live. NovaCare Rehabilitation takes great pride in its involvement with the area's numerous community programs. Company executives are active with the Chamber of Commerce and employees are active with organizations such as the American Red

▶ The NovaCare WorkStrategies™ Program is designed to *Keep America on the Job* by focusing on injury prevention and management.

Cross, the Juvenile Diabetes Foundation, and many others. In 2001, the Arthritis Foundation of Southeastern Pennsylvania recognized NovaCare Rehabilitation as the Corporate Community Leader of the Year for Philadelphia. Another example of NovaCare's dedication to Philadelphia came when Mayor John Street wanted to come up with a plan for Philadelphia to lose "76 tons of fun in 76 days." At the time, Philadelphia had been ranked as the fattest city in America. With only a few hours notice, NovaCare employees helped make arrangements to get the program started and make it a huge success.

The most important way in which NovaCare makes a difference to its neighbors in Philadelphia, or any community where it has a presence, comes in the quality of clinical care and customer service that it provides to its patients and referring customers. The treatment and prevention of musculoskeletal and neuromuscular injuries was the initial foundation of NovaCare Rehabilitation and continues as a major focus. After an initial physical examination by a physician, patients are referred to NovaCare Rehabilitation. At the first visit, a patient undergoes an initial evaluation by a physical therapist and an individualized treatment program is designed to meet the patient's specific rehabilitation needs and goals. Throughout treatment, NovaCare Rehabilitation's clinical team provides ongoing communication to physicians, case managers, and employers creating a "team approach" to rehabilitation.

Since its inception, NovaCare has taken a leadership role in the rehabilitation industry and in 2001, NovaCare introduced a new national offering: The NovaCare WorkStrategies™ Program, which is designed to Keep America on the Job. Each year, employers pay more than $20 billion in workers' compensation costs. Eighty percent of

◀ 297

workplace injuries are due to worker habits and more than half are musculoskeletal (sprains and strains) in nature. The goal of the NovaCare WorkStrategies™ Program is to effectively partner with employers to reduce the costs of work-related injuries by focusing on injury prevention and management. This is accomplished through a proactive and integrated team approach, which includes the employee, the employer, the physician, the case manager, the clinician, and other key team members. NovaCare's WorkStrategies™ services include: functional capacity evaluations, injury prevention training and education, job analyses, on-site or work-site physical therapy, ergonomic assessments, pre-placement and post-offer screenings, return-to-work programs, and work risk analyses. This Program provides employers with a comprehensive approach that is customized to the employer's specific needs and goals, a constant focus on ongoing communication and successful case resolution, and education of management and employees.

Within the Philadelphia community, the company also operates a network of NovaCare Occupational Health Services centers, which are outpatient medical facilities that exclusively specialize in the treatment of work-related injuries, as well as special health testing requirements for employers. NovaCare Occupational Health Services' board-certified physicians are well equipped to handle any non life-threatening injury, such as lacerations, minor burns, strains and sprains, foreign objects in eyes, crush injuries, and chemical exposures. NovaCare Occupational Health Services offers a range of core services, including injury treatment and management; physical

298 ▶

▲ On-Site Rehabilitation Programs place a NovaCare clinician on a company's premises to handle acute injuries and/or to provide a comprehensive injury prevention and management program.

examinations; drug and alcohol testing; and on-site services. This team's goal is to manage each case with the goal of returning injured employees to full duty as quickly and safely as possible.

Recognizing the needs of the individual is always at the center of NovaCare Rehabilitation's relationship with its patients. To an individual who has never been injured before, the idea of outpatient rehabilitation can be daunting. NovaCare Rehabilitation views every patient who walks through the doors of one of its centers as an opportunity to make a positive difference in his or her life. In addition to high-quality clinical care and customer service, the energy, enthusiasm, and passion that NovaCare employees bring to their job benefits the patient. Making the effort to answer patients' questions and address their concerns is also what makes the difference at NovaCare.

This commitment to its patients and referring customers was highlighted when NovaCare Rehabilitation, with the support and encouragement of Select Medical Corporation, embarked upon a Service Culture Initiative. Put into effect in 2001, this program is designed to help maintain the company's trademark clinical and service excellence in the day-to-day activities of everyone involved within the NovaCare

◀ Pre-Placement and Post-Offer Screenings are utilized by companies to successfully match an employee to a job to minimize the risk of injury and to provide the new employee with information to remain healthy at work.

▲ As President of NovaCare Rehabilitation, Edward R. Miersch leads a team committed to making a positive difference everyday through excellence in clinical care and customer service.

organization. Simply stated, the company's service goal is to come together to make a positive difference everyday by providing clinical and service excellence to its patients, customers, and fellow employees. The men and women at NovaCare live up to that service theme by addressing the five service standards of safety, courtesy, teamwork, efficiency, and creating the best possible experience. One of the major advantages that this program provides is a common goal that unites employees at more than 500 locations throughout the country.

Technological advances play an enormous role in any health care field and physical therapy is no exception. Having established its role as one of the leading physical therapy providers in the country is indicative of the success NovaCare has enjoyed; however, having centers spread throughout the country can offer its own set of challenges. In spite of the fact that a large part

▶ NovaCare Rehabilitation partnered with The Philadelphia Eagles to build The NovaCare Complex, a 108,000 square-foot, state-of-the-art complex situated in South Philadelphia.

of the day-to-day business is handled in the local centers, communications between the individual centers and the central offices is a must. NovaCare has gone to great lengths to ensure the ability to quickly communicate and share the latest information and updates. Having access to clinical outcomes data sharing information between different centers is a tremendous asset to the company. The Clinical Outcomes Program at NovaCare measures and reports changes in patient health status, functional clinical outcomes, and patient satisfaction. Outcomes information is tracked, trended, and reported through national and market-specific reports. This program benefits NovaCare's referring customers by providing reports on clinical functional outcomes, which allow physicians, payers, and employers to compare NovaCare outcomes to other providers. Internally, the program promotes clinical excellence, cost-effectiveness, and high-quality service.

The future for NovaCare looks promising on several fronts. Following a well-planned strategy focused on responsible organic growth, NovaCare seeks to expand in areas where the company's reputation has been established. In our society, there will continue to be a growing demand for physical rehabilitation services. As a local, regional, and national leader, NovaCare Rehabilitation will continue to meet the needs of its patients and customers through clinically differentiated programs and a strong commitment to customer service. ℗

▸ Crozer-Keystone Health System

*I*n 1990, the parent companies of Delaware County Memorial Hospital in Drexel Hill and Crozer-Chester Medical Center in Upland merged to form the Crozer-Keystone Health System (CKHS). Building on the belief that these two strong, viable hospitals would enhance the delivery of health care in Delaware County, the Crozer-Keystone Health System has achieved clinical and financial success.

From a historical perspective, generations of patients and their families have relied on the hospitals of the Crozer-Keystone Health System which, combined, have provided more than 400 years of service to the surrounding communities.

Today, Crozer-Keystone is the fourth largest health care provider in the Delaware Valley, caring for two-thirds of the residents of Delaware County. Despite a financially unstable health care climate in Pennsylvania, the Crozer-Keystone Health System utilizes its resources well, to maintain a revenue base of over $600 million a year with a positive bottom line. Each year, the health system admits more than 40,000 inpatients, receives 110,000 emergency department visits, and performs 27,000 surgeries.

Crozer-Keystone Health System employs 7,200 caring people—making it the single largest employer in Delaware County—and is staffed by 2,600 highly specialized nurses and physicians. Fostering the professional development of current and prospective employees, Crozer-Keystone has affiliations with local nursing schools and sponsors or co-sponsors educational programs to train allied health professionals. The system is actively engaged in the training of the next generation of physicians.

In addition to its hospitals, the Crozer-Keystone Health System comprises a network of 200 specialty and primary care physicians across Delaware County; four long-term care facilities; two transitional care centers; Centers for Occupational Health; and two regional cancer centers.

Crozer-Chester Medical Center, which is the health system's largest teaching hospital and tertiary-care facility, houses a nationally renowned burn center, the county's only trauma center, an open-

▲ The Crozer-Keystone Health System, the largest healthcare provider in Delaware County, Pennsylvania, comprises five hospitals, the Healthplex® Sports Club, and dozens of primary, specialty, and subspecialty physician practices throughout the county. More than 7,200 employees and 2,600 doctors and nurses work together to fulfill Crozer-Keystone's mission: to help create a healthy place to live and work and a sound environment in which to build and maintain families.

◀ Crozer's helipad provides entrée to its Trauma Center, Burn Center, and Emergency Services. The Trauma Center, the only designated regional trauma center in Delaware County since 1987, treats 1,300 patients annually. The Trauma Center often works in concert with the multidisciplinary team of the Nathan Speare Regional Burn Treatment Center, which was the first of its kind in the Delaware Valley when it was founded in 1973. The Burn Center, which is an American College of Surgeons-designated site, treats nearly 300 patients from around the region, country, and world each year. It has pioneered cutting-edge methods of burn treatment, such as cultured cell transplantation and daily use of the "shower trolley," which have become the standard of care nationwide.

▲ From open-heart surgery (as seen here) to primary angioplasty, the hospitals of the Crozer-Keystone Health System are on the forefront of cardiac care. Crozer is credited with providing residents in the Delaware County community with the first open heart surgery program, the first cardiac care unit, the first cardiac catheterization unit, and the first cardiac rehabilitation program.

heart surgery program, a highly specialized neonatal intensive care unit, and the Crozer Regional Cancer Center. Delaware County Memorial Hospital (DCMH), the largest of CKHS's community hospitals, is a leader in maternity and neonatal care, as well as cardiac and emergency services. DCMH is also home to a comprehensive SurgiCenter and the Delaware County Regional Cancer Center.

Springfield Hospital provides a full range of acute-care services and wellness care, with emphasis on diabetic treatment, sports medicine, and surgery. Springfield Hospital is complemented by the adjacent 176,000-square-foot Healthplex® Sports Club, which is one of America's largest and most fully integrated health and wellness centers. With 7,000 members and the latest facilities and programming, the Healthplex® is Delaware County's premier health club.

Another of CKHS's community hospitals is Taylor Hospital in Ridley Park, which is best known for the Sleep Disorder Center—the only one of its caliber in the region—and its surgical services and strong primary care base. Community Hospital, a comprehensive outpatient hospital in Chester that provides vital health and

▶ The specialized facilities at the Healthplex® Sports Club, including its comprehensive cardiovascular equipment, help make the club Delaware County's premier health and fitness center. The Healthplex® also offers an experienced staff, a range of specialized classes and leagues for members of all ages, and such amenities as childcare and a full-service spa. And, through its affiliation with the Crozer-Keystone Health System, the Healthplex® offers medically supervised wellness classes for those recovering from injuries or illness.

human services, administers a variety of primary care and mental health services, substance-abuse programs, and women and children's health care programs.

Crozer-Keystone's commitment to community outreach and public health extends beyond the walls of its hospitals. The system provides nearly $18 million in charitable care annually. Every two years, the health system undertakes a community health needs assessment in order to monitor and help improve the health status of Delaware County residents. Ten years of data has shown marked improvement in the county's overall health.

Crozer-Keystone continues to face numerous challenges and opportunities. As a result of a dramatic growth in patient volume and an aging Delaware County population, Crozer-Keystone has increased the number and breadth of its services. Inpatient beds have been added across the system, and construction of new emergency departments at both DCMH and Crozer are currently underway. The health system continues to upgrade its technology and adopt the latest evidence-based medicine practices.

The Crozer-Keystone Health System has been recognized numerous times for its quality of service and clinical effectiveness. The health system has received several awards from the Delaware County Chamber of Commerce for contributions to the community, and is ranked among the nation's Top 100 Integrated Healthcare Networks and Most Wired health systems. Crozer-Keystone has also been honored with many VHA leadership awards and, most recently, recognized as one of five national winners of the American Hospital Association's NOVA Award, a prestigious honor for community outreach.

Outstanding patient care, dedicated staff, cutting-edge technology and modern facilities, and hands-on community service combine to assure that Crozer-Keystone Health System will continue to enrich the lives of Delaware County residents for generations to come. ℗

▶ Universal Health Services, Inc.

*A*lthough it owns and operates more than 100 facilities throughout the United States, Puerto Rico, and France, Universal Health Services, Inc. (UHS) has had its roots in the Philadelphia area for 30 years.

Today, Universal Health Services is a leading hospital management company with more than 100 acute care, behavioral health, ambulatory surgical centers, and radiation oncology centers in the US, Puerto Rico, and France. The company, whose shares are traded on the New York Stock Exchange (symbol UHS) has revenues of more than $3.2 billion in 2002 and employs more than 30,000 people.

UHS owns and operates the largest group of behavioral health hospitals in Pennsylvania, and it recently acquired its first acute care hospital in the Philadelphia suburbs. With 38 hospitals, UHS operates the largest behavioral health division in the United States, all directed from its headquarters just outside of Philadelphia.

When Alan B. Miller, President and CEO of this publicly traded company, founded Universal Health Services, Inc. in 1978, he located the business in the Philadelphia region because of its proximity to both New York City and Washington, D.C. That would give the company access to Wall Street, the financial capital, and the federal regulators and policymakers in our nation's capital.

At the same time, the Philadelphia region has one of the largest concentrations of healthcare institutions, medical schools, universities, and pharmaceutical companies in the United States. That meant that UHS would have a large pool of talented and healthcare-trained employees available to it.

Careful Planning, Strategic Growth

One key to UHS's successful growth and its sustained superior performance is the company's strict adherence to a carefully planned expansion strategy.

▲ **Alan B. Miller, President and CEO.**

When he started UHS, Miller was not new to the healthcare arena. In 1973, he became President of American Medicorp, also located in the Philadelphia area. By 1978, he had turned American Medicorp from a company with financial difficulties into the second-largest hospital management firm in the nation. In fact, Miller was so successful at American Medicorp that the company attracted the attention of Humana Inc., which completed a hostile takeover in 1978. Miller decided to start over and founded Universal Health Services, Inc. later that year.

By concentrating on hospitals located in medium-sized but fast-growing markets, UHS has been able to develop a network of facilities that are important to their communities, provide high-quality medical services, and develop considerable market share. At the same time, the company has continually looked to develop new lines of business, including surgery and radiation oncology centers, and has helped propel its expansion through the investment of capital and recruitment of the best people in the industry.

◀ **Central Montgomery Medical Center.**

▲ **Fairmont Behavioral Health System.**

One of the company's most visible facilities is The George Washington University Hospital in Washington, D.C. When UHS acquired an 80-percent interest in the hospital in 1997, the company committed to building a new state-of-the-art hospital. Today, the new facility is the most technologically advanced hospital in the nation and provides internationally renowned medical care for government officials, foreign leaders, as well as the residents of the Washington, D.C. metropolitan area.

In early 2002, UHS acquired its first acute care hospital in the Philadelphia metropolitan area. Now called Central Montgomery Medical Center, the hospital is located in the suburbs of Philadelphia and serves the fast-growing eastern Montgomery County and central Bucks County region.

When UHS acquired Central Montgomery Medical Center, it immediately began to expand and improve the services offered at the hospital. Within months, the hospital had opened new magnetic resonance imaging (MRI) and interventional radiology suites so that residents could receive the highest quality care in their local community.

The George Washington University Hospital and Central Montgomery Medical Center are just two examples of the strategy that has made UHS so successful. By carefully identifying markets that need high-quality healthcare services and giving the

hospitals the resources to meet that demand, UHS provides patients with excellent medical care. That attracts the best physicians, nurses, and other medical professionals to the hospital staffs, which in turn, has a significant positive impact on the company's financial performance.

Service Excellence Drives UHS

In addition to providing hospitals with the resources they require, Universal Health Services works to ensure that everyone employed by the company has the knowledge and skills they need to help UHS achieve its goals. An important part of that process is the company's *Service Excellence* program.

All UHS employees take part in the program, whether they are at the corporate office in King of Prussia or at any of its hospitals. In short, *Service Excellence* provides all UHS employees with a set of eight standards that guide them as they strive for excellence in everything they do. Among the topics covered by the *Service Excellence* program are personal responsibility, positive attitudes, effectiveness, and teamwork.

Miller started UHS with a simple goal: put patients first and by doing so, the company will drive outstanding returns for its investors. By striving for excellence in everything it does, UHS has created a network of hospitals that are top-rated. That's a fitting achievement for a healthcare company that's based in the home of the nation's first hospital. ℗

◀ 303

▶ **George Washington University Hospital.**

▶ Independence Blue Cross

*T*he tall blue building at 1901 Market Street is home to one of the Philadelphia region's great corporate success stories.

Within the confines of that building, more than 6,500 people serve the health insurance needs of 3 million residents of the area. Another 2,500 work at other facilities throughout the region and the country, bringing total corporate employment to more than 9,600 associates and member enrollment to nearly 4.2 million.

The company is Independence Blue Cross, an $8.3 billion health insurance enterprise currently experiencing its 15th consecutive year of positive financial performance.

The enormity of Independence Blue Cross's importance to its marketplace is best understood by the realization that, during the year 2002, it will pay out more than 41 million claims to cover the health care needs of its members at a cost of more than $6.3 billion. IBC will handle more than 7.1 million customer service inquiries and pay more than $134 million in taxes to federal, state, and local governments.

Its success, however, is not measured only in dollars but by the security it provides to its members and the peace of mind they experience because of membership in a financially strong and caring health insurance company.

The growth and current preeminence of Independence Blue Cross are the result of twelve years of strategic planning and implementation accomplished by professional management and dedicated employees under the direction and leadership of its Chief Executive Officer, G. Fred DiBona, Jr., who assumed the presidency of the company in 1990.

Fully aware of the winds of change and rising costs which were sweeping the health care industry, Fred DiBona and his team streamlined the company's service, diversified its products, and brought it into the era of managed care and technological change. Today, each of its quality award winning managed care products, Personal Choice

▲ A distinguished landmark on the Philadelphia skyline, the Independence Blue Cross building stands 45 stories tall at the corner of 19th and Market Streets.

and Keystone Health Plan East, has membership in excess of 1.1 million area residents and workers.

Through managed care, comprehensive benefit plans have been enriched with wellness and preventive programs which have brought healthier lives to hundreds of thousands of members who have taken advantage of adult immunizations; mammography reminders; cholesterol control guidelines; pediatric care; weight control and smoking cessation programs; and health management assistance to people with diabetes, asthma, congestive heart failure, and pulmonary disease.

◀ At one of many community-centered events sponsored by Independence Blue Cross, CEO G. Fred DiBona, Jr. recognizes two participants of the annual Blue Cross Broad Street Run—a 10-mile road race through the heart of Philadelphia—benefiting the American Cancer Society.

▲ An independent licensee of the Blue Cross and Blue Shield Association, Independence Blue Cross is able to offer its members the security and peace of mind that comes with access to one of the nation's largest networks of physicians and hospitals.

owned subsidiaries reaching into New Jersey and Delaware. As a predominantly regional enterprise, it is one of the area's leading purchasers of goods and services from other local firms.

Of the many factors that have contributed to the success of IBC, none is more important than the role it plays in the communities it serves. It is consistently among the leaders in corporate and employee support of the United Way. Its executives and managers personally serve on the boards of innumerable civic organizations. Its "Blue Crew" volunteer program enlists more than 900 employees and their families to participate in community service efforts such as Rebuilding Together, Christmas in April, Philadelphia Reads, the Ronald McDonald House, the National Adoption Center, Habitat for Humanity, Philadelphia Cares, and numerous others.

After more than 60 years of service, Independence Blue Cross is today a Philadelphia tradition, a financially strong company with a dedicated staff and leadership that constantly pushes for innovation. It is not only a preeminent corporate citizen of the Philadelphia area, but a recognized national leader in the health insurance field and a major contributor to the well-being of its members and its community. ℗

Although very much a commercial success story, Independence Blue Cross never lost its commitment to a social mission which goes back to its founding more than sixty years ago. It is still the "insurer of last resort," accepting all applicants regardless of medical condition, subsidizing premiums to keep them affordable. This year its Caring Foundation, which provides health insurance for poor and needy children through Pennsylvania's CHIP Program, (Children's Health Insurance Program) served the 100,000th child in its twelve-year history. During 2002, Independence Blue Cross, under the guidance of the Commonwealth, has begun a similar program for adults of moderate income and has already signed up several thousand members.

Medicare and Medicaid risk products provide comprehensive health plan coverage, including wellness programs, for eligible people in both government programs.

From an economic standpoint, IBC's impact on the Greater Delaware Valley region is immeasurable, with wholly

◀ 305

▶ After more than 60 years of service in the Philadelphia region, Independence Blue Cross is a Philadelphia tradition—providing health care insurance to over 3 million area residents and employing over 6,500 associates.

▸ Northwestern Human Services

*O*riginally founded in 1967, Northwestern Human Services (NHS) has established itself as a leading community-based behavioral health and human services provider. With programs and facilities also located throughout New Jersey, Washington, D.C., and Virginia, NHS is currently the largest provider of behavioral health and human services throughout Pennsylvania. Offering a full continuum of specialized care, NHS focuses on mental health and drug and alcohol rehabilitation, working with individuals suffering from mental retardation, juvenile justice, and elder care. Every day, the men and women at NHS strive to enable children and adults in their homes, schools, and communities to face challenges and change their lives in the least restrictive setting possible. Helping those most in need, allowing them the opportunity to grow with dignity, and assisting them with moving on to lead happy, fulfilling lives is the passion and mission of every NHS employee. It is what they do best.

Employing over 6,500 men and women, NHS is a strong, committed organization that is dedicated to the enrichment of each and every life of the 50,000 consumers it serves each year.

Today, NHS faces more challenges to its mission than ever before. It is a fact that 50 million Americans face some form of mental illness, that mental retardation touches one in five American families, and more children and adults are plagued by substance abuse problems each year. The number of juveniles incarcerated in the United States each year continues to grow steadily, making it evident that the development of alternative treatment plans is necessary to rehabilitate their lives and create new futures. The increasing number of this nation's elderly and addressing their needs will also continue to be a growing concern for years to come.

In addition to more obvious health-care matters, NHS has had growth issues to deal with as well. As a not-for-profit organization,

▲ **M. Joseph Rocks, Chairman and Chief Executive Officer.**
Photo ©2002 John McGrail

NHS receives almost 98 percent of its revenue from government funds. In the last decade, the company has gone through a major period of expansion. As more consumers began seeking help, the organization began attracting some of the finest practitioners available. The highly trained staff of clinicians, social workers, therapists, and psychiatrists at NHS has met these challenges with a renewed commitment to their goals and are prepared to address the issues and problems that both children and adults face each day. Master's and doctoral level staff develop tailor-made programs to best address each consumer's treatment needs.

While improving treatments and changing the lives of consumers for the better has been critical to the work that NHS has done over the years, the corporation's outdated financial

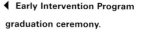

◀ **Early Intervention Program graduation ceremony.**

▲ Larry Parkinson, Ohana House resident.

infrastructure suffered. Until recently NHS lacked the proper business operation structure to accommodate the explosive growth of the prior decade, which in turn threatened the financial stability of the corporation.

Pennsylvania State Senator M. Joseph Rocks assumed the roles of NHS's Board of Trustees chairman in January of 2000 and chief executive officer in June of 2000. An experienced state legislator, Senator Rocks has a history of active involvement in the drafting of healthcare legislation and program funding for disadvantaged and disabled individuals. He has also served as a NHS Board of Trustees member for over 15 years prior to becoming chairman and chief executive officer.

Charged by NHS's Board of Trustees to develop and execute a financial turnaround plan to address the key issues that threatened the corporation's future, Senator Rocks and the newly appointed financial management team began the systematic restructuring of the business operations to restore financial stability to the corporation.

Returning NHS to its "mission philosophy" of core services required the execution of a strategic financial turnaround plan that addressed every aspect of the corporation's $240 million operating

budget. Several non-core businesses that didn't coincide with the primary mission were divested. Tireless hours were dedicated to restructuring the short-term borrowing capacity. An aged accounts receivable problem and an escalating accounts payable were addressed. All facets of the financial structure were analyzed and restructured. By applying sound business acumen, NHS was rescued from impending financial crisis and the financial house rebuilt. Once again NHS is able to live up to its hard-earned reputation as one of the country's premier behavioral health and human services providers.

NHS continues to provide the highest quality of care to our society's most vulnerable individuals. For over 30 years, NHS has been helping those with mental retardation to build life skills that better enable them to enjoy a normal life, teaching men and women with drug and alcohol dependencies to face and overcome their addictions, providing foster homes for children and giving them a chance at a better future, and offering support to our nation's elderly. Today, with its financial stability restored, Northwestern Human Services can continue the pursuit of its primary mission: changing lives one individual at a time. ℗

◄ 3 0 7

▶ NHS staff volunteering at WHYY Telethon.

▸ Penn Eye Care

The Department of Ophthalmology at the University of Pennsylvania Health System was founded in 1874 to provide eye care services to soldiers returning from the Civil War. Since then, Penn Eye Care, as it is referred to today, has continued to play the role of an important component in maintaining the University of Pennsylvania's reputation as one of the United States oldest and most well-respected medical and surgical ophthalmic programs.

The Department of Ophthalmology, housed at Scheie Eye Institute on the Presbyterian Medical Center campus, the Hospital of the University of Pennsylvania, and five other clinical practice sites, is dedicated to continuing this tradition by providing a complete range of medical and surgical eye care services, vision care and optical services, as well as remaining in the forefront of eye and vision research. Coupled with that is an overriding concern for excellence in patient care, education of future ophthalmologists and vision scientists, and the advancement of research to prevent vision loss and blindness.

Over the years, Penn Eye Care has attracted some of the world's foremost experts in ophthalmology and vision, as well as some of the world's leading eye surgeons. The faculty ophthalmologists and scientists have received international recognition for their contributions. Specific acknowledgements include being listed in "Best Doctors of America, Top Docs" in *Philadelphia Magazine*, as well as being invited to take part in lectureships, visiting professorships, and memberships on editorial boards of leading professional journals.

Penn Eye Care ranks second in eye and vision research among the 125 ophthalmology departments at medical schools in the United States. This level of excellence is achieved by a constant awareness of the needs of patients and a continuing dedication to the advancement of ophthalmology.

For well over a century, medicine and medical-related sciences have been among the most rapidly advancing fields. Since the years following the Civil War, Penn Eye Care has continued to capitalize

▲ Penn's Scheie Eye Institute does more eye and vision research than all of the medical schools and eye hospitals in the tri-state area combined.

on and lead many of those advances. Today the organization is in the forefront in developing new technology for evaluation of eye diseases, as well as working to advance treatment of these conditions through improved surgical and laser procedures and leading randomized trials to evaluate new treatments. The University of Pennsylvania Department of Ophthalmology is currently involved in more eye and vision research than all of the medical schools and eye hospitals in the tri-state area together.

One of the most exciting examples of this research is a collaborative effort between scientists at Penn Eye Care, Cornell, and the University of Florida. By employing retinal gene therapy, researchers were able to reverse blindness in three

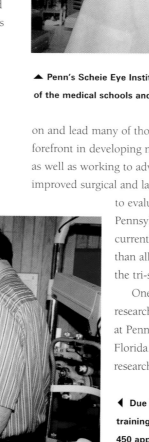

◀ Due in part to highly dedicated faculty, the residency training program at Penn's Scheie Eye Institute attracts 450 applications per year for five positions. The program combines cutting-edge clinical and research education to mentor the future leaders in ophthalmology and vision science.

▲ The same doctors that perform vision research also take care of patients. Therefore, patients at Penn's Scheie Eye Institute benefit first from new discoveries.

treatment too late, *4Sight* staff has combined its efforts to educate the local population about the dangers of diabetic retinopathy and facilitate access to the appropriate healthcare facilities. The goal is to identify individuals at risk during the earliest stage possible—at a time when treatment can be carried out effectively. With more than 1,000 patients enrolled in the local program, *4Sight* expects that it will eventually extend to hundreds of communities across the United States and throughout the world, wherever diabetic blindness is a major problem.

With its core of highly-skilled ophthalmologists and vision scientists, the University of Pennsylvania Department of Ophthalmology continues to plan the growth of its medical/surgical and vision care services, in addition to its eye research. The research endeavors will continue to attract leaders in ophthalmology and vision research to Penn Eye Care and to Philadelphia. Plans are underway to establish new practice sites in the Greater Delaware Valley Community, which will improve eye care services in the local community.

Many people overlook the science behind eye care when considering healthcare issues, in spite of their reliance on their vision. Fortunately for the residents of the Delaware Valley area and the rest of the world, Penn Eye Care does not. Penn Eye Care tirelessly works to find ways to protect, save, and restore vision, and leads the way in eye and vision research. ◉

dogs that had suffered from the condition since birth. More than two years after becoming front-page news in publications around the world, each of the dogs remains sighted in the treated eye. Research for this and other programs continues, preparing for the day when these techniques can be used to save the sight of humans on a broad scale.

Since 1997, Penn Eye Care has been proud to lead *4Sight*, the West Philadelphia Prevention of Blindness Program. *4Sight* is a partnership between the University of Pennsylvania Department of Ophthalmology and the West Philadelphia pastors, public health nurses, community leaders, and other members of the medical establishment. *4Sight* was organized to attempt to reduce blindness from diabetic retinopathy. As most diabetic blindness is the result of the patient receiving

▶ Designed by Kling Lindquist and completed in 1972, the Scheie Eye Institute building's unique shape was inspired by the eye. Today, Scheie continues to serve as the flagship of the Department of Ophthalmology for the University of Pennsylvania Health System.

CHAPTER FIFTEEN

Education

**Philadelphia's staggering dedication to education is exemplified by its
impressive community of public and private schools. From pre-kindergarten
to post-graduate, each school in its own way upholding standards of
excellence and forging paths into the future for today's youth.**

PHILADELPHIA

▸ University of Pennsylvania

As the fourth oldest college and the oldest university in the country, the University of Pennsylvania has a tradition of educational excellence that reaches back to the very foundation of the United States. Today, Penn, an Ivy League institution with an enrollment of more than 21,000 students, is one of America's premier research universities, offering undergraduate, graduate, and professional degrees through its 12 schools.

Penn's faculty and students inspire, demand, and thrive on excellence. Penn regularly places among the top 10 national universities in the U.S. and has a longstanding reputation for excellence in graduate and professional education, with a number of its graduate and professional schools ranked at or near the top in their fields. The Wharton School, the School of Nursing, the School of Arts and Sciences, the Graduate School of Education, the Law School, the School of Medicine, and the School of Veterinary Medicine all rank among the nation's top 10. Penn faculty members have won seven MacArthur Awards, two Pulitzer Prizes, and four Nobel Prizes, including the 2000 Nobel Prize in Chemistry won by Alan MacDiarmid.

The University of Pennsylvania is deeply rooted in Philadelphia, the birthplace of American democracy. The institution's charter was written in 1749 by founder Benjamin Franklin, and the first students enrolled in his "College, Academy, and Charitable School" in 1755. Franklin believed that an institution of higher learning, which Pennsylvania lacked at the time, was necessary for the colony to grow and prosper. From the beginning, the school's curriculum was unusual, placing emphasis on contemporary subjects and non-sectarian instruction.

Faithful to that vision, Penn's faculty generates knowledge that is unconstrained by traditional disciplinary boundaries and combines the exploration of intellectual frontiers with the desire for results useful in the real world. Through these studies, the University enhances its teaching of both theory and practice, as well as the linkages between them. Excellence in instruction and research in a

▲ Penn's urban campus is surprisingly park-like, with plenty of places to meet, socialize, study outdoors, or simply relax.

wide range of professional disciplines in the arts and sciences allows Penn to produce future leaders.

America's first university has a long tradition of academic innovation, beginning with the first professional school in America, the School of Medicine, founded in 1765. Other noteworthy academic firsts at Penn include the first university teaching hospital in America (Hospital of the University of Pennsylvania, 1874) and the world's first business school (Wharton School, 1881). The age of modern computing began with the unveiling of ENIAC, the world's first all-electronic, general-purpose digital computer, at Penn in 1946. In 1997, the nation's first hospital—Pennsylvania Hospital, founded by Franklin in 1751—became part of the Penn family when it joined the University of Pennsylvania Health System.

The field of nanotechnology—engineering at the level of a single atom—holds the promise of novel medical treatments, microscopic computers, and more,

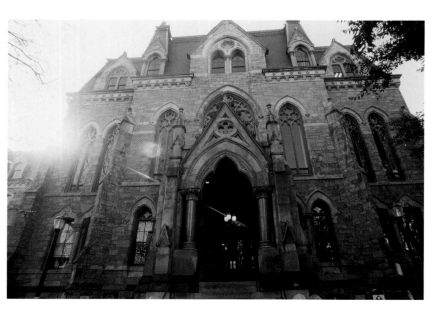

◀ College Hall, built in 1871, is the oldest building on Penn's 262-acre West Philadelphia campus.

312 ▸

and Penn is one of a handful of research universities at the cutting edge of this field, with its Center for Science and Engineering of Nanoscale Systems conducting basic research and the Nanotechnology Institute identifying potential applications for the fruits of that research.

Penn takes particular pride in allowing its students and faculty the freedom to pursue knowledge wherever it may be found, without regard to traditional disciplinary boundaries. The University has actively promoted interdisciplinary academic programs like the Joseph H. Lauder Institute of Management and International Studies and research centers such as the Leonard Davis Institute, which brings faculty from four Penn schools together to study health-care issues. Such close collaborations are possible because all 12 of Penn's schools are on the same West Philadelphia campus.

Penn is among the most selective universities in the country, admitting roughly one in every five applicants to its undergraduate schools each year. Its undergraduate business program is the only one in the Ivy League and is rated among the best in the world. As an Ivy League member, Penn offers its students the opportunity to excel on the playing field within the context of the overall academic experience. Penn features 20 men's and 14 women's intercollegiate athletic teams, making it one of the broadest athletic programs in the nation.

▲ Sculptor George Lundeen captured Penn's founder, Benjamin Franklin, at rest in this sculpture affectionately known as "Ben on the Bench," a popular photo spot on campus.

▼ Penn's residential college houses, three of which are located in the Quadrangle, the University's oldest dormitory, promote the integration of academic and social life.

313

The University campus is home to a vibrant mix of artistic and cultural activities as well. The University of Pennsylvania Museum of Archaeology and Anthropology, founded in 1887, is one of the country's premier museums devoted to archaeology and world cultures, and the Institute of Contemporary Art regularly showcases the best of modern and postmodern art. The professional theater, dance, and music offerings of the Penn Presents series at the Annenberg Center and Irvine Auditorium are augmented by a rich array of student performing arts groups. Penn's 262-acre West Philadelphia campus is also home to a number of architectural landmarks, including Frank Furness' innovative University Library of 1891 (now the Fisher Fine Arts Library); Louis I. Kahn's Richards Medical Research Laboratory; Hill College House, designed by Eero Saarinen; and Houston Hall, the first student union in the United States, opened in 1896.

In addition to providing first-rate education and research, Penn has maintained a continuing tradition of community awareness and involvement. Penn has always been an important force, not only in the city's intellectual and educational life, but also in its economic and cultural well-being. The University is the largest private employer in the city of Philadelphia and the fourth-largest private employer in the Commonwealth of Pennsylvania, providing the area's citizens with valuable jobs. Penn graduates have gone on to serve the city, the region, and the nation. Penn research has helped spark economic development in the region; in fiscal year 2000, Penn's Center for Technology Transfer helped launch four new start-up companies in the Delaware Valley.

▲ Penn Relays, held every April, is the oldest and largest amateur track meet in America, dating back to 1895.

Penn has worked to develop strong ties to its home community of West Philadelphia and the city as a whole. The University has implemented a series of programs—called the West Philadelphia Initiatives—to improve the neighborhood surrounding its campus. Working with community groups, Penn has invested in new retail development, construction, purchasing, and education in the neighborhood, including a new neighborhood public school operated with the assistance of Penn's Graduate School of Education. Penn mortgage incentives have encouraged new homeowners to put down roots in the neighborhood. Other partnership programs, like the West Philadelphia Improvement Corps community school program, put the University's intellectual resources at the service of community residents to help develop skills and solve problems.

On a more individual level, members of the faculty and staff hold various offices throughout the nation's collegiate community, as well as supporting and taking part in a variety of local organizations and programs.

In dealing with an institution as old as the University of Pennsylvania, one has to take notice of the changes that have come about as it has evolved with the times. For much of its history, Penn drew the bulk of its students from Philadelphia and the surrounding region, even though its School of Medicine's stature attracted students from all over the United States. That began to change around the turn of the century, when the opening of the Quadrangle Dormitory in

◀ Juniors at Penn celebrate their passage to senior year on Hey Day, an annual University tradition.

▲ Penn has invested heavily in state-of-the-art laboratory facilities for medical, scientific, and engineering research.

courses that use real-world problem solving as a way to test theories and teach citizenship, Penn's present-day academic programs continue to embody Franklin's spirit of practical innovation.

Under President Judith Rodin's leadership, Penn has enjoyed significant growth in its academic reputation, in its endowment, and in student interest. The University's strategic plan for the next five years, "Building on Excellence: The Next Agenda," seeks to maintain those gains through recruiting talented young faculty members, channeling resources to bring all of its academic departments into the top ranks in their fields, identifying and promoting new opportunities for interdisciplinary research, and building on the improved ties to the community established under the West Philadelphia Initiatives. The plan also calls on Penn to take maximum advantage of its location in the heart of one of America's largest cities to promote both academic study of urban issues and the continued revitalization of its home neighborhood and city. New construction projects currently under way, such as Jon M. Huntsman Hall, the new classroom and office facility for the Wharton School, will allow Penn to consolidate academic facilities and departmental offices, thus opening up other space on campus for new uses.

In the end, Penn's people are what make it successful. The intellectual curiosity, energy, and talent of the students, the strength of the faculty, and the capability and dedication of the staff together have produced an academic institution that is among the finest in the world, and one that is proud to call Philadelphia its home. ◗

◀ 315

1895 allowed the University to house students on its campus. Today, the University attracts students from all 50 states and six continents, with more than 3,000 international students attending the University in a typical year. On average, 1,200 to 1,300 Penn students participate each year in one of Penn's 60 study-abroad programs in 41 countries. Penn is a far more diverse place than it was in 1879, when the first African-American students enrolled for classes, or in 1882, when women first enrolled in Penn's graduate programs. Women today make up almost half of Penn's student body, and nearly 30 percent of full-time students are African-American, Asian-American, or Latino.

What has remained constant throughout Penn's history is the commitment to combining practical knowledge and theoretical understanding embodied in Franklin's oft-quoted statement that students in his academy would "learn everything that is useful and everything that is ornamental." From continuing education programs for working professionals to academically based community service

▶ Penn's commitment to academic excellence means students have the opportunity to study and do research with some of the world's finest scholars, including MacArthur Fellows, Pulitzer and Nobel Prize winners.

▶ La Salle University

*L*a Salle University is an independent, coeducational university founded in 1863 by the Christian Brothers, a Catholic order dedicated to teaching and career preparation. The University is committed to academic excellence and individualized attention in a values-based, inter-faith educational community.

Located just minutes from Center City Philadelphia on a beautiful 100-acre campus, La Salle University's main campus includes 12 acres of woods and gardens, the restored 18th century home of American portrait painter Charles Willson Peale, and one of the finest college art museums on the East Coast. The University's Bucks County Center is located in Newtown, Pennsylvania.

Ranked among the country's top schools by *U.S. News & World Report*, *Barron's, Money*, and *The New York Times*, La Salle has more than 40,000 alumni, most of whom continue to live in the Delaware Valley. La Salle alumni credit the University's purposeful liberal arts approach for improving their thinking and reasoning, problem solving, and written and oral communication skills, as well as preparing them for a life of learning and rewarding personal lives. These deep roots in the community and a commitment to educational excellence have firmly established the University as a valuable part of the Philadelphia metropolitan area.

The University currently offers undergraduate concentrations in almost 60 academic areas within its three schools: Arts and Sciences, Business Administration, and Nursing. These range in focus from the standard programs of study to high-tech areas such as Digital Arts and Multimedia Design, as well as Integrated Science, Business and Technology. La Salle is also extremely proud of its E-Commerce Institute, the first institute of its kind in the nation, which is aimed at educating all students, regardless of their major, about e-commerce as an important business tool. Additionally, La Salle prides itself on offering more than a dozen graduate programs, including the University's first doctoral program: clinical psychology.

▲ **A focus on values and ethics, as well as respect for the individual, are at the core of a Christian Brothers' education.** Photo ©2002 John McGrail

The University's population is approximately 5,500 students, including 3,200 full-time undergraduates (about 85% of whom are resident students) and 800 part-time undergraduates, as well as 1,600 graduate students. Most classes average 20 students, and the student-faculty ratio is 16-to-1.

One of the University's defining characteristics is its use of its city location. Its identity as a Philadelphia school affects the curriculum, stimulates and inspires the faculty, and provides opportunities for recreation, entertainment, employment, and community service for students. Because it practices what it believes as a Christian Brothers' university, La Salle serves as a moral compass for its students and a dutiful neighbor in its community.

La Salle has a long-standing commitment to community service, particularly in Northwest and North Philadelphia. The University offers a broad range of

◀ **Students and faculty on "The Quad."**
Photo ©2002 John McGrail

▲ **La Salle basketball team in a playoff game of the 2002 Atlantic 10 Championship.** Photo ©2002 John McGrail

services to benefit people who reside in the neighborhoods proximate to the main campus, including La Salle's Neighborhood Nursing Center and about 30 outreach programs. Volunteers include faculty, staff, and students. Nearly half of the University's full-time students are involved in service-related programs.

La Salle derives its name from the patron saint of teachers, John Baptist de La Salle, a priest and educational innovator who founded the Christian Brothers in 17th century France. For over 300 years, the order has been known for its dedicated teaching and devotion to students.

A nationally recognized Honors Program praised by the National Collegiate Honors Council for being "a very special sort not available to larger, general universities" is available for La Salle's most gifted learners.

Academically, La Salle's graduates have distinguished themselves in the nation's best graduate, law, and medical schools. And they

boast an extraordinary record for winning Fulbright Fellowships and other prestigious postgraduate awards. Over the past 20 years, 96 percent of those students who were recommended by La Salle were offered entry into medical schools. A national survey ranks La Salle 7th out of 256 schools of its type as the undergraduate point of origin of doctoral degree recipients over a 75-year period. The University is ranked 10th by Standard & Poor's among liberal arts colleges in the number of graduates who are top corporate leaders.

Professors with a passion for teaching and mentoring touch La Salle students' hearts and spirits, as well as their minds. Through challenging small classes where dynamic discussion takes place, the La Salle faculty ensures all motivated students succeed in an environment of mutual respect.

La Salle is a total learning community with an appreciation for the multiple ways of learning ranging from the seminar room and hands-on experiential learning—like internships—to active participation in more than 80 on-campus clubs and organizations.

The University fields 23 NCAA Division I sports teams including 11 for men (baseball, basketball, crew, cross country, football, golf, soccer, swimming, tennis, and indoor and outdoor track and field) and 12 for women (basketball, crew, cross country, field hockey, lacrosse, soccer, softball, swimming, tennis, indoor and outdoor track and field, and volleyball). More than 500 undergraduates participate in intercollegiate varsity sports and more than 1,000 in intramural sports at La Salle.

La Salle goes well beyond simply preparing students for meaningful careers and success in graduate studies. The University provides graduates with the skills they need to have a positive impact on the social, political, professional, and moral challenges of contemporary society. ℗

◀ 317

▶ **Students on tennis courts below the Connelly Library. Hayman Center at far left.** Photo ©2002 John McGrail

CHAPTER SIXTEEN

Real Estate & Development

**Philadelphia, the City of Neighborhoods, has communities defined and
bound by tradition, heritage, and purpose. Whether home is Center City or
a suburban neighborhood, Philadelphia offers the ideal environment for
every person and business.** Photo ©2002 John McGrail

▸ The Rubenstein Company, L.P.

*C*ommercial real estate investment and development isn't something that one readily associates with rocket science, but this unlikely combination is part of the history of The Rubenstein Company. Founder and Chairman, Mark E. Rubenstein, could have followed either path. He is an engineer by profession, holding both an undergraduate and master's degree in mechanical engineering from Johns Hopkins University, where he later taught theoretical mechanics. However, after involvement in some family real estate matters, he discovered a genuine interest in real estate. Mark chose to step away from his budding high-level science career to found The Rubenstein Company in July of 1969. He never looked back.

Since then, under the leadership of Mark and his son, David B. Rubenstein, the company's current President and Chief Executive Officer, The Rubenstein Company has grown from an office of three people to more than 150 employees. The company owns an impressive portfolio of trophy and high-quality commercial office buildings throughout the East Coast. While much has changed since opening its doors in 1969, the company has held firmly to two major founding philosophies. First, the company understands the importance of, and strongly relies on, the quality of its relationships—with its tenants, equity partners, lenders, suppliers, and contractors. Over time, business relationships frequently become partnerships, and then friendships. Second, the company applies a very patient, conservative, detailed, and long-term strategy to every project in which it becomes involved. It asks, "What is the best thing to do for the long-term

▲ **Mark and David Rubenstein.**

enhancement of this property?" Investments in the future are made because of this long-term perspective, which is always beneficial to tenants.

Through the years, one tenant at a time, the company has developed a well-earned reputation for a quality of property management that is second to none. Because the firm itself performs the management and leasing of each property, and because of the company's incredible attention to detail, Rubenstein ensures the quality of every service provided to its tenants. Tenants rarely leave the company's portfolio, knowing they can expect only the best from their current location and property. With Rubenstein as their landlord, they are free to concentrate on their own business without real estate worries.

Despite The Rubenstein Company's growth and success, the firm retains the feel and values of a family-run business. Every day Rubenstein buys lunch for all of its employees, and everyone in the company, at all levels, has lunch together. This tradition has been extremely important in nurturing a friendly atmosphere among a group of highly motivated individuals, allowing them to develop into a team that stresses perfection in everything the company does.

The company also has capitalized by utilizing the skills of some of the best professionals in the industry. Members of the Rubenstein management team have the ability to make their own decisions, and

◀ **One Logan Square.**

▲ **Two Logan Square.**

have a strong personal drive to serve and to achieve. These are characteristics that The Rubenstein Company wants and needs to ensure the level of service that its tenants have come to expect.

Another virtue that differentiates Rubenstein from its competition is its willingness to approach every acquisition target as a probable long-term investment. This approach is somewhat rare in the industry. When The Rubenstein Company prepares to acquire a new asset, it conducts an extremely thorough, due diligence process, stressing, based on Mark's background, the importance of the building's technology. If a building's systems aren't of the highest quality, the company immediately plans an upgrade. Capital improvement and renovation programs are designed, and cost-saving initiatives are set in motion. While this often means putting money into areas of operation that are not necessarily visible to the tenant's eye, it better ensures future cost-effective and problem-free

▶ **Radnor Corp. Center.**

building services. Tenants notice the immediate positive changes when their buildings are acquired by The Rubenstein Company.

A final critical factor to the success of The Rubenstein Company has been its home base—the city of Philadelphia itself. While the company owns property throughout the East Coast, and despite a business desire to diversify regionally, the company always comes back to the city it knows best. Philadelphia, for The Rubenstein Company, has been a very wise investment. The company believes strongly in the business vitality of Philadelphia, in the quality of its cultural institutions, in its regional beauty, in its people and their productivity, and in the city's future. The Rubenstein Company is dedicated to, and actively supports this growth and continues to invest in creating a better business climate for Philadelphia businesses.

The Rubenstein family has been a major supporter of the Philadelphia Museum of Art, MCP/Hahnemann University Hospital, the Children's Hospital of Philadelphia, and certain of the city's many universities. Senior Rubenstein managers participate on a wide range of civic boards and organizations.

The future plans of The Rubenstein Company involve patient, controlled, intelligent investment and expansion into other geographic markets while continuing to raise its visibility in its home city of Philadelphia. Competitors have come to recognize Rubenstein as a quiet, very smart, very professional company, while its tenants, vendors, equity partners, and lenders understand that they will always get the treatment they want and deserve from one of the nation's finest real estate companies. ☉

◀ 321

▸ Turner Construction

*T*urner Construction Company was founded in 1902 by Henry C. Turner and DeForrest H. Dixon. Early on, the company distinguished itself as a front-runner in the market of reinforced concrete. Over the years, the company would grow and expand, not only in terms of size, but also in the areas of product involvement.

Today Turner employs over 4,700 men and women in 42 offices throughout the country and has established a broader geographic presence in the United States than any other construction company. From pre-construction services through construction management and general contracting services, Turner possesses unparalleled experience in its field, by combining the accessibility and support of a local firm with the strength and resources of a national corporation. Turner is able to provide a complete range of construction and program management services in all segments of the building market, running the gamut of project types, including hospitals, airports, office buildings, and sports facilities. The size and scope of Turner Construction allows the company to complete an average of more than 1,000 projects each year. These ventures range in size and complexity from less than $1 million to well over $300 million.

During its long history in Philadelphia, the company has taken part in a long list of memorable projects, including the Bell Atlantic Tower, Mellon Bank Center, Strawbridge & Clothier, Four Seasons Hotel, the Philadelphia Electric Company high-rise, Commerce Squares one and two, 10 and 11 Penn Center, as well as Franklin Field. As we settle into the 21st century things haven't changed, Turner still remains in the forefront of the industry; building some of the most exciting projects in Philadelphia. Some of the more notable projects are the National Constitution Center, Philadelphia's US Airways International Airport—International Terminal, and Lincoln Financial Field (Philadelphia Eagles Stadium), which are currently under construction. Employing over 200 people, Turner's

▲ **Bell Atlantic Tower (foreground) and Mellon Bank Center (background).**

Philadelphia office is poised to continue its' long tradition of contribution to the architectural landscape of Philadelphia while maintaining their commitment to the communities in which they build.

Turner's impact on the community goes far deeper than the high rises and stadiums it has helped to build. Realizing that success begins at an early age, Turner has become a major supporter of numerous education programs. Since 1999, Turner has been a sponsor of the City Year Program, an organization that promotes community involvement in high school graduates. After graduation, young men and women dedicate themselves to a year of service to the community. A graduate's year can involve anything from mentoring grade school children to establishing project based learning opportunities. Turner is also heavily involved in the ACE-

◀ **University of Pennsylvania—Sansom common.**

▲ **KPMG.**

mentoring program for the CHAD School, a charter high school for architecture and design. Professionals from Turner teach a series of seminars at the school, providing young people with a look at career opportunities in construction that they might not be familiar with, enlightening and motivating students to work toward careers in architecture, construction, engineering, and other related fields. The year concludes with a final presentation and a graduation ceremony. Similar programs have also been developed for the Adaire Elementary School and on a more sophisticated level the George

Washington Carver High School. In addition, Turner is involved in developing, sponsoring, and managing an annual golf outing for Girard College. A former orphanage, Girard is now a school for disadvantaged children who would otherwise not get the opportunities provided by a private school education. Turner's golf outings have raised more than $330,000 dollars for Girard since 2000. By lending aid to these schools, as well as other charitable organizations, Turner Construction strives to help build strong foundations for tomorrow's leaders.

Turner Construction has established itself as one of the finest firms in its industry for a number of reasons. First and foremost is the quality of the people that Turner seeks to employ. While companies in every industry are constantly looking to hire and keep good people on staff, Turner succeeds. The number of highly skilled men and women employed by Turner would be hard-pressed for any construction company to match. There seems to be a feeling of dedication that is exhibited by every member of Turner Construction, from the highest levels of the management team to the newest members of the staff. It's not uncommon to see people spend their entire careers with the company.

A comprehensive focused effort has gone into establishing Turner as one of the most efficient companies in the industry. The organization and structure of each office is based off of a single pattern, and company wide-computer and information systems that make it easier for data to be passed from one office to another.

◀ 3 2 3

▼ **Lincoln Financial Field.**

Where size is often considered to be detrimental to a company's efficiency, Turner is able to use its size and the shared experiences of many of their offices to make itself even more efficient.

Throughout its existence, Turner Construction has demonstrated an ability to adapt itself to the changing times and continually evolving needs of its clients. A great many things have changed for Turner since its' founding over one hundred years ago. Where the company originally acted as a contractor, employing the carpenters, laborers, mechanical workers, pipe fitters, and electricians, Turner now takes on more of a professional managerial role. Rather than doing the actual onsite labor, Turner employees now find themselves tackling the huge organizational challenges that are involved in any major construction project.

Another obvious change has been the firm's ever-increasing utilization of information technology. In a relatively short time, computers have become an integral part of the construction management process. This has visibly reduced the management manpower requirement of each project. Continuing advances in computers and company software provide project managers better ways of monitoring almost every part of each project's construction more efficiently than ever before.

What may be the most important factors to Turner's continued success are the aspects of the company that haven't changed at all. While it might appear that the Turner of today, with a staff of over 4,500 completing more than $6 billion of construction annually, bears little resemblance to the operation begun by Henry Turner in 1902, the company continues to remain closely tied to the values and goals it was founded on.

▲ **Temple University Hospital.**

Henry Turner once said, "A promise made is a promise kept," a statement that reflected his attitude on how his company should approach each project. Never losing sight of that vision is what has allowed Turner Construction to grow into the industry leader it is today. Equally important is the deep-seated tradition of social responsibility and fair play that is recognized by all. Turner's EEO and affirmative action programs are widely praised and have become models for much of the construction industry. The men and women of Turner Construction take pride in such recognition, feeling that it has contributed to the perception of Turner as the best in its industry. Maintaining that reputation is also something they are proud of.

All of these factors have contributed to creating the recipe for success of Turner Construction. Turner and individual staff members have made significant contributions to the American construction industry, while its long history has provided the company with a reputation of cost-effective construction, project management

◀ **Cingular.**

▲ **Wildwoods Convention Center.**

Throughout the course of his career, Henry C. Turner would refer to his clients as "respected friends." His philosophies regarding integrity, concern for quality, and service to clients are reflected in Turner's mission statement, but also in the way the company continues to conduct itself. Having recently celebrated its 100th anniversary, Turner is preparing itself for its second century of business. Through teamwork and partnering, a strong sense of purpose, and a commitment to getting it right the first time, Turner Construction Company will continue to be the leader in providing building construction services. ℗

experience, and a list of long-standing relationships. Turner-built projects are constantly being recognized for superior construction performance by national and local chapters of the Associated General Contractors of America and other organizations. Most importantly, Turner's quality of product and service has resulted in more than 60 percent of the company's business coming from clients who have worked with Turner in the past.

Turner construction has made it a mission to: "be the recognized leader in providing building construction services, both nationally and in every location in which Turner operates. We will achieve this by consistently exceeding our commitments and the expectations of our clients, design professionals, subcontractors, vendors, and the community at large. These services will be delivered by a team oriented, responsive, innovative, reliable, ethical, and skilled staff who participate in world-class training and development programs, and benefit from the career employment opportunity."

▶ **Philadelphia International Airport, Terminal B/C.**

▸ Brandywine Realty Trust

*S*ince 1988, when it changed over from Linpro Specified Properties, Brandywine Realty Trust worked hard to plant its roots deeper into the Greater Philadelphia region. With the transition to Brandywine, the company continued to expand its holdings from just four properties until it has become the Mid-Atlantic region's premiere full-service real estate company. Brandywine Realty Trust is a completely integrated real estate operating company, organized as a real estate investment trust, and is involved in the ownership, management, leasing, acquisition, and development of office and industrial properties, primarily in the suburban areas of the Mid-Atlantic United States. With a steadily growing portfolio that included 20.3 million square feet in 2001, Brandywine Realty Trust is recognized as the largest landlord in one of the largest real estate markets in the nation with more than 25 percent of the market share of the suburban Philadelphia office market. The company is headquartered in Plymouth Meeting, Pennsylvania, and has regional offices in Mount Laurel, New Jersey, and Richmond, Virginia.

Brandywine Realty Trust is positioned to meet the needs of virtually any business. The company currently holds the highest concentration of office properties and key development parcels of any company in the region. These properties are all located in much sought-after, high-exposure areas that provide timeless appeal to tenants who are able to take advantage of the company's sizeable market share by being offered excellent locations, amenities, and flexibility.

While the majority of companies in a variety of fields are constantly working to expand their holdings and operations to a national or even global marketplace, Brandywine Realty Trust has focused on a decidedly concentrated area of operations. In choosing to focus on developing and strengthening its standing in the Greater Philadelphia marketplace, Brandywine has put itself in a position that will allow it to continue to lead this marketplace.

▲ Cira Centre (rendering), 30th and Arch Streets, Philadelphia, Pennsylvania.

This targeted geographic focus provides the company a deep understanding of the real estate climate and business community, giving Brandywine Realty Trust a significant competitive advantage. The company's extensive market knowledge and financial strength gives Brandywine the resources it needs to take advantage of opportunities to meet the needs of its tenant base.

Reliance on solid business fundamentals has always played an important role in Brandywine Realty Trust's success. With a company strategy that includes operating in markets with high barriers to entry, Brandywine is poised to continue its market leadership and dominance. Due to the large number and wide variety of its holdings, Brandywine Realty Trust can accommodate the needs of any type of corporate client.

Brandywine also is extremely conscious of who it selects as tenants for its various properties. Brandywine Realty Trust possesses a portfolio that

◀ 100 Brandywine Boulevard, Newtown, Pennsylvania.

▲ **400 Berwyn Park, Berwyn, Pennsylvania.**

leadership, customer service, development expertise, and charitable giving. It is through the hard work of our team of professionals and our own passion for excellence that Brandywine Realty Trust has been able to maintain its position as the number one landlord in the suburban Philadelphia marketplace," noted Gerard H. Sweeney, President and CEO of Brandywine.

Brandywine Realty Trust prides itself on the capacity of its development team to deliver an unprecedented breadth of experience, as well as a vast amount of resources, to each and every project. Enduring quality, responsiveness to tenant needs, a team effort in building the company's market share, and maintaining high occupancy rates throughout its portfolio continue to drive Brandywine's development focus.

One of the most recent innovations that Brandywine has brought to its properties is e-Tenants. The first of its kind, the program came

contains a balanced cross-section of the Mid-Atlantic market. Tenants of varying business types, sizes, and leasing terms can be seen in Brandywine holdings. Since there is no shortage of businesses that wish to locate to a Brandywine facility, the company is able to be highly selective of its potential tenants, yet maintain its steady growth.

An efficient operating platform always has been vital to Brandywine Realty Trust. This consists of maintaining full integration of the regional offices and constantly working to increase and expand the company's already extensive knowledge of the local market, thus ensuring that Brandywine will continue to stay a step ahead of its competitors.

The final fundamental element of the Brandywine success story is its highly motivated team of professionals. Brandywine employees are among the best talent in the real estate industry. Employees share the vision, mission, and values that have made their company the leader it is today. Hiring the best employees, challenging them to achieve, and keeping them happy is another skill that Brandywine has cultivated over the years. The fact that the company has been honored as one of the best mid-sized companies to work for in the state of Pennsylvania is a credit to Brandywine's unique combination of company strength and entrepreneurial spirit.

"I take a tremendous amount of personal pride in knowing that Brandywine Realty Trust has set the example for community

▶ **Three Christina Centre, Wilmington, Delaware.**

online in May of 2000. e-Tenants provides commercial real estate tenants with a value-added amenity program available via the Internet. The process offers a cache of online services including 24/7 concierge and personal assistant services, an expeditious service request feature, a pre-qualified directory of exclusive business discounts, and office relocation assistance, just to name a few. Currently e-Tenants has been adopted by 100 percent of Brandywine's tenant companies and over 6,600 individuals. While there have been several attempts on the part of other companies to reproduce the e-Tenants model, none have been able to achieve what e-Tenants has folded into a single-source tenant amenity. A separate but wholly owned company of Brandywine Realty Trust, e-Tenants is available to other national and regional commercial real estate landlords that continually strive to distinguish their portfolio and provide extraordinary service.

Brandywine Realty Trust possesses extensive capabilities that give it the assurance of an uncompromised capacity to satisfy the space requirements of a steadily growing tenant base. Brandywine also has amassed impressive land holdings in order to accommodate future development opportunities. These holdings are located throughout the company's target markets, and the large majority of them are adjacent to properties already owned by Brandywine Realty Trust. The land offers the company room to grow and will

▲ Arboretum III, Richmond, Virginia.

accommodate well over four million square feet of office and industrial space, giving Brandywine and its tenants even more room to evolve.

In an attempt to identify an opportunity that could significantly impact the region, in May 2002, Brandywine Realty Trust announced that it was awarded the rights to develop the Cira Centre designed by Cesar Pelli Associates. Pelli Associates is recognized the world over for their involvement in a number of the world's highest quality office developments. Development of this site is at Amtrak's 30th Street Station in the University City section of downtown Philadelphia. "With this development, we see the ability to create a neighborhood; an extraordinary environment; a place that is vibrant, exciting, and has the ability to positively impact the basic foundation of University City, as well as appealing to tenants from both within and outside the region," said Mr. Sweeney.

Brandywine has become adept at applying fresh, innovative strategies to create new value for the tenants of its properties. Alternatives such as office renovation, adaptive reuse, and new construction offer the greatest long-term solutions for some of the

◀ 2000 Lenox Drive, Lawrenceville, New Jersey.

many challenges that real estate companies face, as well as enabling the company to preserve open space that becomes increasingly valuable as the region continues to grow and prosper. At the same time, Brandywine works to balance development with ecological preservation by incorporating the most energy- and resource-efficient materials and systems in its facilities. The company takes these steps, proving its awareness of where and what it plans to develop, minimizing the impact of its projects on the natural environment.

Brandywine Realty Trust, in addition to being a strong corporate member of the Greater Philadelphia community, has taken an active role in key civic and charitable organizations, including the National Association of Industrial and Office Properties (NAIOP). Many members of the staff at Brandywine play active roles within the organization, while several company executives dedicate their time filling important positions in the national organization. The company also has led the way in fundraising efforts for non-profit charities that include Habitat for Humanity, Race for the Cure, Gift for Kids, Walk to Cure Diabetes, the Salvation Army, and the Multiple Sclerosis foundation, as well as a number of other altruistic organizations, and hosts numerous blood drives throughout the year.

All of these factors add up to creating a company that is focused on providing unparalleled service to its valued customer base. Brandywine Realty Trust employs a fully deployed management staff that strives to anticipate its customers' needs and provides powerful tools in order to help each tenant achieve his or her business goals. The direct result of all the hard work and dedication of the executives and staff of Brandywine Realty Trust has been the establishment of one of the highest tenant retention rates in the industry. ℗

▲ **401 Plymouth Road, Plymouth Meeting, Pennsylvania.**

◀ 3 2 9

▶ **200 Berwyn Park, Berwyn, Pennsylvania.**

▶ Ewing Cole Cherry Brott

For over forty years, Ewing Cole Cherry Brott has been providing architecture, engineering, interior design, and planning services to clients nationally and internationally. Alexander Ewing founded the firm in 1961 with the goal to provide quality design and construction consulting services to clients throughout the Delaware Valley. Today, Ewing Cole Cherry Brott is a full-service firm of over 270 design professionals, headquartered in Philadelphia, Pennsylvania with offices in Washington, DC; Cleveland, Ohio; and Los Angeles, California.

The firm went through several name changes before becoming Ewing Cole Cherry Brott in 1993. Although the name has changed to reflect additional partners, the firm's commitment to design excellence remained the same.

Ewing Cole Cherry Brott is the second largest A/E firm in Philadelphia and ranks among the Top 100 A/E firms in the world. Ewing Cole's portfolio includes a diverse collection of projects in the healthcare, academic, cultural, research and development, sports and entertainment, corporate interior, and government markets. Providing a wide range of services to multiple markets has allowed Ewing Cole Cherry Brott to weather the economic vicissitudes and enjoy steady growth over its four-decade history.

The firm's early years were focused primarily in the healthcare market, and today, Ewing Cole Cherry Brott has worked with almost every healthcare institution within a one hundred mile radius of its office in Philadelphia's Independence Mall. The experience gained in the healthcare field provided valuable infrastructure and design talent that prepared the firm for diversification that began in the 1970s.

Ewing Cole Cherry Brott has designed large, complex projects for many of the region's leading businesses and institutions, including Fox Chase Cancer Center, Children's Hospital of Philadelphia, Wyeth Pharmaceuticals, Rohm and Haas, the Philadelphia Phillies, University

▲ **Fox Chase Cancer Center, Philadelphia, Pennsylvania.** Photo by Tom Bernard

of Pennsylvania, Thomas Jefferson University Hospital, the Philadelphia Museum of Art, Franklin Institute, Delaware Investments, Wolf Block Schorr and Solis-Cohen, and Kvaerner Philadelphia Shipyard.

The Kvaerner Philadelphia Shipyard project is representative of the firm's ability to manage complicated and technologically sophisticated projects. Ewing Cole Cherry Brott managed, designed, and engineered the first new shipyard built in the United States since World War II in record time and within an extremely aggressive schedule. The project revitalized the shipbuilding business in the city and created over 10,000 new jobs for Philadelphia.

Another high profile Ewing Cole project is the Philadelphia Phillies new ballpark. When it opens in April of 2004, the Philadelphia Center City skyline will be the backdrop for the open-air ballpark featuring natural grass and a dirt playing field that combines the essence of Philadelphia's rich tradition of sports architecture with an unmistakably modern 21st century style.

◀ **Kvaerner Philadelphia Shipyard, Philadelphia, Pennsylvania.** Photo by Jeffrey Totaro

▲ **New Phillies Ballpark, Philadelphia, Pennsylvania.**
Courtesy of Ewing Cole/AEI Digital

Ewing Cole has been working for Fox Chase Cancer Center since 1980. Tremendous growth, coupled with the need to bring research and patient care together led to Ewing Cole's most recent project for Fox Chase, the Cancer Prevention Pavilion. The Pavilion houses the Research Institute for Cancer Prevention, the first comprehensive program of its kind in the nation, dedicated to preventing cancer. This advanced research facility allows scientists to integrate their work with clinical trials and risk assessment programs. Ewing Cole is designing projects that integrate medical advances with environments that provide compassionate patient care.

An example of Ewing Cole's interior design expertise is represented in the recent relocation of the Delaware Investments headquarter offices into two connecting buildings in downtown Philadelphia. Programming and test fits were utilized to select the new facility which now occupies approximately 450,000 square-feet. It includes such amenities as a state-of-the-art training center and auditorium, lunchroom, computer room, trading desk, and investor center.

▶ **Singapore Turf Club, Kranji, Singapore.**
Photo by Erhard Pfeiffer

Ewing Cole's design expertise has been recognized with several awards. Most recently the Boardwalk Hall (formerly the Historic Atlantic City Convention Hall) received the 2002 New Jersey Historic Preservation Award, the 2002 *Building Magazine's* Modernization Award, and was also named 2001 Renovation Project of the Year by *New York Construction News*. The firm has received the NAVFAC Commander's Award and Construction Specification Institute's Environmental Sensitivity Award for our work at Washington Navy Yard's Building 33; and the Air Mobility Command Design Award for the design of the McGuire Ambulatory Health Care Center at McGuire Air Force Base. In addition, our lighting design practice is the recipient of thirteen International Illumination Design Awards, Philadelphia Section.

Ewing Cole understands that in order to attract and retain the very best design professionals, it is important to mentor, develop, and enhance the skills of its professionals. To support this goal, the firm holds in-house seminars where team members present their project to the entire firm, encouraging a cross fertilization of design ideas. AIA Continuing Education credits, Engineering Review meetings, and software training classes are held regularly to keep all design professionals abreast of the latest technological advances in the industry.

◀ 331

While Ewing Cole's origins were focused on serving a regional client base, today the firm views expansion as a critical tenant of its future. In addition to Philadelphia, Ewing Cole also has offices in Cleveland, Ohio, Washington, DC (whose client list includes projects for the National Institutes of Health, the Smithsonian Institution, the National Gallery of Art, and the Holocaust Museum) and, most recently, Los Angeles, California.

While Ewing Cole's origins were focused on serving a regional client base, today the firm views expansion as a critical tenet of its future and has expanded to include offices in Cleveland, Ohio; Washington, D.C.; and Los Angeles, California. Ewing Cole's national presence, experience, and design expertise were instrumental in recently being awarded a project to assist the American Red Cross on its ten-year, $1 billion expansion program across the United States. ℗

▶ General Building Contractors Association

*I*n the early 1700s, a group of builders from Philadelphia founded their own trade association with the intention of protecting their businesses and insuring their reputations by enforcing certain rules about doing business and upholding standards in quality. Currently the oldest and one of the most respected associations of its kind in the United States, the modern outgrowth of that original group is known as the General Building Contractors Association. Today's GBCA is infinitely more complex and deals with a variety of issues the founders of the original trade organization never could have imagined. From the beginning, GBCA has been determined to protect the interests of its members and, over the course of its long history, has become an integral part of the city's landscape.

GBCA is primarily an association of contractors engaged in commercial building. Because commercial construction is an industry where numerous companies are often necessary to complete a single project, it is not practical for labor unions to negotiate contracts with each individual contractor in the Philadelphia region. GBCA is able to simplify the process by negotiating and administering collective bargaining agreements, on behalf of management, with all of the industry's basic trades.

The GBCA is also involved in a variety of other programs that benefit its members. Utilizing the resources provided by the Industry Advancement Program, the GBCA sponsors a very ambitious education program, which includes "Buildup," a program that goes into effect at the 5th grade level and helps to inform children about the construction industry. GBCA is a major supporter of the Charter High School for Architecture and Design (CHAD), as well as several apprentice training programs jointly administered with the unions.

The association has developed an extremely successful annual building awards program, which recognizes the quality and skill of its contractor members. It also runs a Mentor-Protégé Initiative, which pairs member construction firms with emerging construction firms in the Philadelphia area.

GBCA takes on a number of other roles, including advising its members on safety issues, OSHA citation handling, working closely

▲ **GBCA Headquarters at 36 South 18th Street, Philadelphia, Pennsylvania.**
Photo by Barry Halkin

with the American Institute of Architects on contract provisions, monitoring legislation, and lobbying on behalf of its members in state and local government settings.

Since it was first established, the GBCA has served as a forum for the contractors of Philadelphia to discuss the different issues of importance in the construction industry. GBCA is an extremely reliable source of information to the community. By maintaining a mutually beneficial, non-adversarial relationship with organized labor, the association prides itself in its labor/management cooperative efforts. As the industry continues to change and become more and more complex, the GBCA will continue to search for new and innovative ways to adapt and improve its service to its members, helping them to build a better Philadelphia. ℗

◀ **Future constructors listen attentively to Philip Radomski, Vice Chairman of GBCA's Board of Directors, during an on-site BuildUp! class.**
Photo ©2002 John McGrail

CHAPTER SEVENTEEN

Sports

There is something hypnotic about the hold sports have over the people of Philadelphia. Here one finds more knowledgeable, dedicated, and enthusiastic sports fans per capita than most other places on earth.

Photo ©2002 John McGrail

▶ Philadelphia Phillies

A **world-class ballpark in Philadelphia!** The 43,000-seat, state-of-the-art Phillies Ballpark is undoubtedly the ultimate baseball and entertainment experience. Featuring natural grass, a dirt playing field, a scenic view of the Philadelphia skyline, an open-air atmosphere, and more, the Phillies Ballpark is an exciting destination for all fans.

The Ballpark is located on a 21-acre site in South Philadelphia on the north side of Pattison Avenue, between 11th and Darien Streets. This new venue, which opens in April 2004, combines the essence of Philadelphia's rich tradition of sports architecture with an unmistakably modern 21st century style.

Designed To Be The Very Best

As fans approach the Ballpark, they are immediately greeted with a breathtaking view of a Philadelphia-style sports-facility clad in red steel, brick, and stone. At home plate, third base, and first base, there are 50-foot high glass enclosed towers that glow at night when lighted. When walking towards the corner plazas, the steel framed seating bowl and glass towers flank the primary entrances and are a key visual element in the Ballpark's architecture. This remarkable sight is certain to become one of the most well known landmarks in Philadelphia.

Adding to the Ballpark's many fan-specific design elements is an unique opportunity to catch a glimpse of the field from outside the gates. This design was enabled by a walk-around open-air concourse that was intentionally created to keep fans connected to the game at all times. So when fans enter the gates and approach the main concourse, the enticing preview of the grass-and-dirt field quickly comes to full view.

The main concourse, just a few feet from each gated entrance, is located at street level—no more ramps to access this very popular area! The four primary entrances lead directly to the airy main concourse and an open view of the playing field. Since the field is located below ground level, nearly half of the fans entering the Ballpark step down to their seats.

One of the many features that makes the Ballpark exceptional is its intimate environment, created by two leading architectural firms: Ewing Cole Cherry Brott (ECCB), Philadelphia, Pennsylvania, and HOK Sport+Venue+Event (HOK SVE), Kansas City, Missouri. With the goals of placing fans closer to the action and maximizing sightlines to the field, the architects decided to combine "bowl" style seating with a field that is recessed 23 feet below street level. Inspired by the classic plans of Baker Bowl, home of the Phillies until 1938, and Connie Mack Stadium, formerly Shibe Park, which housed the team until 1971, the seating bowl features a cantilevered

structure—another design element that ensures fans are placed right on top of the action. Just the fact that the Phillies Ballpark could fit inside Veterans Stadium—with plenty of room to spare—clearly indicates how intimate the Ballpark truly is.

Playing Field Facts

The architects orientated the playing field with home plate situated in the southern part of the Ballpark site and opened up the outfield area to capture the Philadelphia Center City skyline. What an awesome experience to watch a Phillies game and see the sun set on the beautiful downtown Philadelphia skyline!

To have a Ballpark that is world-class includes having field dimensions that are entertaining for fans and a playing field that is fair to both pitchers and hitters. Taking this into account, the Phillies once again encouraged ECCB & HOK SVE to develop a uniquely shaped outfield wall that creates a new and fun dynamic to fielding balls. The result is a distinctive shape in the wall just left of center field, where unique angles create a corner with distances that extend from 381 feet to 385 feet and reduce to 369 feet at the left field power alley. Just left of center field, the angled center field wall that is 6 feet high creates a corner with a wall that is 19 feet high—establishing the deepest part of the field at 409 feet.

This is no doubt a fair ballpark for pitchers and hitters, with dimensions of straightaway center at 401 feet, the power alleys at 369 feet, left field at 329 feet, and right field at 330 feet. A favorite among fans is left field—where many enjoy watching players climb the 8-foot wall right before their eyes.

There are those times, too, when fans are treated to exciting pitcher's duels—which are more likely to be experienced when the wind is blowing hard from the north and the batters are hitting the ball high into the air. For those fans who want to increase their chances of catching a home run ball, they make sure to bring their glove on a warm night when the wind is blowing from the south and position themselves in the direction of the wind.

The overall field geometry of the Ballpark is based on straight lines and is angular, and the shape of the field between the foul poles is reminiscent of Shibe Park. Fans are closer to every swing of the bat since the distance from home plate to the backstop is 49 1/2 feet—that's 10 feet closer than what fans are accustomed to at Veterans Stadium. The distance from each dugout to the nearest baseline is 51 feet.

It's Much More Than A Ballpark

In addition to all the Phillies' action on the field, there's also plenty of action off the field. Take the festive outfield entertainment area which spans the entire outfield concourse. From the left field scoreboard entrance to the right field seats, fans can experience family-fun amenities, lively entertainment, and enhanced concessions offering a variety of delicious foods and refreshments. This area definitely makes a trip to the Ballpark an incredible experience.

Also located within the Ballpark are four larger-than-life bronze statues honoring Phillies legends Mike Schmidt, Steve Carlton, Robin Roberts, and Richie Ashburn. Created by world-renowned sculptor Zenos Frudakis, these amazing life-like replicas will no doubt be cherished by baseball fans for years to come.

Another unique characteristic is the rooftop bleacher seats. These fun bleacher seats are located on the roof of the outfield entertainment buildings and have a clear view of the baseball field. In fact, during the design stages of the Phillies Ballpark, fans indicated their interest to have bleacher seats incorporated into the architecture of the facility—in an effort to be reminiscent of Shibe Park/Connie Mack Stadium, where many fans enjoyed major league games from their rooftops on 20th Street. These seats are definitely a fan favorite, and are sure to be a top seating choice.

The bullpen viewing area, a highly sought after location, is designed so all can see their favorite pitchers warming up, talking strategies, or anxiously waiting to get the call. It's just another way to get fans closer to the action, which means no more guessing who's up in the bullpen—so fans, just leave those binoculars at home. These bi-level bullpens were designed to enhance the fans' experience as the pitchers prepare for their grand entrance to the natural grass and dirt field.

Many fans enjoy walking around the Ballpark and stopping at the Special Viewing Area to soak up the sights. At this specific place, all can watch the ballgame and catch a glimpse of the spectacular Center City Philadelphia skyline. This viewing area, created by a unique opening in the upper level bowl, is located on the first base side of the Ballpark and is a must see.

Food And Fun

Of course at the Ballpark everyone always gets the munchies, so why not try one of the many tasty food options—from traditional ballpark fare, such as hotdogs, popcorn, and peanuts, to food with plenty of Philadelphia flavor, such as cheese steaks, pretzels, water, ice, and more. For those who like to grab a quick bite and eat in their seats, there is a variety of food offered throughout the open-air concourses and in the outfield entertainment area.

Fans who prefer a seated environment dine at one of the two restaurants: Scoreboard Restaurant and Sports Pub Cafe. The Scoreboard Restaurant is the perfect location for food and fun. Here fans are able to take their family, friends, and clients to dinner or lunch—and never miss a pitch. Located at the northwest corner entrance inside the scoreboard, this unique bi-level restaurant offers two different views: one perspective directly of the field and the other of the Center City Philadelphia skyline.

Another popular eating spot with a more relaxed atmosphere is the Sports Pub Cafe. Located in the southwest corner of the Ballpark, the Sports Pub Cafe is bustling with action. Here fans enjoy delicious food and mingle with friends before, during, and after the game. Plus, there are large screen televisions—keeping everyone connected to the ballgame.

Adding to the unlimited entertainment opportunities offered at the Ballpark are 72 world-class suites, the Diamond seating area, and the unique Club areas. These areas were specifically designed to be a perfect fit for those with premium needs for entertaining.

This Ballpark is not just another home for the Phillies—it's the only place in Philadelphia where fans can have the ultimate baseball and entertainment experience. From watching your favorite Phillies pitcher take the mound on a natural grass and dirt field, to bringing the family for an afternoon of fun in the outfield entertainment area, to catching a home run down the left field power alley—all are guaranteed to have a great time, at any place in the Ballpark.

Fans will no doubt treasure every experience and look forward to creating new memories with each visit to the Phillies Ballpark for years to come.

This editorial was printed in 2002, prior to the opening of the New Ballpark in 2004. Go to phillies.com for updated information on the Phillies Ballpark.

Special Features

▲ It's more than just a Ballpark—there's delicious food, great entertainment and activities, and much more.

Measuring Up for Success!
Wall Distances & Heights

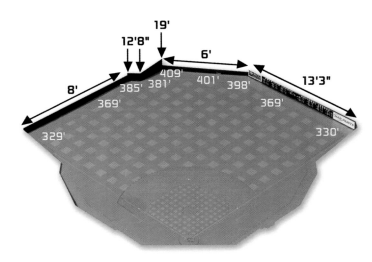

▲ Phillies New Ballpark: unique field dimensions and a playing field that's fair to both pitchers and hitters.

▼ View of the northwest plaza entrance located near the festive outfield entertainment area and Scoreboard Restaurant.

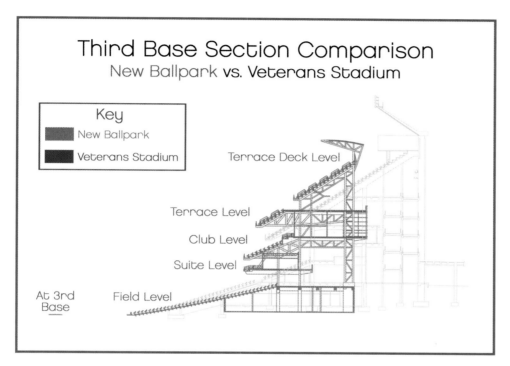

Third Base Section Comparison
New Ballpark vs. Veterans Stadium

Key
New Ballpark
Veterans Stadium

Terrace Deck Level

Terrace Level

Club Level

Suite Level

At 3rd Base   Field Level

◀ **Enjoy being closer to the action! This intimate New Ballpark can actually fit inside of Veterans Stadium.**

▼ **A fun day in the sun at the Phillies Ballpark.**

▸ The Philadelphia Eagles

*I*t was an experience that Jeffrey Lurie won't forget. The Philadelphia Eagles had just defeated the Bears in the NFC Divisional Playoff game and advanced to the NFC Championship game.

The thrill of victory was just as great as the challenge ahead. The Eagles were to next face the St. Louis Rams and the winner would advance to the Super Bowl.

And Lurie, the Eagles' Chairman/CEO, was as excited as any long-time fan.

"It culminated in a victory where you said, 'We're going to the NFC title game. We're one of the two best teams in the conference and if we win next week, we're in the Super Bowl.'"

"There's little that can be a bigger high than that," he added. "From what we've been able to build, with all the work this organization puts in year-round—the players, the coaches, the entire organization—it was just a moment when I felt, 'Boy, we've achieved a lot and there's so much more we're going to achieve.'

"That feeling, that's why you want to own a team, work for a team, or be a fan of a team. It was a moment of real pride, real excitement."

The wonderful journey that was 2001 ended the following Sunday in St. Louis, but it dampened neither Philadelphia's enthusiasm for the Eagles or Lurie's commitment to the team and to the city. Indeed, both passions are as strong as ever and the results are impressive.

From 1995—Lurie's first full season as owner—through 2001, the Eagles earned four trips to the playoffs. Only Miami, Green Bay, and San Francisco reached the postseason more often in that span. From 2000-2001, the Eagles won 22 games, second only to St. Louis in the entire NFL.

On the field, the Eagles are young and growing and considered one of the favorites in the NFL in the near future. Off the field, the

▲ Quarterback Donovan McNabb (5) is among the league's most electrifying talents.

Eagles are now thought of as one of the most dynamic and progressive organizations in all of sports.

Lurie can look out of his office at the sparkling NovaCare Complex and see the team's new stadium, Lincoln Financial Field, racing toward its August, 2003 completion. The South Philadelphia landscape has changed, and the Eagles are dominating the scene.

"I'm very pleased with the direction of the organization," said Lurie. "It takes a real commitment to doing what we believe in, and we're very focused on being the best sports franchise possible, both on and off the field."

In fact, that is just what the Eagles are doing. While the 2001 season was capped by a trip to the NFC title game and a berth

◀ Pro Bowl defensive end Hugh Douglas (53), who is as quick with a quip as he is when rushing the quarterback, helped Eagles Youth Partnership launch the Eagles Book Mobile with a $50,000 contribution.

in the Pro Bowl for eight Eagles, the club's success off the field was just as striking and no less planned for.

The winter and spring of 2001 indeed marked the beginning of a new era in Eagles history.

In March of that year, the club formally opened its $37 million NovaCare Complex, a new corporate headquarters/training facility. The 108,000 square-foot facility is among the largest—and most cutting edge—in sports.

Just three months later, the team broke ground on what will be the crown jewel of sports and entertainment venues, Lincoln Financial Field.

Upon purchasing the Eagles, Lurie stated, unequivocally, that a new, state-of-the-art stadium would be a key component in building the Eagles into an elite franchise.

"I've said so often," added Lurie, "winning the Super Bowl is the ultimate goal of this organization. Stadiums and training facilities, however, are a vital element in the success and stability of franchises on both a present and long-term basis. As an organization, you want to assemble the best staff and the best players, but you also have to provide them with the best facilities and environment in which to achieve success.

"That's what we want to do with Lincoln Financial Field and what we've already done with the NovaCare Complex. With each venue we are making a dramatic leap, literally going from worst to first. Both will be striking in terms of their architecture and amenities, and both will be seen as icons not only of the Eagles, but also of Philadelphia. As Mayor John Street has said, "To move forward as a world-class city, we need world-class stadiums.' Now, with Lincoln Financial Field, a venue that will be unparalleled in its design, its

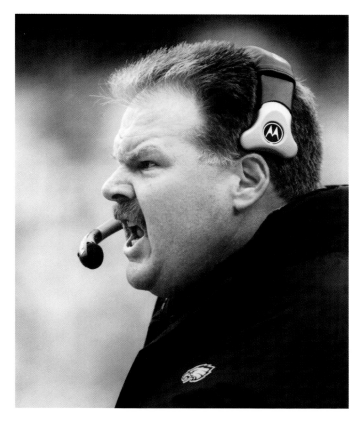

▲ Head Coach Andy Reid led his team to the playoffs in 2000 and, a year later, to the NFC Championship Game.

amenities, and its fan accommodations, the dynamism surrounding the Philadelphia Eagles—along with the image of the city of Philadelphia—will be elevated to new heights."

Added team President Joe Banner, "The new stadium, with its dramatic qualities and flexibility, is certain to enhance the image and climate of—not to mention the economic activity within—the Philadelphia region. The Army-Navy Game—which generates enormous revenues for the city—is just one example of a major event that belongs in Philadelphia. In terms of what it will mean to the club in a macro sense, it will enable us to be competitive financially while at the same time further defining us as a first-class organization.

"Our commitment to making the NovaCare Complex the best day-to-day headquarters in the league reflected our desire to succeed by providing our players and staff with what many observers have already called the best possible working environment in the NFL. Ultimately, our investment in Lincoln Financial Field will send a message about how driven we are with regard to achieving success and about how committed we are to enhancing the comfort and enjoyment of our fans."

◀ With a team contending for a Super Bowl title and with a new, amenity-filled, state-of-the-art stadium opening in 2003, Eagles fans—long known as the most passionate in America—have lots to cheer about.

Lincoln Financial Field

The new stadium will bring the fans so much closer to the field. It will provide them with dramatically improved sight lines and the most state-of-the-art amenities and services. In terms of technological enhancements, Lincoln Financial Field will represent a world of difference from what fans have experienced at The Vet and even from what is available in some of the newest facilities around the country.

The entire building is designed from a fan's perspective and with a fan's day-of-game experience in mind, from the time they drive into the lots to the time they leave. Outside of the fact that the new stadium and The Vet will have roughly the same number of seats (66,000), that's where the similarities end. The new stadium will be unique and spectacular in its own right, yet comfortable and accommodating.

Compared to The Vet, Lincoln Financial Field will feature twice as many seats in prime, sideline locations and 20 percent more seating in the lower bowl. The Eagles' new home will also feature 162 luxury suites and over 8,000 club seats. High-tech, experiential elements such as a distributed sound system and the biggest, most technologically advanced video boards in operation will entertain fans in a dramatic, positive "in-your-face" style. Outside, a 100,000 square-feet plaza will provide fans with an element never-before-seen at Philadelphia sporting venues—a large, centralized area for pre and post-game activities.

"The partnership between Lincoln Financial Group and the Eagles is one forged from similar visions and shared philosophies," said Lurie. "If we could have gone to the drawing board and designed a partner, Lincoln Financial Group would have been the one for a variety of reasons. From a business perspective, we are thrilled to be associated with one of the nation's leading financial services companies. And from a community standpoint, we are very proud to be associated with a Fortune 300 company that, like us, makes its home here in Philadelphia and is committed to making this city a better place.

"Lincoln Financial Group is a leader in its field. And in terms of being an active, caring corporate citizen, they are a leader in the

The Eagles are literally going from worst to first with the opening of their two new homes, Lincoln Financial Field and the NovaCare Complex. Each will be striking in terms of their architecture and amenities, and both will be seen as icons not only for the Eagles, but for Philadelphia as well.

community, having made it a priority to participate in the civic, cultural, and educational affairs of the region."

Eagles Youth Partnership

The Eagles' off-the-field success includes more than just the opening of a new stadium and corporate headquarters. Indeed, Lurie, who was named NFL Owner of the Year by *The Sporting News* in 1995 and by Fred Edelstein's *Pro Football Insider* in 2000, has described his philosophy of ownership as a "partnership between the city, the fans, and the team." As such, one of Lurie's primary objectives early on was the formation of Eagles Youth Partnership, the team's non-profit, charitable wing.

Established in 1995 by Lurie and his wife, Christina, Eagles Youth Partnership (EYP) has become a difference making—and award winning—venture. Moreover, EYP has developed into one of the most innovative and dynamic non-profits in Philadelphia and the NFL.

The mission of Eagles Youth Partnership is to enhance opportunities and improve the quality of life for children in the Greater Philadelphia region through health and education partnerships. The strategy for achieving that goal involves teaming the Eagles and their players with corporate and community partners in a "game plan" that delivers services, grants, incentives, and messages to children in a way that positively influences their lives.

◀ Twice named NFL owner of the year, Jeffrey Lurie, has overseen the Eagles' rise to prominence on and off the field. With his team contending for a championship and with the club's charitable wing, Eagles Youth Partnership, making a positive impact in the lives of children, the Eagles clearly rank among the NFL's elite clubs.

"We are in a position where we can be a catalyst for change," said Lurie. "People look to the sports teams as leaders. We can try to make a better life for more people…We really can make a difference."

EYP makes a difference in education by operating programs like the Eagles Bookmobile—which visits underserved children in schools, shelters, libraries, recreation centers, summer programs, and parks and provides them with free books—and by providing grants that seed new initiatives and enhance existing reading and after-school programs. Through the Eagles Top Achiever Awards program, the Eagles also recognize academic excellence.

EYP tackles health problems that block children from achieving their potential by implementing such programs as the Eagles Eye Mobile, which in its first six years of operation, provided free eye exams for more than 6,200 children and free prescription eyeglasses to those who were found to need them.

EYP also partners with numerous community groups each year on an annual day of service during which the entire Eagles organization builds a playground in an underserved community. To date, Eagles players, staff, coaches, and management have worked together with neighborhood adults and children to landscape, paint murals, inlay tile mosaic, and build play structures in six sections of the Philadelphia area. A grant from Eagles Youth Partnership covers the cost of each community build. ℗

◀ Each year, Eagles Youth Partnership and the entire Eagles organization join forces with community groups to build a playground in an underserved section of Philadelphia.

CHAPTER EIGHTEEN

Marketplace

King of Prussia Mall, the largest mall east of the Mississippi and the
second largest in the country, joins other retail establishments and service
industries of the Greater Philadelphia area as a vital part of the economy as
well as the quality of life throughout the Delaware Valley.
Photo ©2002 John McGrail

▶ Marriott Residence Inn

*W*eary travelers on the road will oftentimes settle for any hotel that may have a vacancy for a good night's rest. But at the Marriott Residence Inn of Philadelphia, those travelers will find much more than just a hot shower and a warm bed. It is here that guests experience the great service and comfortable atmosphere that have helped make Marriott one of the true giants in the hotel industry today.

Opened in 1993, this extended stay hotel near the airport caters to the needs of those people who are on short or long term assignments, relocating, or even during home damage and repair. The Marriott Residence Inn features two different suite types to satisfy each customer's needs. The first type is the studio suite, which is similar to an efficiency apartment with everything contained in one area. A comfortable sitting area with a large oversize working desk, the bedroom, and the bathroom occupy this area. The two-bedroom suites contain a kitchen in the center alongside a cozy living room and fireplace. On either side of this common area are two bedrooms that close off from the kitchen and living room, each equipped with its own bathroom.

Each of the 102 suites have kitchens that are fully equipped with full-sized refrigerators, microwaves, dishes, silverware, dishwashers, and coffee pots to make every guest's visit one of the most relaxing and productive stays that they could ever experience in a hotel setting. Each of these roomy suites are generally 50 percent larger than traditional hotel rooms, with the studio suites measuring approximately

▲ **The hotel consists of 17 buildings.** Photo ©2002 John McGrail

▼ **Gatehouse/Lobby Area where breakfast and socials are served.**

▲ **Studio Suite.** Photo ©2002 John McGrail

bagels, yogurt, fruits, and juices serve as the staples of a wide array of breakfast items, offering all that a guest could possibly ask for. There is also an evening social hour in the gatehouse Monday through Thursday, serving hors d'oeuvres to its guests after a hard day's work, as well as a manager's reception once a week. The manager's reception is a full-fledged dinner with complimentary beer and wine. Everything from veal parmesan and spaghetti to barbecued chicken is served at the manager's reception dinners and the weekly event has proven to be one of the hotel's most successful endeavors, with some guests actually planning their stay around the delicious and filling meals.

But there's more to the Marriott Residence Inn besides extra-large rooms and free dinners. The hotel and its 35 employees play a large role in the community with several charitable donations, as well as manpower devoted to organizations in the city that benefit greatly from the hotel's generosity. The Children's Miracle Network is one charity that has benefited from the devotion of the staff at the Marriott Residence Inn. Each holiday season, the employees stuff stockings and purchase gifts for small children to donate to the Salvation Army, a selfless act that brings so much

650 square feet, while the two-bedroom suites occupy 850 square feet of space. For those that will be spending more than a night at the hotel, this allotment of room and space gives each guest the closest experience to being at home as possible.

Guests are also welcome to partake in a complimentary hot breakfast buffet every morning that expands on the traditional continental breakfasts that most hotels are able to offer. Such items as

▼ **Main Entrance.** Photo ©2002 John McGrail

▲ **Gatehouse Lobby.**

joy to so many faces. Blood drives for the American Red Cross have been sponsored at the hotel in the past and will continue to play a large role in the future. In addition, Marriott sponsors a program called Spirit to Serve, which finds Marriott employees working alongside local organizations to help with city projects. Everything from cleaning up various lots around town to lending a hand in painting or constructing buildings is part of this wonderful program. On the local level, the full-service Marriott Hotels have lobbied with state officials in order to boost tourism in the state following the tragic events of September 11, 2001. Letters have been penned to congressmen, asking them to join the fight for tourism to help increase business in the hotel industry. Serving as a champion to causes that affect the company directly and indirectly, the people behind the Marriott name are continuously striving to make a difference in both the industry and the community as a whole.

There is little wonder how the Marriott chain has managed to climb to the top rungs of the hotel ladder. Whether it's a cozy evening curled up by the fireplace with a good book or a delightful dinner for two, the staff at the Marriott Residence Inn of

▶ **Swimming Pool and Spa Area.**

Philadelphia believes that if they can give each of their guests room to relax, room to work, and room to breathe, those customers will come back again and again. Add to that the desire to help out their fellow man and to keep selflessly dedicating their own time and energy to making sure that Philadelphia remains one of the most vibrant and exciting cities in the country, and you've discovered the secret to this hotel's success. ℗

▲ **Aerial View.** Photo ©2002 John McGrail

▶ **Two-bedroom suite.**

Photo ©2002 John McGrail

▸ B101

ndependence and innovation have been synonymous with Philadelphia since the time of Benjamin Franklin and the Revolutionary War. So it's no coincidence that the city's longstanding radio icon WBEB 101 FM has built its success in the industry and in the Philadelphia community on these very principles.

B101, as it is commonly referred to, is Philadelphia's highest rated radio station and, in an age of consolidation and media conglomerates, remains the only locally owned, independent radio station in a major U.S. market.

The station's roots can be traced back to 1957 when Founder and Partner David Kurtz first applied to the FCC for a broadcast license. The FCC granted the license in 1962 and WDVR (Delaware Valley Radio) 101.1 FM was born. Soon after, in 1963, shortly before the station went on the air, Kurtz was joined by station President and Partner Jerry Lee. Together they made a commitment to run their station with an entrepreneurial spirit, a passion for radio, and a desire to make the industry and the community better for their efforts.

Their first decision as a team was to broadcast Jerry's custom-designed "Beautiful Music" format, playing only songs that were familiar favorites. The unique format quickly paid off. Within four months of going on the air in May of 1963, 101.1 FM became the number one FM station in Philadelphia.

▲ Jerry Lee with the Bee Bus. A fleet of station vans with uniformed Bee Crew and Buzzbee the mascot show up all over the Delaware Valley with year-round promotions and prize giveaways.

A Station of Firsts

Philadelphia's top station soon established itself as the highest rated and top billing FM station in the country. At a time when AM was king, Jerry Lee and David Kurtz built their FM station into a huge success. It was the first FM station to bill one million dollars in a year and, by most accounts, established the viability of the FM band in radio.

The desire of the station's leadership to continually push the envelope has led to many innovations that have shaped the radio industry to this day. With the groundbreaking "Beautiful Music for Beautiful People" advertisements, the radio station was the first to produce a professional TV commercial. It was also one of the first radio stations to use celebrity spokespersons in television spots. The practice has become standard in the industry. B101 has used spokespersons such as Patrick O' Neal, Robert Urich, Teri Garr, and most recently, Candice Bergen.

After changing the call letters to WEAZ and the station's name to "Eazy-101," Jerry Lee initiated another marketing coup. In what's been called "The Radio Project," the station became the first to give listeners custom-designed radios tuned to a single station. Most recently B101 became the first radio station to provide links to the Web sites of each and every on-air advertiser.

B101 has always seemed to be one step ahead of the curve. When EAZY 101 was at the

◀ B-101's major annual charity event is the Stocking Stuffer program, which gives holiday stockings filled with toys to needy kids. Many schools participate, and last year over 50,000 stockings were delivered through the Salvation Army.

▲ Buzzbee has become one of the two most recognized mascots in the city and a big favorite of kids.

top of the Philadelphia market as an easy listening format station, Lee and Kurtz stunned the industry by changing the format to adult contemporary. After the format change the station would be known as EZ-101. The move paid off as EZ-101 was soon recognized as one of the top ten adult contemporary stations in the country. The willingness of Jerry Lee and David Kurtz to change when it is not the obvious or even popular choice has driven the station's continued growth in Philadelphia and the industry.

The Bee has Philadelphia Abuzz

Lee and Kurtz made another bold move in 1993 when EZ-101 changed to B101.1 FM. The focus of the station is now "all music, very little talk." B101 adopted Buzzbee as a mascot, making him Philadelphia's only radio mascot. The new mascot gives the station the ability to be more visible and active in the community. Buzzbee and the station's fleet of vans makes appearances and donations at events, fundraisers, and hospitals

▶ Following September 11, General Manager Blaise Howard and Jerry Lee donated $10,000 in the name of station clients to the Salvation Army New York Disaster Fund.

and is in line with the station's mission of giving back to the community.

The new mascot was not the only thing to change when the station became B101. The audience focus shifted to women. At a time when men were still thought by many to be the key demographic for advertisers, B101 did extensive research and determined that spending patterns were changing and women were emerging as family decision makers. The new focus has allowed B101 to carve out a new niche for the station with advertisers and deliver to a very desirable and concentrated audience. With groundbreaking programming like the public affairs show "The Woman's File," B101 has developed the largest and most loyal female audience in the Philadelphia market, far outdistancing the nearest competitor.

B101 has continued to grow and thrive with its new focus. The public affairs program, "Left, Right, Center," won a prestigious Pennsylvania Association of Broadcasters award for best locally-produced program and the Pennsylvania Association of Broadcasters named Jerry Lee Broadcaster of the Year in 1997.

With B101's tremendous success it has been the target of many acquisition attempts by large radio station groups or media conglomerates. The radio industry has been a frenzy of acquisitions and mergers for many years, but B101 remains the only locally owned independent radio station in a major U.S. market. From a financial standpoint it would be easy for Kurtz and Lee to sell, but they don't for two reasons—after all these years they still have a passion for radio and the station gives them the forum to make a difference in the community and with future generations of people.

"As broadcasters we not only have the ability to reach the public but a responsibility to use our voice to positively affect the society in

which we live," said Jerry Lee. "David and I have always taken that responsibility very seriously and have done our best to drive positive change by using the station and its resources."

The Station That Gives Back

With B101, community involvement isn't a hollow promise. The station and its owners have been involved in social programs at the local, national, and international levels. Jerry Lee created the Broadcast Industry Council to Improve American Productivity—an organization that has spearheaded national campaigns for literacy, productivity, and exports. The station's long-standing success has allowed Lee and Kurtz to continually grow their charitable initiatives. Working with the Salvation Army, B101 started an annual toy drive that has collected millions of dollars in toys for needy children.

Most recently Lee and Kurtz have turned their resources to crime fighting research and initiatives. In 2001, the University of Pennsylvania dedicated the Jerry Lee Center of Criminology.

▲ Jerry Lee, Philadelphia District Attorney Lynn Abraham, and former Attorney General Janet Reno celebrating the dedication of the Jerry Lee Center of Criminology at The University of Pennsylvania.
Photo by Toohey Brown

The center, the first research-based crime fighting organization of its kind, has attracted some of the top criminologists in the world and is the site of groundbreaking research projects and forums on the prevention of crime and terrorism. It is recognized as one of the top crime research centers in the world. Its largest current project is a $3.5 million contract with the English government to introduce and test "restorative justice" for serious adult offenses in London, Oxfordshire, and the Newcastle area, Northumbria.

Jerry Lee is just as passionate about crime fighting as he is about radio. He takes a very hands-on approach and serves on the board of several top national and international criminology organizations. He is the only non-criminologist who is a voting member of the Campbell Crime and Justice Group, an organization made up of the 14 top criminologists and Lee. He has also been instrumental in bringing to the center the Crime Justice Journalist Group, whose mission it is to inform crime reporters of which prevention programs work and which don't.

The Jerry Lee Center is the culmination of years of hard work and community mindedness by Jerry Lee, David Kurtz, and the whole B101 team. Kurtz and Lee have stayed true to their original vision. They built a very successful radio station and have made a difference in both the industry and their community.

◀ Running the morning show from a laptop: DJ Chris McCoy, Program Director Chris Conley, and Jerry Lee in the new digital studio.

Competing against huge media companies and radio groups, the locally owned B101 remains one of the top radio stations in Philadelphia and the country.

And no matter how large and successful B101 becomes it still embodies the spirit of the city in which it resides. The innovation and independence that are the symbols of Philadelphia are still the backbone of its most successful radio station, Philadelphia's own B101. ℗

▲ In an era of corporate giant radio, B-101 is still owned and operated by the founding partners, David L. Kurtz and Jerry Lee.

The Future Is Now

With all the success B101 and its owners have had they are not resting on their laurels. Every day the station is pushing for the next big idea. B101 utilizes the Internet to give advertisers easier access to their audience and greater opportunities for revenue. The station also continues to make significant investments in research and development as a means to drive programming success and gain a deeper insight into its audience's mindset. It is this ability to use technological advances and unconventional thinking that has continually given B101 a leg up on its competition.

When others have said that an independent station can no longer be successful in a major market, B101 continues to beat the odds.

▶ Improving inner city education is one of Jerry Lee's major interests as exemplified by the high school achieving students of The Gesu School.

▶ City of Philadelphia

*L*ong before anyone had even considered the idea of an independent nation in North America, Philadelphia was growing, establishing itself in the earliest chapters of American history. The city was founded in 1682 by William Penn, an English Quaker who dreamed of a community where others of his faith could find freedom of worship, as well as the opportunity to govern themselves and develop their own way of life. Penn had given his original settlers orders to found their great town in a place "where it is most navigable, high, dry, and healthy."

The location that would become Philadelphia was all of that, quickly evolving into a bustling center of trade, rivaling New York by the turn of the century. A rapidly growing economy, an attitude of religious tolerance, and Penn's rather radical policies, which allowed common citizens to take part in their government, as well as offering them the ability to practice their own religions, soon attracted thousands of English, German, and Scotch-Irish to the burgeoning colony. By the 1770s, due to its location and the savvy of the local businessmen, Philadelphia was among the three most important centers of business in the British Empire, as well as the political, economic, and military center of the North American colonies.

Considered to be the birthplace of American government, Philadelphia was witness to some of the most important moments in the birth of the United States. While originally in favor of reconciliation with Britain, the citizens of Philadelphia and the Commonwealth of Pennsylvania were among the most dedicated to the cause when it became obvious that peace was no longer possible. The city would be the site where the Declaration of Independence was signed in 1776 and the Constitution of the United States was adopted in 1787. It also would serve as the fledgling nation's capital from 1790 to 1800. Today, Philadelphia stands as a city with several faces, proudly celebrating its past, enjoying its continuing development, and eagerly anticipating the future.

▲ Philadelphia's City Hall, topped by the statue of William Penn by Alexander Milne Calder, as seen from the Swann Memorial Fountain at Logan Circle, with sculpture by Alexander Stirling Calder—son of Alexander Milne Calder and father of Alexander Calder, creator of mobile sculptures. Photo by Richard McMullin

Since its founding, Philadelphia's potential as a port, coupled with a healthful climate, made it an ideal capital for the growing colony. Today, location remains vital to the success of Philadelphia, but for different reasons.

Still important as a seaport, Philadelphia's role as one of the primary doorways to the United States has grown with the capabilities of the Philadelphia International Airport. A hub of US Airways, Philadelphia International Airport is one of the busiest airports in the country, welcoming guests and bringing in cargo from all over the world. Additionally, the city is centrally located between New York and Washington, D.C., and has excellent railway and highway systems, making it easily

◀ Independence Hall, where the Declaration of Independence was signed and the U.S. Constitution was created, shown at the City's official July 4th Independence Day celebration, including the presentation of the Philadelphia Liberty Medal. Photo by Richard McMullin

▲ The sky over the Philadelphia Museum of Art brilliantly illuminated with fireworks concluding Philadelphia's Fourth of July Celebration.
Photo by Richard McMullin

accessible from anywhere in the northeastern and southeastern United States.

This easy access continues to be one of the many characteristics that make Philadelphia appealing to companies that are looking into new areas for expansion. Extremely business-friendly city and state governments are willing to work to continue expanding the area's business and industrial base by providing tax breaks and other incentives to new companies. The second largest city on the East Coast, the population of the Greater Philadelphia metropolitan area now exceeds five million and continues to grow, providing a tremendous opportunity as far as potential customers and clients are concerned.

▶ Philadelphia's annual celebration of America's birthday in America's birthplace—the multi-day Sunoco Welcome America! series of events—features the spectacular "Pennsylvania-Memories Last A Lifetime" July 4th Parade on the Benjamin Franklin Parkway, with City Hall in the background. Photo by Richard McMullin

As well as providing profitable markets for businesses, Philadelphia is also home to more first-rate colleges and universities than anyplace else in the country, except for New York City. These highly respected institutions are an invaluable resource for employers in that they help provide an intelligent workforce with educations that are second to none.

Visitors to Philadelphia are able to find an endless variety of attractions to occupy their time. They can walk the same streets that Benjamin Franklin and the other founding fathers walked as they explore America's most historic square mile, visiting the Liberty Bell, Independence Hall, and the Betsy Ross House, among others. They can visit world-famous museums such as the Philadelphia Museum of Art, the Rodin Museum, The Barnes Foundation, The Franklin Institute Science Museum, and the Pennsylvania Academy of Natural Sciences, as well as experiencing some of the most prominent performing arts companies and touring presentations in the brand-new Kimmel Center for the Performing Arts, the permanent home of the Philadelphia Orchestra. Guests also can enjoy some of the city's world-class restaurants, the trend-setting shops and malls, or vibrant downtown nightlife. Sports fans find themselves immediately at home, cheering any one of Philadelphia's eight professional teams or premier sporting events, while many eagerly anticipate the completion of the new professional baseball and football stadiums now under construction.

In spite of its size, Philadelphia remains a city of neighborhoods, determined to take care of its neighbors and its children and constantly working to provide the highest quality of life in the safest environment possible. Philadelphia, the place that LOVES YOU BACK©, continues to seek out ways to grow and develop, looking after its own while welcoming newcomers into its community. ℗

◀ 355

▶ Philadelphia Convention & Visitors Bureau

The Philadelphia Convention & Visitors Bureau (PCVB) is the official sales arm for the City of Philadelphia, including marketing Philadelphia nationally and internationally as a first-tier destination for conventions, meetings, and tourism.

The PCVB, a 1,100-member, nonprofit organization, assists meeting planners, tour operators, and visitors with all aspects of meeting and touring in Philadelphia and serves as the main liaison to the city's hospitality community. The PCVB has a Board of Directors representing the travel industry that is made up of hospitality, business, civic, and government leaders.

Greater Philadelphia Health Care Congress: Due to the wide range of health-care institutions and research centers in Philadelphia, health-care related conventions account for more than one-third of all conventions held in Philadelphia each year. The Greater Philadelphia Health Care Congress, a PCVB-pioneered division made up of health-care professionals from the Philadelphia region, has played an integral role in bringing health-care conventions to Philadelphia. From 1993-2012, health-care conventions account for more than 1.5 million definite room nights valued at $525 million in delegate spending.

Philadelphia's ample meeting space and convenient hotels coupled with first-class dining, attractions, and shopping make it a great destination for groups of all sizes. The city is fit to accommodate the needs of corporate and mid-sized meetings, as well as citywide conventions, providing big city excitement with hometown charm. The PCVB's hallmark services, including Convention Sales, Convention Services, and Marketing Communications, provide first-class attention every step of the way to a successful corporate meeting or convention in Philadelphia.

▲ **The Pennsylvania Convention Center, the second-largest convention center in the Northeast, offers more than 440,000 square feet of exhibit space and the highest ratio of meeting room space to exhibit space in the country. The 1.3 million square-foot facility opened in 1993 and covers six downtown city blocks, central to retail, business, and cultural areas in the city.**

The PCVB's performance in servicing meetings and conventions has earned it many prestigious industry awards over the years, including being honored eight years in a row with the Gold Service Award from *Meetings & Conventions* magazine and with a 2001 Top Destination Award from *Facilities & Destinations* magazine. In addition to assisting with the planning of citywide conventions, the PCVB also serves as a one-stop-shop for corporate and small meeting planners who are looking to meet in Philadelphia.

Since 1993, more than 660 groups have met or plan to meet at the Pennsylvania Convention Center in Philadelphia, resulting in

◀ **Philadelphia, the nation's birthplace, is a colonial city with a modern outlook. This "city of neighborhoods" showcases many renowned historical landmarks, a thriving arts community, exciting restaurants and nightclubs, well-loved sports teams, and much more.**

▲ Be sure to visit Philadelphia's Chinatown where the elaborately designed "Chinese Friendship Gate" awaits visitors ready to explore the richness of various Asian cultures and cuisines.

Multicultural Affairs Congress: The Multicultural Affairs Congress (MAC), a division of the Philadelphia Convention & Visitors Bureau, is composed of ethnically diverse members representing a cross-section of Philadelphia's business, government, cultural, hospitality, and civic communities. MAC works to increase Philadelphia's share of national multicultural meetings and conventions, including support and promotion of multicultural institutions and attractions and increased educational and business opportunities for people of color. Since its inception in 1987, MAC has generated more than $500 million in meetings and convention business for the city. The department has been instrumental in helping to increase the number of minorities working in management positions at Philadelphia's leading hotels by more than 600 percent since its inception.

more than 5.7 million definite room nights and generating an average of $200 million in delegate spending per year. In 2002, Philadelphia hosted a record number of citywide conventions.

The Tourism Sales and Services Department of the PCVB develops and implements sales programs domestically and internationally in order to promote Philadelphia as a tourism destination. The department sells Philadelphia as a destination domestically to tour operators, group leaders, automobile clubs (AAA), wholesalers, and travel agents. The department's sales efforts, along with major tourism developments in the city, have led to the return of many operators for overnight stays. In 2002, the PCVB launched a $1.2 million international consumer marketing campaign with funding from the Delaware River Port Authority. The international efforts focus on Philadelphia's four primary markets—the United Kingdom, Germany, France, and Italy, as well as other parts of Europe, South America, and Asia.

Through a concerted effort by the PCVB, its Board, and members, Philadelphia continues to rise as a prime destination for meetings, conventions, and tourism. For more information on the Philadelphia Convention & Visitors Bureau or hosting a meeting in Philadelphia, call 1-800- CALL-PHL, or logon to www.pcvb.org. ℗

Philadelphia Sports Congress: Building on the past successes of significant events, including the NCAA Women's Final Four, NBA All-Star 2002, and the ESPN X Games, the Philadelphia Sports Congress sells Philadelphia and the region as a sports destination. This division of the Philadelphia Convention & Visitors Bureau is responsible for attracting, developing, and promoting sports-related events and conventions to the city.

◀ 3 5 7

▶ The stunning Grand Hall of the Pennsylvania Convention Center is a century-old train shed. This Victorian shed is the sole surviving single-span train shed in the nation and links exhibit halls to additional meeting and banquet space.

▸ Four Seasons Hotel

Opened in July of 1983, Four Seasons Hotel, Philadelphia, has been providing guests with the finest in luxury accommodations in the hotel market for almost 20 years. Located on the Benjamin Franklin Parkway, considered one of Philadelphia's most beautiful streets, Four Seasons lies near many of the city's greatest attractions. Visitors can view lovely fountains and statuary as they walk to visit some of the city's premier museums and cultural institutions or fashionable shopping, business, and financial districts.

Four Seasons, designed by A. Eugene Kohn, is situated on the axis of the Parkway in the Logan Square neighborhood. While the building maintains a character all its own, it fits in well with the elegant nature of its surroundings. The hotel features 364 rooms, including 92 Four Seasons Executive Suites, six extra large suites, and the Presidential Suite. Guests can choose one of four magnificent views: the Swann Memorial Fountain, the Parkway, City Hall and the skyline, or Four Seasons' beautifully landscaped courtyard. The rooms themselves are spacious, furnished with a large armoire, wing chair, an ottoman, and an oversized desk—all done in the Federal Period style commonly used by Philadelphia cabinetmakers. Blended with this historic feel is an assortment of twenty-first century luxuries: updated telephone system with two lines, dataports, voicemail, and high-speed Internet access; remote controlled cable TV with Spectradyne; clock radios; in-room safes; and lockable closets.

In addition to deluxe accommodations, Four Seasons offers a wide variety of exceptional amenities. A fully equipped health spa is

▲ **Four Seasons Hotel Philadelphia's location reflects the dynamism of the city. Commerce, culture, and entertainment are all steps away.**

available to guests, featuring a 45 x 18-foot swimming pool, a Jacuzzi, a sauna, an exercise room completely outfitted with Universal exercise equipment, and luxurious men and women's locker rooms. Guests can treat themselves to massages, facials, and other assorted body treatments. Twenty-four hour concierge service provides guests with everything from making dinner and theater reservations to issuing messages. Guests also have access to a full-service business center, secretarial support, and can be provided with medical help or child-care.

Moreover, a variety of dining options are available to guests— whether it be dinner at the nationally renowned Fountain Restaurant, cocktails in the sophisticated Swann Lounge and Café, a pleasant out-of-doors meal at the Courtyard Café, or enjoying a quiet meal in his or her own room, guests get the very best that Philadelphia has to offer without even leaving the hotel.

The only 18-time AAA Five Diamond Award winning hotel in Pennsylvania, Four Seasons Hotel has built a tradition of excellence spanning nearly two decades. Continuing and improving upon this tradition is the premier desire of the management and staff, guaranteeing the enjoyment of Philadelphia visitors for many years to come. ℗

◀ **The Fountain Restaurant is regarded as the city's best, with number one ratings for food, decor, service, popularity in the Zagat Survey. Romantic views of the Swann Memorial Fountain enhance the experience.**

▶ Strawbridge's

For over 130 years, Strawbridge's has been offering the citizens of Philadelphia the finest in apparel and accessories for men, women, and children, home fashions, furniture, gifts, and cookware. Visitors are provided with services ranging from on-line wedding registry to alterations and gift-wrap.

Strawbridge's first store was opened in 1868 by merchants Justus C. Strawbridge and Isaac H. Clothier at the corner of Eighth and Market Streets in downtown Philadelphia. Strawbridge had gained experience by operating a dry goods store in the same location.

The flagship store at Eighth and Market would become a destination for shoppers from Pennsylvania, New Jersey, and Delaware. In the 1930s Strawbridge & Clothier would become one of the first retailers in the country to open stores in the suburbs. The company remained family owned and operated until it was purchased by the May Department Stores Company. The name was changed to Strawbridge's, but customers continue to get the same top-quality products and the same great service they've always been accustomed to receiving.

Today there are 20 Strawbridge's stores employing 5,500 associates in three states on the East Coast. Every man and woman who helps make up the Strawbridge's team does his or her best to make the shopper's experience as convenient and enjoyable as possible. They do this through a dedication to identifying and meeting the needs of each customer in a relaxed and friendly atmosphere. The company itself provides the very best in fashion, quality, and value, as well as the most pleasant surroundings possible. One example of

▲ Strawbridge's at 8th and Market Streets. Life-size scene of the Cratchit home from Charles Dickens' "A Christmas Carol" Exhibit.

this is the full-scale replica of Charles Dickens' "A Christmas Carol," located at Strawbridge's at Eighth and Market. For decades, visitors have flocked to the exhibit, the only one of its kind, which stays open throughout the holiday season.

In addition to being one of the nation's premier retail chains, every Strawbridge's establishment strives to be a worthy member the community. Through its involvement with numerous non-profit and civic organizations such as Race for the Cure, The Philadelphia Museum of Art, The Children's Hospital of Philadelphia, Boy's and Girl's Club, The Kimmel Center for the Performing Arts, St. Francis De Sales Elementary School, and The Rena Rowan House, the company works diligently to help maintain and improve the quality of life in the areas where it does business.

The future looks bright for Strawbridge's, with new store openings and renovations of existing stores always on the horizon. By continuing the longtime tradition of strong business management and support of its community, Strawbridge's ensures its customers another century of retail excellence. ℗

◀ 359

◀ Strawbridge's in Moorestown, New Jersey. Opened in November 1999.

▸ Hotel Windsor

*T*n 1998, the newly renovated Hotel Windsor opened its doors to the public. Formerly an apartment complex, the new hotel offered visitors a unique option in regards to guest accommodations. Located within 15 minutes of the Philadelphia International Airport and less than a mile from the 30th Street Train Station, the Hotel Windsor is the perfect choice for business and leisure travelers alike.

Philadelphia is a city with a rich history, yet remains firmly rooted in the modern world. The Hotel Windsor is situated perfectly for visitors to see both of these faces. Within a few short blocks, guests can find Philadelphia's world-renowned art museums and sprawling green parks. Easy access to public transportation also provides a simple means of visiting the historic sites that are a little farther out of the way, and a prime downtown location puts visitors within blocks of the city's trend setting restaurants and shops.

One of the many characteristics that separate the Hotel Windsor from other luxury hotels is its ability to meet the needs of permanent residents, as well as temporary guests. It is able to fill this dual role because of the rooms. The Windsor is unique because of its status as an all suite accommodation. Guests or residents receive their choice of accommodations: standard suites, studios, or one-bedroom apartments. Each space is very large and has fully-operational kitchens, allowing the guest a level of comfort not to be found in a standard hotel. Aside from the size and quality of the rooms, guest are provided with a long list of amenities that include well-lit, oversized work spaces; dual port phones; voicemail; cable TV with HBO; large walk-in closets; a 24-hour, fully equipped fitness center; a roof-top pool with sundeck; same day laundry service; guest laundry facilities; 24-hour concierge and business services; as well as two critically acclaimed restaurants, Gianni's Bistro and Peacock on the Parkway.

An independent hotel, operating under the corporate umbrella of Potomac Hospitality, the Hotel Windsor isn't your usual cookie-

▲ **The spectacular view of City Hall from the Hotel Windsor.**

cutter hotel. The thoughtful staff at the Hotel Windsor is always looking for the opportunity to increase the number and quality of services offered to each guest, regardless of whether they are visitors or permanent residents. Large comfortable suites, luxurious amenities and services, a prime downtown location, easy access to the entire city, and reasonable rates combine to make The Hotel Windsor an ideal home away from home for almost anyone. ℗

◀ **Spacious living area of a one-bedroom suite.**

▸ Enterprise Index

ACE INA
1601 Chestnut Street
Two Liberty Place
Philadelphia, Pennsylvania 19103
Phone: (215)640-1000
www.ace-ina.com
Pages 266-269

Advanta
Welsh & McKean Roads
Spring House, Philadelphia 19477
Phone: (215)444-5370
Fax: (215)444-5075
E-mail: lbrechtmarr@advanta.com
www.advanta.com
Pages 250-251

American International Group
1700 Market Street
Suite 200
Philadelphia, Pennsylvania 19103
Phone: (215)255-6000
www.aig.com
Page 280

B101
10 Presidential Boulevard
Bala Cynwyd, Pennsylvania 19004
Phone: (610)667-8400
Fax: (610)667-6795
E-mail: blaiseh@101-fm.com
www.b101radio.com
Pages 350-353

Ben Franklin Technology Partners of Southeastern Pennsylvania
11 Penn Center, Suite 1100
1835 Market Street
Philadelphia, Pennsylvania 19103
Phone: (215)972-6700
Fax: (215)972-5588
E-mail: roseann@sep.benfranklin.org
www.sep.benfranklin.org
Page 225

Beneficial Savings Bank
510 Walnut Street
Philadelphia, Pennsylvania 19106
Phone: (215)864-6000
E-mail: info@beneficialsavingsbank.com
www.beneficialsavings.com
Pages 238-243

Brandywine Realty Trust
401 Plymouth Road
Suite 500
Plymouth Meeting, Pennsylvania 19462
Phone: (610)325-5600
Fax: (610)325-5622
E-mail: mimi.brown@brandywinerealty.com
www.brandywinerealty.com
Pages 326-329

Chester County Aviation
1 Earhart Drive
Suite 1
Coatesville, Pennsylvania 19320
Phone: (610)384-9000
Fax: (610)384-7083
www.chestercountyaviation.com
Page 224

The Children's Hospital of Philadelphia
34th Street and Civic Center Boulevard
Philadelphia, Pennsylvania 19104
Phone: (215)590-1000
www.chop.edu
Pages 284-287

City of Philadelphia
1515 Arch Street
12th Floor
Philadelphia, Pennsylvania 19102
Phone: (215)683-2063
Fax: (215)683-2099
E-mail: bonnie.grant@phila.gov
www.phila.gov
Pages 354-355

Commerce Bank
Corporate Headquarters
1701 Route 70 East
Cherry Hill, New Jersey 08034
Phone: (888)751-9000
Fax: (856)778-3375
E-mail: customerservice@yesbank.com
www.commerceonline.com
Page 256

Crozer-Keystone Health System
Healthplex Pavilion II
100 West Sproul Road
Springfield, Pennsylvania 19064
Phone: (610)338-8200
Fax: (610)328-8231
E-mail: crozer@crozer.org
www.crozer.org
Pages 300-301

Delaware Valley Industrial Resource Center (DVIRC)
2905 Southampton Road
Philadelphia, Pennsylvania 19154
Phone: (215)464-8550
Fax: (215)464-8570
www.dvirc.org
Page 235

Doyle Consulting Group, Inc.
2005 Market Street
Suite 3510
Philadelphia, Pennsylvania 19103
Phone: (215)561-0510
Fax: (215)561-3736
E-mail: mullin@doyleconsultinggroup.com
www.doylegroupinc.com
Pages 270-271

Duane Morris LLP
One Liberty Place
Philadelphia, Pennsylvania 19103
Phone: (215)979-1000
Fax: (215)979-1020
www.duanemorris.com
Pages 274-275

ESM Productions
340 North 12th Street
Suite 404
Philadelphia, Pennsylvania 19107
Phone: (215)925-2566
Fax: (215)829-4645
E-mail: smirkin@esmproductions.com
www.esmproductions.com
Page 226

Ewing Colc Cherry Brott
100 North 6th Street
Philadelphia, Pennsylvania 19106
Phone: (215)923-2020
Fax: (215)574-0952
E-mail: info@ewingcole.com
www.ewingcole.com
Pages 330-331

First Union/Wachovia
1339 Chestnut Street
Philadelphia, Pennsylvania 19107
Phone: (215)985-6000
Fax: (267)321-7701
www.wachovia.com
Pages 248-249

Four Seasons Hotel
One Logan Square
Philadelphia, Pennsylvania 19103
Phone: (215)963-1500
Fax: (215)963-9506
www.fourseasons.com/philadelphia
Page 358

General Building Contractors Association
36 South 18th Street
Philadelphia, Pennsylvania 19103
Phone: (215)568-7015
Fax: (215)568-3115
E-mail: jnickerson@hotmail.com
www.gbca.net
Page 332

The Graham Company
One Penn Square West
Philadelphia, Pennsylvania 19102
Phone: (215)567-6300
Fax: (215)569-3025
www.grahamco.com
Pages 244-245

The Greater Philadelphia Chamber of Commerce
200 South Broad Street
Suite 700
Philadelphia, Pennsylvania 19102-3896
Phone: (215)545-1234
Fax: (215)790-3600
www.philachamber.com
Pages 252-253

Greater Philadelphia Venture Group
200 South Broad Street
Suite 700
Philadelphia, Pennsylvania 19102
Phone: (215)790-3689
Fax: (215)790-3601
www.gpvg.com
Pages 276-277

Hotel Windsor
1700 Benjamin Franklin Parkway
Philadelphia, Pennsylvania 19103
Phone: (215)981-5678
Fax: (215)981-5684
E-mail: sales@windsorhotel.com
www.windsorhotel.com
Page 360

Independence Blue Cross
1901 Market Street
Philadelphia, Pennsylvania 19103
Phone: (215)241-2075
Fax: (215)241-0403
E-mail: christopher.cashman@ibx.com
www.ibx.com
Pages 304-305

Innovation Philadelphia
2600 Centre Square West
1500 Market Street
Philadelphia, Pennsylvania 19102
Phone: (215)496-8110
Fax: (215)320-1991
E-mail: ipweb@ipphila.com
www.ipphila.com
Pages 222-223

Janney Montgomery Scott LLC
1801 Market Street
Philadelphia, Pennsylvania 19103
Phone: (215)665-6000
Fax: (215)587-9819
www.jmsonline.com
Page 278

Jefferson Health System
259 North Radnor-Chester Road
Radnor, Pennsylvania 19087-5261
Phone: (610)225-6200
E-mail: holtp@mlhs.org
www.jeffersonhealth.org
Pages 288-291

La Salle University
1900 West Olney Avenue
Philadelphia, Pennsylvania 19141
Phone: (215)951-1000
www.lasalle.edu
Pages 316-317

Lexicomm International Ltd.
501 Washington Lane
Jenkintown, Pennsylvania 19046
Phone: (215)989-5000
Fax: (215)989-5001
E-mail: nsmoler@lexicomm.com
www.lexicomm.com
Page 279

Lincoln Financial Group
Centre Square West Tower
1500 Market Street
39th Floor
Philadelphia, Pennsylvania 19102
Phone: (215)448-1401
Fax: (215)448-3962
E-mail: amongan@lfg.com
www.lfg.com
Page 258

Marriott Residence Inn
4630 Island Avenue
Philadelphia, Pennsylvania 19153
Phone: (215)492-1611
Fax: (215)492-1665
E-mail: nick.katsikis@marriott.com
www.marriott.com
Pages 346-349

McDonald's East Division
Centre Square
1500 Market Street
Suite 3500
Philadelphia, Pennsylvania 19102
Phone: (215)814-9090
Fax: (215)405-8440
www.mcdonalds.com
Pages 246-247

Northwestern Human Services
620 Germantown Pike
Lafayette Hill, Pennsylvania 19444
Phone: (610)260-4600
Fax: (610)260-4591
www.nhsonline.org
Pages 306-307

NovaCare Rehabilitation
680 American Avenue
King of Prussia, Pennsylvania 19406
Phone: (610)992-7200
Fax: (610)265-6049
www.novacare.com
Pages 296-299

PECO, An Exelon Company
2301 Market Street
Philadelphia, Pennsylvania 19103
Phone: (800)494-4000
www.peco.com
Pages 220-221

Penn Eye Care
Scheie Eye Institute
51 North 39th Street
Philadelphia, Pennsylvania 19104
Phone: (215)662-9886
Fax: (215)662-1721
E-mail: szkolnim@uphs.upenn.edu
www.pennhealth.com Keyword: Eyes
Pages 308-309

Philadelphia Convention & Visitors Bureau
1515 Market Street
Suite 2020
Philadelphia, Pennsylvania 19102
Phone: (215)636-3300
Fax: (215)636-3327
www.pcvb.org
Pages 356-357

The Philadelphia Eagles
NovaCare Complex
One NovaCare Way
Philadelphia, Pennsylvania 19145
Phone: (215)463-2500
Fax: (215)339-6745 or 5464
E-mail: howard@eagles.nfl.com
www.philadelphiaeagles.com
Pages 340-343

Philadelphia International Airport
Executive Office, Terminal E
Philadelphia International Airport
Philadelphia, Pennsylvania 19153
Phone: (215)937-5499
Fax: (215)937-5495
www.phl.org
Pages 218-219

Philadelphia Phillies
Veterans Stadium
3501 South Broad Street
Philadelphia, Pennsylvania 19148
Phone: (215)463-1000
Fax: (215)463-9878
E-mail: tickets@phillies.mlb.com
www.phillies.com
Pages 336-339

Public Financial Management
Two Logan Square
18th and Arch Streets
Suite 1600
Philadelphia, Pennsylvania 19103-2770
Phone: (215)567-6100
Fax: (215)567-4180
E-mail: info@publicfm.com
www.pfm.com
Pages 262-265

Rohm and Haas
100 Independence Mall West
Philadelphia, Pennsylvania 19106-2399
Phone: (215)592-3000
Fax: (215)592-3377
www.rohmhaas.com
Page 234

The Rubenstein Company, L.P.
4100 One commerce Square
2005 Market Street
Philadelphia, Pennsylvania 19103
Phone: (215)563-3558
Fax: (215)563-4110
www.trclp.com
Pages 320-321

Strawbridge's
685 North Glebe Road
Arlington, Virginia 22203-2199
Phone: (703)524-1200
www.strawbridges.com
Page 359

Sunoco, Inc.
Ten Penn Center
1801 Market Street
Philadelphia, Pennsylvania 19103-1699
Phone: (215)977-3000
www.sunocoinc.com
Pages 230-231

The TASA Group
1166 DeKalb Pike
Blue Bell, Pennsylvania 19422-1853
Phone: (800)523-2319
Fax: (800)329-8272
E-mail: experts@tasanet.com
www.tasanet.com
Page 254

BIOGRAPHIES

Marion Laffey Fox, Author, Special Introduction

Philadelphia journalist Marion Laffey Fox, a graduate of the University of Pennsylvania, is active in civic and cultural affairs. A former guide in the Historic Houses of Fairmount Park, she has lectured on travel, decorative arts, design, architecture, and costume.

Author of *Philadelphia: World Class!* in 1997, and co-author of *It's Your Body—Know What the Doctor Ordered* with Dr. Truman J. Schnabel, Jr., Fox has contributed to newspapers and magazines such as *The Christian Science Monitor, USA Today, Town & Country, House Beautiful, Architectural Digest, Travel & Leisure, Country Inns, Art & Antiques, Forbes FYI,* and *The Tatler.* In addition, she is a senior contributing editor to *Southern Accents* and contributing editor to *Coastal Living, Santa Barbara,* and *Newport Life* magazines.

Fox has served on the boards of numerous local and national organizations including the Lankenau Hospital Foundation. She is member of the Academy of Music Ball Program committee and the Franklin Institute Bower Awards Committee.

Kurt Niland, Author

Born in New Haven, Connecticut, Kurt Niland regards his lifelong interest in geography, anthropology, political science, and literature as a culmination of his experiences living in several states, Southeast Asia, and Europe. He attended New Mexico State University, the University of New Mexico, and Auburn University at Montgomery, where he graduated as top student of English and Philosophy in 1993 with a degree in English and a minor in International Studies.

Kurt's writing, covering a broad range of subjects, has appeared in numerous journals, academic magazines, and books, including *Notes and Queries* (Oxford); *Critical Matrix* (Princeton); *The Papers of the Bibliographical Society of America* (University of South Carolina), *The Triangle* (Sigma Tau Delta), and several others. He was the first winner of the Clifford J. Durr Lecture Series Award recognizing writing excellence, and he was also Alabama's only college student to receive a Younger Scholars Award from the National Endowment for the Humanities, which resulted in a grant to research the life of King James V at Yale University. Kurt is also author of *The Spirit of the Place,* a book showcasing the chefs, restaurants, and recipes of Florida's Emerald Coast. In addition to writing, Kurt has lectured to high schools and universities on a number of topics including Buddhism, the socio-political relationship of Thailand and Cambodia, the presence of erotic poetry in Puritan New England, and the writings of Flannery O'Connor and Ben Jonson.

A resident of Montgomery, Alabama, Kurt has been an editor and writer for Community Communications, Inc. for the last six years.

John McGrail, Photographer

John McGrail is a native Philadelphian. Upon graduation from La Salle University, he was commissioned as an officer in the U.S. Army. McGrail served as a paratrooper in the 82nd Airborne Division during the Vietnam era. While in the Army he took up photography as a hobby and later earned a second bachelor's degree with honors from Brooks Institute of Photography in Santa Barbara.

Based in New York City for ten years, John traveled internationally on magazine assignments. He has shot for *Life, Time, Fortune, Business Week, Discover, Scientific American, Sports Illustrated, People, Smithsonian, Travel & Leisure,* and many other national and foreign publications. McGrail's work has been published in more than 80 countries.

John moved his family back to the Philadelphia region in 1986. He has developed several specialties such as aerial, maritime, and portraiture for his work with regional corporations and design firms. His panoramic work can be seen in permanent exhibits at several national parks. He created wall-sized mural images for the Independence Seaport Museum. WCAU-TV News has featured a profile on Mr. McGrail and he has earned awards from the Philadelphia Art Directors Club. He was the feature photographer for the 1997 book *Philadelphia: World Class!,* also published by CCI.

The McGrails make their home in Bucks County. John can be contacted through his web site: www.johnmcgrail.com.

▸ Bibliography

Beers, Dorothy Gondos, "The Centennial City, 1865-1876," in *Philadelphia: A 300-Year History*, edited by Russell F. Weigly. New York: W.W. Norton & Company, 1982.

Bellwether Report, "Philadelphia ranks among top tech regions," *Technology Times*, October, 2001, 10.

Bellwether Report, "Reports show Philadelphia ranks among America's top high tech regions," *Technology Times*, February, 2002, 14.

Bellwether Technology Partnership. *Greater Philadelphia's Technology Sector: A Regional Overview*. Philadelphia, 2001.

Benn, Tracy Jean, ed., *The 2002 Greater Philadelphia Story*. Philadelphia: The Greater Philadelphia Chamber of Commerce, 2002.

Booker, Janice, *Philly Firsts*. Philadelphia: Camino Books, 1999.

Bronner, Edwin B., "Village into Town, 1701-1746," in *Philadelphia: A 300-Year History*, edited by Russell F. Weigly. New York: W.W. Norton & Company, 1982.

Burt, Nathaniel and Wallace E. Davies, "The Iron Age, 1876-1905," in *Philadelphia: A 300-Year History*, edited by Russell F. Weigly. New York: W.W. Norton & Company, 1982.

Clark, Joseph F., Jr., and Dennis J., "Rally and Relapse, 1946-1968," in *Philadelphia: A 300-Year History*, edited by Russell F. Weigly. New York: W.W. Norton & Company, 1982.

Dunn, Mary Maples and Richard S., "The Founding, 1681-1701," in *Philadelphia: A 300-Year History*, edited by Russell F. Weigly. New York: W.W. Norton & Company, 1982.

Federal Reserve Bank of Philadelphia Research Department. *The Industrial Evolution: Two Decades of Change in the Philadelphia Metro Area's Economy*. Philadelphia, 2002.

Geffen, Elizabeth M., "Industrial Development and Social Crisis, 1841-1865," in *Philadelphia: A 300-Year History*, edited by Russell F. Weigly. New York: W.W. Norton & Company, 1982.

George, John, "Tapping into the Human Genome Project," *Philadelphia Business Journal*, 5-11 May, 2000, 4.

Greater Philadelphia Chamber of Commerce. *Major Employers of the Greater Philadelphia Region*. Philadelphia, 2000.

Kostelni, Natalie, "Report: Merck plans huge lab," *Philadelphia Business Journal*, 4-10 August, 2000, 1.

McCalla, John, "Ridge: Tech's $750M man," *Philadelphia Business Journal*, 4-10 May, 2001, 1.

Peco Energy. *Greater Philadelphia: An Economic Development Statistical Profile*. Philadelphia, 2002.

Peco Energy, Economic and Business Development Department. "Greater Philadelphia Welcomes Biotech Health Care Cash Infusion," *Communique*, Philadelphia, Summer/Fall, 2001, 1.

Pinkenson, Sharon, ed. *The Greater Philadelphia Film and Video Guide*. Philadelphia: The Greater Philadelphia Film Office, 2001.

Selected Demographic Data for the Greater Philadelphia Region, Philadelphia: Greater Philadelphia Chamber of Commerce, 2001.

Thayer, Theodore, "Town into City, 1746-1783," in *Philadelphia: A 300-Year History*, edited by Russell F. Weigly. New York: W.W. Norton & Company, 1982.

Tinkcom, Harry M., "The Revolutionary City, 1765-1783," in *Philadelphia: A 300-Year History*, edited by Russell F. Weigly. New York: W.W. Norton & Company, 1982.

Tinkcom, Margaret B., "Depression and War, 1929-1946," in *Philadelphia: A 300-Year History*, edited by Russell F. Weigly. New York: W.W. Norton & Company, 1982.

Weigley, Russell F., "The Border City in a Civil War, 1854-1865," in *Philadelphia: A 300-Year History*, edited by Russell F. Weigly. New York: W.W. Norton & Company, 1982.

▶ Index